laneman
publishing

Chasing
Dreams

**An obsession
with catching
big fish**

by **Tony Miles**

Chasing Dreams - a limited edition book.
Published in 2001 by Laneman Publishing
5 Lyons Court, Dorking, Surrey RH4 1AB
© Tony Miles 2001

British Library Cataloguing in Publication Data

A catalogue record for this book is available from the
British Library.

ISBN 1-901717-07-0

Illustrations by Pete Curtis
Design and production by Lane Design.
Telephone: 01306 875154

Printed in Great Britain.

Contents

Introduction

For over forty years of my life, I have been dedicated to the pursuit of big fish, and within these pages are chronicled the highlights of those years. My angling enjoyment has always been enhanced by the pleasure I get from sharing my thoughts and experiences with others through the written word, and I hope you derive as much entertainment from these pages as I did in recollection of many special moments.

While big fish angling is often a solitary pursuit, its enjoyment is magnified by being able to share successes and failures with special people, and in this respect I am extremely fortunate in having so many top class anglers as friends. They are now so numerous that it would be impossible to name them all, so I have to content myself with highlighting a few men. Top of the list, of course, has to come Trefor West. He and I have been close friends now for over thirty years, and that has never wavered. It is a friendship that I value highly. Close behind come all the other members of the Coventry Group, principally Merv Wilkinson, Mick Nicholls, Phil Smith and Terry Jones. A special thanks is also extended to Graham Marsden, a fine angler, great writer, good friend and one who I owe a special debt of gratitude for encouraging my first tentative steps towards computer literacy. The same sentiments must go to Dave Plummer and his lovely wife Linda, who, for so many years, made their home available to me whenever I fished in Norfolk

As I have matured as an angler and writer, many younger, up and coming big fish men have made my acquaintance and become good friends. Many are stunningly successful anglers in their own right, and I am learning from them all the time. To Matthew Bodily, Adrian Busby, Martin Bowler, Matt Hayes, Stuart

Adrian Busby.

Stef Horak.

Trefor West.

Phil Smith.

Morgan, Guy Robb, Simon Lush and Stef Horak I extend my greetings, and thanks, as I do to the hundreds of readers who contact me through my regular writing and internet connection with www.fishingwarehouse.co.uk.

It would also be remiss of me not to thank the many tackle dealers who regularly provide me with products. Can I therefore make special mention and give special thanks to Drennan International, Relum, Korda Products, Solar Tackle, Century Rods, Leeda and Shimano. And I must not forget Double T, the company now run so successfully by my old mate Trefor West.

Bait manufacturers have also not been slow at coming forward in providing materials for my experiments over the years, and I owe a debt of gratitude to SBS, Richworth, Rod Hutchinson, Nutrabaits and John Baker. Special thanks must also go to David Moss-Allison. When Trefor and I were developing our Pulse Rods and Action Baits ventures, David acted as our business manager, handling all the boring administration with admirable aplomb.

For one who has been so prolific a writer over the years, it was inevitable that an autobiography of this type would contain some material that had appeared previously. I am grateful, therefore, for permission from Simon Roff and Stu

Martin Bowler.

Matthew Bodily.

Dexter of Coarse Fisherman, and Jim Baxter of Sheffield Angling Star, to use extracts of articles in this manuscript.

Lastly, I must thank Paul Selman and Stephen Lane of Laneman Publishing, who agreed to publish this book so enthusiastically, and who have since invited me on board their exciting new project on the Internet. Having been mightily impressed with the superb quality of their previous books, I am delighted to be associated with such a professional organisation.

If any of you have my previous books, you will know that I have dedicated them to my wife Fran. Those that know me will not be surprised that I am doing exactly the same thing with this work. We have now been married 35 years and no man could have had greater support in fulfilling his dreams than I have from Fran.

Once again, with unashamed love and affection, I dedicate this book to my wife.

Tony Miles
March 2001

Merv Wilkinson.

Graham Marsden.

My wife Fran.

Early Days

I remember clearly the first day I ever went fishing. I was thirteen years old, on holiday from school, and a friend Dave and I had been persuaded to go with his father to the local canal. Dave's dad had recently taken up the sport again after a long lay off. I can't say I was particularly looking forward to the experience, it sounded very boring, and so I only tagged along on sufferance.

To be honest, I would have been content exploring the adjacent woods and climbing trees, but old Alf insisted Dave and I learn how to fish for ourselves, and set us up with ancient greenheart rods, centrepin reels, assorted floats and hooks to nylon. Apparently, we were fishing for roach, and he showed me how to plumb the depth, set the float and so on. Within an hour I was casting passably well. Following instructions, my float was near the rushes on the far bank, with a single maggot impaled on a size 16 under a horrendous bulbous float.

Dave and I were side by side, and presently we began catching a succession of tiny gudgeon, which lacked the strength to pull the float under. Whenever the float started to bob about, we struck. And then my float did go right under, but this time when I lifted the rod point, something pulled back. It was our first roach, probably no more than six ounces, but I can remember the excitement of that moment even now. When the time came to pack up, we had caught a few more smaller roach, and I had to admit that I had really enjoyed it. I wanted to go again.

Over the next two years, Dave and I really got into our fishing, going on our push bikes to the local river Leam, the Oxford canal and Napton reservoirs. We were never to catch big fish, and by the end of the season in March 1959 my six ounce roach was still the biggest fish we'd had. The Leam had given us hundreds of gudgeon and tiny roach and dace, the canals transparent little skimmers and infant perch, and the reservoirs nothing. We were totally lost there!

And then in May 1959, my mother fuelled my budding angling career by giving me a surprise birthday present. I

was fifteen, and that copy of Still Water Angling by Richard Walker changed my life for ever. I read it from cover to cover, not once but many times, and although the chapters on Redmire were my favourite, the one on catching big fish by design had the most profound effect. I now knew the direction I wanted my fishing to take.

Returning a tench to Fawsley in 1966.

On June 16th, Dave and I went with his dad to the canal once again, but this time I was determined to catch something bigger than the usual run of bits, and sat there for what seemed like hours with a big worm on the end while Dave was happily taking little bream. And then the float shot away, and I eventually landed a perch of 1lb 4oz. I only had one more bite that day, just before we packed up, and pulled out of a very big fish. There was an expanse of golden flank, and then it was gone; almost certainly a common carp. I remember being delighted with the perch, even though I'd landed but the one fish. Dave and Alf had accumulated probably fifty small fish between them, but I would not have swapped. My early specimen hunter's mentality had been born.

Good chub and perch from Claydon Brook in 1964.

A couple of weeks later, Dave and I embarked on our first ever night fishing trip, much to the worry of our mothers. The night fishing descriptions in Still Water Angling sounded really exciting. What they didn't say, though, was how bloody cold it got! That was the first time I ever tried legering, having read about dough bobbins, and I'll never forget that bit of bread shooting in the air in the early hours as a big roach of 1lb 6oz engulfed my flake hookbait. Dave sat all night with a light on his float, happily knocking out small bream, but I was now increasingly a big fish or bust angler.

Napton Reservoirs - early sixties.

In October of that year, my lifetime passion for chub was kindled when I took two of 1lb 8oz each on cheese extracted from my sandwiches from the Leam, and the same month I stood in awe as an adult angler photographed a big perch from the river. He said it weighed three pounds. To my impressionable eyes, it looked monstrous.

By the following summer, Dave and I had formed a close friendship with two brothers, Ken and Maurice, whose father farmed 120 acres between Coventry and Banbury. They were both keen anglers too, and knew some different, interesting waters. One was Fawsley Park lake, and in late June 1960 I was to see my first tench. It weighed all of a pound, caught by Ken, but I thought I'd never seen or felt such a beautiful fish in my life. The trip to Fawsley was interesting. Dave and I had biked to Ken's farm, about 18 miles, and hitched our bikes with ropes to the back of Ken's motorbike. With Maurice on the pillion, Ken towed us to Fawsley, another ten miles away! God knows what the police would have made of it, but luckily we never got our collars felt and emerged unscathed. After that first trip to Fawsley, we fished it regularly, and I was to take my first few tench, to over 4lb plus good roach to 1lb

Two good Cherwell chub, 1968.

Landing small pike from Claydon Brook in 1966.

10oz. I also took several good eels, to nearly 4lb, but detested the things. In that, I've never changed!

Billy Lane's tackle shop in Coventry was always a hive of information, and we met one interesting old boy who told us about the big bream of the Oxford canal near Napton, and how to catch them with lift floats. He also told us about a farm pond with big rudd, and how he had been catching roach up to nearly two pounds from the reservoirs. We spoke for over an hour and he really fired us up. We couldn't wait to get cracking, and the first target was the bream. I close my eyes now and I can still see the swims, on a wide bend in the canal, where the far bank was a mass of reeds. We had been told to lay on among the reeds with big pieces of bread flake, and use plenty of groundbait.

Our pocket money had run to two pounds of Kestrel breadcrumbs apiece on the first session, a blistering hot July day, and we had the encouragement of very early success. Within an hour of starting, Dave caught a bream of 2lb 8oz, and by the time we packed up at dark, he'd had three more and I'd managed two, best exactly three pounds.

Next day, we went to the farm pond. Our informant had told us to fish big worms, and this we did, catching so many micro perch we lost count. All morning, though, big fish periodically broke surface right out in the middle. In the end, I cannibalised a sandwich, pinched a great chunk of bread and butter on the end, and lobbed the float out as far as I could. Exactly ten seconds later, it vanished, and within a few more moments Dave and I were staring at the first rudd we'd ever seen. Exactly a pound it weighed and, although we fished that pond many more times afterwards, we never caught another.

The big roach at Napton reservoirs were a completely different ball game, however. You had to have a little angling sophistication to catch them, and one hot afternoon in late June 1961, the four of us were lolling in the sun, enjoying yet another roach blank, when Ken said his dad was taking him and Maurice to a farm near Buckingham where a river ran through that contained massive roach. Apparently the farmer allowed limited camping on his fields, to people he knew, and had agreed that the two lads could spend two weeks of the summer holiday there. This sounded like paradise, and we begged to go along as well. Within two days, it was organised, and mid July saw us all pile into the back of Ken's dad's big van for the journey to the Claydon Brook, as the river was called.

Once there, we were introduced to Mr Crooke, a stern but kindly old countryman, who welcomed us warmly but threatened dire reprisals if gates were left open or crops trampled. There was also his housekeeper, Miss Bryant, who took us under her wing, and for a fortnight supplied us with unlimited quantities of fresh milk, eggs and cakes, in return for bowls full of crayfish each night. Mr Crooke adored boiled crays, and we caught hundreds in an hour in the little weir, using drop nets baited with dead fish. That first visit, we set up three tents, two for sleeping and a big bell tent for cooking and general socialising.

That fortnight was magical. On the second morning, Dave and I were up at the crack of dawn, and took roach up to 1lb 15oz on laid on flake. Every day, we saw giant chub, but couldn't catch them until the middle of the second week when Dave eventually landed a monstrous fish of 4lb 8oz on a huge lump of Danish Blue. I remember fetching that cheese from Buckingham. We had asked the shopkeeper for the smelliest cheese he

Landing a Thames fish.

My first ever barbel, from Rushey Weir.

had, and he produced this foul smelling lump from the back room. It was probably in a smell proof cage! Rank doesn't even start to describe it, but that big chub seemed to like it well enough. Ken wasn't so impressed though. When we brought the cheese into camp, he was asleep in the sun, dead to the world. He was trying to grow a moustache at the time, a wispy excuse of a thing, and Dave very gently smeared some of the liquefying cheese on the whiskers. After he'd eventually woken up, Ken continually sniffed the air all day, convinced that Mr Crooke was applying a strange fertiliser on the back fields.

I also remember a practical joke that Dave and I organised that could have had tragic circumstances, looking back on it. At the time, though, it was hilarious and we were helpless with laughter for hours.

Alongside the field where we were pitched, a very quiet lane led from the small village of Padbury to the main Buckingham road and every early morning before dawn a post woman would come cycling down that lane, ringing her bell like mad. She was really irritating. As it happened, Dave had brought with him a plastic skeleton about four feet high, that he'd acquired from a joke shop, plus some luminous paint, with the express intention of having some kind of laugh with it. It came to us in a flash of inspiration.

It was getting dusk, the lane was quiet, and Dave and I strung the painted skeleton across the narrow lane on fishing line between two trees, and pulled it tight so that it hung there in crucifix fashion. As soon as it was completely dark, it looked absolutely gruesome. All night long we sat behind the hedge, giggling. Sure enough, about an hour before dawn, there she was, turning into the lane, bell ringing as usual. Seconds later, there was the most blood curdling scream, and then she went past us like the wind. I have never before or since seen a cyclist's legs a blur. In hindsight, the poor old dear could have had a coronary. But it was so funny. I laughed so much I was crying.

That trip in 1961 was the forerunner to many glorious years on the river, as you will read later, and by 1966 I had many big fish to my credit, specially chub and perch. But I had never really got to grips with stillwaters. That was to change in July, when, after enrolling on a new college course, I met a character called Ray Brown, a real extrovert who was familiar with all the Midland reservoirs. Ray was catching good tench and bream from several waters, but his main interest lay in the pike fishing. He'd had several good doubles. Ray and I

A Marlborough double. Note the thin polythene round the 36" brolly!!

began fishing together regularly, my school friends having fallen by the wayside, and I introduced Ray to the river fishing I was getting to grips with while he took me to several of his still water fisheries. A notable trip I'll never forget is a day on Hollowell, when we had over forty pike between us off the dam.

In the mid sixties, the angling press was full of references to the new concept of the specimen group, following Dick Walker's writings about the advantage of pooled knowledge for the common good. I remember one article vividly, by Peter Butler of the London group, in which he was talking about a campaign they had conducted for the big roach and bream of the London reservoirs. That feature had a profound impact on me and at that moment I decided to start a specimen group of my own, in Coventry. In the close season of 1967, I outlined my idea to Ray, and he thought it was equally exciting. Before making any decision, we contacted Pete Rayment, of the newly formed Birmingham Specimen Hunters, and Dave Ball, of the Leicester Specimen Group and Anguilla Club, for their advice, and had a meeting with Pete at my house, when he outlined how the Birmingham Group operated. We liked what we heard, and in May 1967 placed the first advertisement for members in Angling Times.

Mick Jelfs, now sadly deceased, with Marlborough 21 pounder.

Returning Irish tench in 1968.

I was surprised that the advert only elicited one reply, but it was from the right man, Merv Wilkinson. Ray and I arranged to meet Merv for the first time in July on the banks of a local carp lake, from where I had just fluked a 19lb mirror on a floating bread roll. After only a few minutes chatting to Merv, I knew that here was a man who would be the backbone of the new group. He was 31 years old compared to my 23, and vastly experienced whereas I was still an enthusiastic beginner, despite having by now some very big fish to my credit. Most importantly, Merv knew lots of people, many different waters, and was an angling innovator in every sense. I have many times said publicly that to Merv both Trefor and I owe an incalculable debt. Without his early guidance, neither he nor I would be the anglers we are today. One of the most important weeks in my angling career took place in May 1968, on Lough Ree in southern Ireland, when I fished with Merv for the big tench and rudd. I learned a lot, caught plenty of big rudd and tench, had plenty of laughs, and cemented a friendship that would last for life.

With Merv on board, the group grew quickly through his contacts. Within weeks, we had recruited Terry Jones, a local chub fanatic, and then, a month or so later, Phil Smith, the same age as me, techniques as rough round the edges as mine were, but as keen as mustard. The following summer, in June 1968, Trefor West, Mick Nicholls, Mick Jelfs and Bill Robinson joined, and together we turned the Coventry Specimen Group into one of the most successful big fish organisations that has ever existed.

The group as such did not actually hold together for more than a few years, partnerships forming to follow different paths. In the late sixties, I fished with Mick Jelfs for two summers, in our joint pursuit of Marlborough carp, and then, in the early seventies, Trefor West and I commenced our close friendship that still endures to this day. Phil Smith and Merv fished together for many

Trefor with a Cuttle Mill common.

My first Marlborough carp, 1969.

years, while Mick Nicholls developed into one of the most awesome trout anglers I've ever known, as well as being a top class all rounder. Phil Smith pointed something out to me the other day. All the married men that belonged to the group in the late sixties are still with their wives, with the sad exception of Mick Jelfs who died suddenly at a very early age. In these days of marriage collapses because of fishing, that has to be some kind of record.

From childhood, I had nurtured an ambition to be a writer, and in 1967 decided to pen my first feature. I had been having great success with small stream perch under algae in hot conditions, and when the article was complete, I cheekily sent it to Dick Walker for his comments. Within two days, it was back with me, carefully edited, and in Dick's covering letter he told me that he thought I had the makings of an angling writer, and that he had asked Jack Thorndike, editor of Angling Times, to publish it for me. The feature eventually appeared in August 1967 and not for one moment did I realise that would be the first of nearly 1000 features and a dozen books to follow in the next 33 years.

A brace of Irish rudd.

Two Special Chub

A Personal Best

My first summer of fishing the lovely Claydon Brook, a tributary of the Upper Great Ouse just outside Buckingham, was concentrated mostly on the big roach the river contained, principally in the long, lily covered straight above the mill house.

Below the mill, to the country lane bridge, the river was totally choked with rushes and lilies, apart from one or two tiny gaps. Although we had been told the river contained some huge chub, fishing for them was all but impossible because of the dense foliage. Despite that, we had managed a handful of good fish, to just over five pounds, by the early winter of 1961, when the stream was dredged.

With the benefit of hindsight, and having witnessed the devastation that other dredging has created elsewhere, that 1961 work was very sympathetic to the environment. No trees were uprooted, no bends straightened. All that was done was to remove much of the choking vegetation to open up a quite delightful fishery. In the summer of 1962, with the inevitable scars starting to heal, a delightful new fishery had emerged, with many areas fishable for the first time.

That summer was tremendously exciting, because I was to discover quite how big some of those chub were. On one memorable June day, after a successful early perching session, I wandered back to my car, parked alongside the road bridge, but stopped before leaving the field to peer into the clear gravel run under the near bank. There was usually a shoal of good chub in that swim plus the occasional fish to over five pounds, but today there was but one fish in residence. But what a fish! Before my astonished gaze, there drifted the most colossal chub I had ever seen. Here was a fish I was convinced had to be seven pounds.

Ten minutes later, I was back in position with freelining gear, incorporating six pound line and a size four hook adorned with the biggest black slug I had in my box. After all these years, I can still remember trembling as I prepared to swing the bait over the marginal vegetation, and it was a miracle that the cast was perfect, the slug alighting with a good plop a couple of yards above the fish.

I held my breath as the bait trundled down the steady flow to settle no more than a foot from the chub's nose. The fish never moved, and I firmly believe that had I twitched the bait suddenly upstream I would have induced an immediate take. But I didn't, and the fish left the swim after registering only the slightest interest. I left the bait to lie still, and about five minutes later the fish was approaching it again. With my eyes glued expectantly to the approaching giant, I never noticed the jack pike engulfing my bait, and by then it was too late. It was only when the rod flew over the marginal rushes that I realised what was occurring. The chub disappeared. I have never liked jack pike since!

A predictable mistake a month later led to my ruining another chance at the monster, a mistake born out of impatience, and a very important, if hard, lesson learned. Once again, I had found the fish in the same swim, this

Returning early five pounder to Claydon Brook.

time in the company of the normally resident shoal. The chub were reasonably scattered and I had attempted a selective cast at the big one with double freelined lobworm. Although the cast was accurate enough, a supercharged two pounder had seen the lobs hit the surface, and had obviously made up its mind that nothing was going to beat him to dinner! He must have taken those lobs at 30mph, and the bite was impressive if the fish itself wasn't. Trouble was, it did nothing to calm the nerves of the big one, and he was off downstream in a great puff of silt. Foiled again.

Summer drifted into autumn, and then, one afternoon in early October, there was the chub again, slowly emerging from thick rushes under the opposite bank, almost directly under the road bridge. He was on his own, and this time I managed to get everything right. A double lobworm offering landed almost on his head, and he took them with an angry swirl, before rocketing back into the rushes from whence he came. Within seconds, he was stuck solid.

Keeping calm, I waded slowly across river, going over both waders in the process, until I stood alongside the hole in the rushes where the chub had entered. Carefully, I ran my hand down the line, freeing it from the stems as I did so. Eventually, the line lifted out of the snags and I was temporarily in contact with the fish again. On feeling renewed pressure, the chub shot out the other side of the rush bed, and then the line parted. I looked at the limp line fluttering back towards me and, at that moment, had never felt as gutted in my angling career. Later, after a soothing cup of tea, I vowed that I would not rest until that chub lay in my weigh bag.

Catching that fish became an increasing obsession, and I fished hard until December 1962, but I was never again to find it. The autumn rains lifted the level, making visual contact impossible, and although several good chub were caught from the swim, I was not to bank the one I was after. And then came the big freeze, and for those of you who are too young to remember, it started snowing on Boxing Day, continued unabated for almost two days and then the temperature sank to well below zero. And there it stayed until early March. I remember becoming so acclimatised to the cold that, on the rare days when the temperature climbed to just sub zero at midday, it felt quite warm and I walked around in shirt sleeves.

Fishing virtually came to a standstill. During the early days of the freeze, I did manage to fish through the ice on my local River Leam for a while, but as the ice thickened that also became a waste of time. Many waters were wiped out by the extreme conditions, and dozens more suffered massive, although not total, fish kills. Throughout this period, I was concerned about the fish on my beloved Claydon Brook, a very shallow tributary which could suffer badly. I was particularly concerned about my special adversary. Would he survive the winter so that we could do battle again?

My early forays in June 1963 were not encouraging so far as the big one was

concerned, although I did manage a new personal best on opening day, a clonker of 5lb 10oz on slug. For several weeks, I searched to no avail. Then, on a never to be forgotten day in August, I peered over the parapet of the small road bridge just after dawn, and spotted six chub lying in a huddle over

Another 'five' from the brook.

the gravel at the head of the run, under the overhanging branches of a dwarf willow. In the middle of the group was my old friend. He looked massive.

For ages that morning, I was in a frenzy of indecision. With the six chub in a fairly tight group, the odds were stacked against me that the big one would be first to a bait. I had gone down that road before and was not about to repeat the mistakes of the past. Eventually, I came to a decision, albeit a difficult one. I forced myself to ignore the fish until later in the day, when they would be more likely to be spread around, and spent the morning perch fishing.

At about 2.00pm, my date with destiny arrived. Creeping back into position by the bridge, hidden behind head high rushes, I spotted the leviathan over clear gravel in mid-river. About two yards nearer my bank, another good chub basked in the midday sun, but there was no sign of the other four fish. I felt it was now or never, and flicked out a freelined double lobworm hookbait, intending that it should land a yard or so upstream of my quarry. Nervous energy, however, played a malicious little trick on my casting arm, because, instead of landing in front of the big one, the lobs fell well short and actually landed between the two chub, closer if anything to the smaller fish. My heart sank as both fish darted forward, convinced the target fish would be beaten to the bait. For once, however, I was lucky. At the last moment, the smaller chub veered away, leaving the way clear for the monster to engulf the lobs at top speed, and then power away irresistibly to my left, into a bed of marginal lilies.

Following the loss of the chub in similar circumstances the previous summer, I had stepped up my gear to 8lb line and a size 2 hook, and now proceeded to take full advantage of the power reserve that gave me. From the word go, I applied intense pressure and the chub was literally heaved out of the cabbages before he could tie me up. Foiled in that, the fish rocketed across stream to the rushes that had witnessed last year's disaster. Again, however, I had learned my lesson well, and the reel was clamped hard as the fish strained every sinew to enter the foliage. Right on the edge of sanctuary, he rolled frantically, and at that moment the battle was won. I was from then on in total control, and a few moments later my elation spilled over as I heaved my prize ashore.

I kneeled staring at that chub for ages, drinking in the moment. In truth, it was obviously an old fish, with several scales missing and being badly scarred on one flank, especially on the root of the tail where there was an ugly flesh wound, long healed. It was also quite lean, possibly because of a legacy of a long cold winter with almost no feeding, although enormously long, and I firmly believe that, had I made that chub's acquaintance a couple of years earlier, it would have gone well over seven pounds. As it was, the fish bottomed the scales to 6lb 12oz.

To this day, that old warrior remains my personal best chub, 37 years after the event, and will always retain a very special place in my heart.

An Old Friend

In the summer of 1964, I was heavily into the big roach of the Claydon Brook, taking many nice fish to 1lb 14oz on stewed wheat, laying on alongside lily pads. It was mid-morning in August and I had taken two good roach when a massive chub materialised over the bait. For ten minutes or more, it fed in the swim, without ever looking likely to take my hookbait, before disappearing once more into the undergrowth.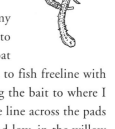

Having located that chub, which I thought certainly 6lb, my interest temporarily waned with the roach and I determined to put that chub in my net. With that in mind, I put aside the float rod, armed as it was with 2lb line, and rigged my second rod to fish freeline with 6lb line and a size 4, baited with two lobs. Carefully lowering the bait to where I had seen the chub first enter the swim, and laying most of the line across the pads where it could not be seen, I settled down to wait, quietly and low, in the willow herb.

After half an hour, I was having persistent trouble with a pair of swans who had discovered my bed of wheat, and the damn things would insist on crossing and re-crossing the little clearing. Soon the inevitable happened, or so I thought. I had been expecting one of the birds to foul the line at any moment, and so I gave out a curse as the line suddenly tightened and the rod top flew round. However, when something heavy surged downstream and the two swans serenely continued swimming upstream, it was obviously a case of misdiagnosis.

Belatedly, I got my act together. In a matter of seconds, the big chub had surged completely through the cabbage patch, miraculously taking the line through without it snagging, and was now charging around in the shallows about twenty yards away. The battle was over in less than two minutes, the chub having fought with little intelligence, and I was soon weighing my second biggest chub ever. It didn't quite make six pounds, scaling 5lb 14oz, but what an immaculate specimen!

Unlike my 6lb 12oz fish, this latest capture was a typical Upper Ouse specimen, short, fat and pristine. The feature that made the fish quite easily recognisable was a slightly deformed top lip, almost like a piscine hair lip.

In July 1966, the river was perfect for summer chubbing with natural baits, low, clear and weedy. With clear blue sky and hot sun, visibility was excellent, even for my short sighted eyes, and I was taking a couple of good fish most days after I had finished with my early morning perching.

On this one very special day, I had decided to go chubbing from the off, and had settled into the bridge pool well before daybreak. Once again, I was on my favourite bait of the time, double lobworm, freelined. Just as dawn was breaking, a good pull had heralded the arrival of the first fish of the day, a chunky 4lb 10oz specimen.

Once it was fully light, I could see there were no other big chub in residence. I moved down to a lovely bend in the river which I had labelled the rushes swim, on account of the dense reeds in mid-river that had bent over to form a dark tunnel. Under this tunnel was a clear gravel run about a yard wide and five yards long, terminating in a much deeper hole. That run was a favourite haunt of chub, which felt safe in their secluded home. There was no way of fishing that swim from the bank because of the set of the foliage, the only way being to get in the river and flick baits up into the tunnel itself, under the rush canopy. Fishing that way, I managed to extricate two more nice fish, including another well over four pounds, and then it was a trek further downstream in search of fresh targets.

By late morning, I was ensconced in my favourite chub swim, an area I called Thorn Bushes, because of the six yard run of dense blackthorns that adorned the opposite bank. Those bushes protruded out from the bank to form a far bank run, and as lilies stretched from the near bank to mid-river, there was a very narrow band of clear water to land a bait. I'd had lots of good chub and perch from here over the years, casting through little gaps in the branches at both the upstream and downstream extremities. In this way, I could present baits right under the foliage.

My first cast was to the downstream branches, and the take was literally instantaneous. As soon as the lobs hit the water, the surface erupted and a four and a half pounder was subsequently landed in short order. With the disturbance that fish created I felt there was no point trying a second cast. I moved immediately to the upstream end and once again my cast was perfect, the lobs sailing through the tiny gap in the branches to land in the dark water almost under the opposite bank.

Although there was no immediate response, the cast had been so perfect that I decided to allow the bait to lie still for a few minutes, while I broke out my flask and sandwiches. For ten minutes or so, I sat in silent bliss, alone in the country with just the kingfishers and moorhens for company. That scenario was paradise then and it is now.

The effects of my early start and the hot sun soon began to make my eyes droop, but my reverie was rudely interrupted when the line suddenly lifted sharply and then tightened. The rod lurched forward on the rest and then a big chub shot from under the branches and dived into the mid-river cabbages. As it rolled, I could see it was a whacker and my heart was in my mouth until it was safely captive in the net mesh. As I lifted it clear the first thing I noticed was that distorted top lip. Here was my friend of two years ago, looking fatter than ever and weighing an immensely pleasing 6lb 4oz.

To ensure that the day was made even more memorable, I was back in the same swim two hours later. Fishing exactly the same way, I was to take my last fish of the day, another cracker of 5lb 4oz, making that July day of 1966 the first time I ever took two chub of over five pounds in a day. Even now, 34 years after the event, the details of that special day are vivid in my memory.

We must all have gone fishing from time to time when we wished we hadn't bothered as soon as we arrive. Whether that be through worries at work or at home, or health problems, sometimes we can't get into it, whatever we try. That's how I felt one miserable day in January 1967, just after New Year.

I'd been quite ill over the festive period, spending several days in bed, and felt that some fresh air in the country may be just the tonic I needed. Not long after my arrival at the Brook, I knew that I had made a mistake, being violently sick in the undergrowth not long after I had arrived on the bank. Common sense dictated that I ought to return home straight away but, as I felt quite light headed, I decided

4lb 10oz chub & 3lb 2oz perch, summer 1966.

to sit quietly for an hour or so to clear my head. To ward off the now steady, cold drizzle, I erected my umbrella in the upper Thorn Bushes swim, directed a legered lob hookbait under the far bank trees, and then sat back to relax, rod on rest. I would be doing no dashing about today.

Unusually for that swim under normal winter conditions, there was no activity from perch and for several hours I sat there unmoving, with intermittent waves of stomach cramps making the whole event one of controlled misery. By lunchtime, with nothing having passed my lips except hot tea, I was feeling marginally better and starting to take an interest in the fishing. After having recast the lobs as far under the foliage as possible, I retreated further under my brolly as the rain got progressively heavier, and then the rod shot off the rest. I have seen barbel bites less fierce. The fight winter chub give is often far more impressive than their summer performance, and this was no exception as the battle ebbed and flowed under the blackthorn branches. Fortunately, despite the daunting appearance of the swim, there were no sunken branches or exposed roots to foul things up, and I was soon landing a big chub which I again recognised instantly as my old friend from six months previously. Once again, he weighed 6lb 4oz, and as soon as I had weighed and returned him, I packed up. I was back home hours earlier than planned, with another massive chub capture under my belt, but this time almost by default.

I said earlier that when I had the fish at 6lb 4oz the first time, it was the first occasion that I had ever taken a brace of chub exceeding five pounds. What must the odds be of the second such occasion involving exactly the same fish. That is

My wife, Fran, with chub of 5lb 10oz.

exactly what happened in February 1971. On a cold day's wandering chubbing, with legered crust, I'd taken a couple of fours early on and arrived at my favourite Thorn Bushes swims around midday. I had two bites from there in fairly quick succession, from fish of 5lb 4oz and 5lb 14oz. The bigger one was my old friend, now going back in condition, and by an amazing coincidence the other fish was the same five pounder that had accompanied him in 1966. That day, I had four chub for 19lb 15oz, which is some average.

Little did I realise it at the time, but that session was one of the last times I was to seriously target the Claydon Brook chub for many years. Not long after that catch, the bore hole that supplied water to the then new town Milton Keynes was brought into service, dropping the level dramatically, and the perch disease struck. The fishery I had loved for ten years deteriorated rapidly and I was soon to move to pastures new. I look back on those ten years as among the most important in my development as a specimen hunter, and I am not ashamed to admit that I often think back to those good times with a tear in my eye. Without wishing to be over sentimental, I am 56 years of age now, with my best years behind me. Not long before his death, I met Tom Williams on the banks of his beloved Hampshire Avon and one thing he said has stuck with me. He said that, as you get old, the only thing you have left to look forward to is nostalgia. I feel I have many, many more big fish in me yet, God willing, but do find myself reminiscing more and more about past sessions the older I get. In those quiet moments, I often think of a friendly old chub with a deformed top lip.

TC Tench

During our formative years of carp fishing in the late sixties, Trefor and I were regular visitors to Marlborough Pool in Oxfordshire, and the journey took us past an appealing looking gravel pit, surprisingly scenic despite being sandwiched between two main roads. The pit appeared totally neglected, and although there were rumours of big bream, we never actually took the time to investigate further. Having no real interest in bream at the time, the water was one of those we intended to have a look at but never got round to.

By the mid-seventies, our summer target had switched to tench, principally at the water that is still a Mecca today, Sywell in Northamptonshire. In those days, Sywell had just started producing the odd six pounder, which was a gigantic tench then, and that was our target at the start of the incredible summer of 1976. Only a few weeks into the campaign we had both increased our personal best to 5lb 10oz and, although a six pounder still proved elusive, we were pleased with our progress.

And then came an evening I will never forget. I was sitting in Trefor's lounge, talking fishing, when the phone rang. It was a young friend of ours, Martin, who fished Marlborough extensively, and regularly reported his carping exploits to us. I heard Trefor say, "How big?" I assumed Martin had taken a good carp. But it wasn't a carp Martin had taken, but a tench, and what a tench. From that neglected gravel pit we had never bothered to investigate, Martin had banked a colossal tench of 7lb 14oz. He also told us of another fish to John Knowles of over eight pounds. At the time, the tench record stood at 8lb 8oz, and very rarely were sevens reported and never eights. So to hear of two fish averaging over eight pounds in a day, with one only an ounce or two off the record, was stunning.

Trefor and I realised that here was a water that was very special indeed, and we wasted no time in drawing up plans for the following season. Martin had invited us down to share in the fishing there and then, but we both felt it right to let him continue to reap the rewards for his efforts for the rest of the current season without interference from us. We would commence our operations in June 1977.

Trefor returning a 7 pounder.

The water actually did not have an official name, as it was never intended as a fishery but a site for depositing dredge spoil from the Thames. Those few who were fishing the water had tacit approval from the owners, Thames Conservancy, and so had known it as the Thames Conservancy Pit, which quickly became TC Pit.

When Trefor and I investigated the legality of the fishing, the Thames Conservancy stance was that, although not officially allowed, they turned a blind eye to anglers' activities so long as there was no trouble on the water.

The few anglers who were fishing TC before our association in June 1977 were guarding the fishing jealously, which was perfectly understandable, and there is no doubt that the presence of two intruders from Coventry was resented. It took only two weeks of the new season for that resentment to surface, and although I have no wish to expand on that here, I can tell you that it took several months before we could fish TC in relative harmony with other anglers.

Our first session had produced very little, but on the second Friday Trefor arrived at dusk, after a Cherwell chubbing session, and settled into a swim very close to the access to the water, as much for convenience as anything else. He would not be fishing at night, being badly in need of sleep, but commence tenching at dawn.

Shortly after daybreak, Trefor landed a magnificent tench of 7lb 2oz, a fish that would have been beyond our wildest dreams twelve months previously. When he came round my house and gave me the news, I determined that I would fish the same swim from Wednesday until Saturday the following week. Trefor had a barbel trip planned.

In the event, I was unable to fish there, two youngsters on their summer holidays being encamped in the swim. But I did discover another good looking area about fifty yards away and eagerly set up camp.

The few days that followed were idyllic, and although I was not to emulate Trefor with a monster tench, I had several cracking fish to well over five pounds and at least saw a definite six before it did me in the rushes. The session was also memorable for a bite I can see even now. I remember filling the kettle just as the swingtip on the left-hand rod shot up. The next second, the rod hurtled forward dragging the front rest completely out of the ground. I literally catapulted myself off my seat, grasping the rod butt in mid-air as it was about to vanish into the lake, and then held on from my kneeling position in the margins as yards of line whistled off the spool. What an electrifying scrap that was, from a male barely reaching 4lb!

For the remainder of that 1977 summer, we fished TC regularly, never catching anything above average and I began my campaign on June 16th 1978 still searching for my elusive six pounder. I had cut a new swim from a thicket of alders the previous day, to avoid the possibility of fishing a prebaited swim, which Trefor had done inadvertently when he took his seven pounder. Just let anyone accuse me of swim jumping this year!

The swim featured an interesting gravel bar at about thirty yards, and on the evening of the 15th I introduced two tins of sweetcorn along this bar, together with

First catch on flavoured maggots, 5lb 12oz, 5lb 14oz and 7lb 1oz.

breadcrumbs, chopped worms and flake samples. Fishing would begin at first light.

In the dawn mist, a large piece of flake was cast out on the left hand rod, the right being baited with lobworm, and I settled down to wait, a fresh cup of tea very welcome in the early morning chill. Several hours passed uneventfully, and by mid-morning my hay fever was giving me hell, the weather having become oppressively hot and humid.

In late morning, I had my first sign of a bite, a very twitchy affair on a piece of flake, which never developed into anything positive. Ten minutes later, I decided to scale down the bait size on that rod and rebaited with two grains of corn. I'd only just reset the swingtip after the cast when it shot up and the rod slid forward in the rest, as a big tench kited to my left. It was a memorable, pulsating scrap, with the tench twice weeding me, but eventually she was mine. As that superb fish slid over the net rim, I knew that my search for a six pounder was over. For a

My 7lb 12oz fish taken in 1979.

moment, my incessant sneezing and running eyes were forgotten, as I confirmed 6lb 15oz and the euphoria of the moment took over.

That afternoon, my planned three day tench session was curtailed early as the pollen count rose to a level where I could hardly breathe because of allergic asthma. On the drive home, despite feeling so rough, I was delighted to have passed another milestone.

In the same way that Trefor's early seven pounder of 1977 was the biggest of that season, my 6lb 15oz fish was the biggest of 1978, and it was not to be until 1979 that either of us connected with another TC mega-tench. I had spent the opening few days on my own, taking a string of five pounders, and remarkably having TC pit to myself. On my second session the following week, I had intended to fish the same swim, but thick drifting algae blowing straight into my pitch forced a rethink. I scanned the water with my binoculars, and noticed rolling activity about fifty yards out from the shallows, some two hundred yards down the bank to my left. That was all the invitation I needed, and began to ferry my gear into this new position.

When I arrived at the section of bank adjacent to the bulk of the activity, it was very overgrown and required a little work to create a big enough area to set my camp and make myself comfortable, without destroying the ambience of the scene. All the while this was going on, tench rolled occasionally, and some of the backs were impressive, even at fifty yards range.

Initially, I decided against baiting, as I knew where the fish were, and went in simply with loaded feeders. However, despite continued activity, no bites resulted, and at the approach of dusk I introduced a quantity of loose feed by continual casting with an open-ended feeder. Before retiring for the dark hours (these were the days before Optonics and tench fishing was carried out in daylight only, with swingtips), I float fished in the margins with lobs until it was too dark to see, and in an exciting hour took several nice tench, to 5lb 14oz.

I was fishing again at dawn, with matched feeder rigs, using a bunch of maggots on one and a full sized lob on the other. After missing several bites on maggots that were nothing more than nudges on the tip, I decided on a bait change, replacing the maggots with a large piece of flake, changing the hook from a 12 to a 6. This amendment did the trick, and within minutes of recasting, I was away. Once again, a big TC fish was kiting to my left, taking it through a soft weedbed, but I was able to avoid becoming snagged. Several heavy thumps told me that this was a tench out of the ordinary, and, sure enough, a few minutes later, I looked on with bated breath as Rolf Wobekking, who was now fishing nearby, carefully weighed a tench for me that he had already estimated at eight pounds. When he announced 7lb 12oz, I was speechless. Never in my wildest dreams had I expected to catch such a huge tench in my lifetime.

Looking back on it now, that big fish contributed to the explosion in popularity of TC in the seasons that followed, together with a sudden rush of big bream that fell to the late Tony Charlett. The change was all too apparent on June 16th 1980, as there were many new faces on the bank. Trefor and I had settled into the swim from which I had taken my seven pounder, for the first week, and we had decided on a massive baiting campaign. We used a hundredweight of breadcrumbs, thousands of lobs and dozens of flake samples, and maintained the baiting accuracy by the simple expedient of Trefor swimming out, towing a baby bath full of feed while I directed operations from the bank. These were the days before the use of boats on pits was commonplace. That opening week, we had an incredible catch of big tench, with most of the fish over 5lb and several sixes and sevens, with Trefor surpassing my best by an ounce, at 7lb 13oz. He also lost, on the Thursday

night, a big bream, which was so greatly to influence our future fishing at TC. One of the new faces, Dave Boulstridge of Coventry, also made his own niche in TC folklore with the biggest fish then landed, an incredibly conditioned, hump backed tench of 8lb 12oz.

My last tench session of the 1980 summer was interesting, in that I landed a new personal best to equal Trefor's, catching the same fish twice in a matter of a few hours. I had located a clear gravel hump, only about eighteen inches under the surface in an otherwise weedy corner of the pit, at about fifty yards range. The hump was several yards wide and after a

Dave Boulstridge with Humpy, a giant of 8lb 12oz.

The biggest TC fish I ever saw, 9lb 7oz to Alan Rawden, unfortunately foul hooked.

few attempts I had managed to position a hookbait at each extremity of the feature. The right hand rod presented double maggot on a 12 while flake was the offering on the other. Both were feeder rigs.

At about mid-morning I had a screamer on the maggots and after an exhilarating tussle in and out of the weed beds eventually netted a very big tench, a fish which sported two unmistakable parallel scars on its flank just below the dorsal. I shouted to Trefor, who was fishing nearby, and he did the honours with the camera, as well as confirming a weight to equal his best. Congratulations received, I slipped the fish back into the water, and switched easily into contented mode.

Several hours passed without further incident and then, on impulse, I decided on one margin fished bait. Winding in the flake rod, I rebaited with a large lively lobworm and placed the bait only feet from the bank in a clear depression just over the marginal rushes. After adjusting the rod rests, I put the kettle on and relaxed once again. Minutes later, the rod top hammered round, just like a barbel bite, and I found myself attached to another powerful adversary. After another enjoyable fight, a big tench rolled into the net. The first thing I noticed was those scars. Just to be certain I examined and weighed the fish. Sure enough, there was the previous hook mark and the fish still weighed 7lb 13oz. It must be unique for a personal best fish to be caught twice in one day.

Although I was to take several six pounders in the year that followed, 1981, the season was dedicated to bream fishing, as you will read later, and I never did the tench justice. In fact, our fishing was designed to avoid tench bites, if possible. In the summer of 1982, however, I was once again targeting those lovely TC tench, eight pounds being the barrier to beat. That was one target that was never achieved, 7lb 13oz remaining my biggest ever TC fish.

The tench fishing in 1982, although still good, was changing in two ways. Firstly, the vastly increased angling pressure meant that the fish were wising up to anglers' baits much more rapidly, which led in turn to fewer and more indecisive bites. Secondly, the average size of the tench started to drop quite noticeably, with three and even two pounders appearing regularly.

In 1982 I started my experiments with flavoured baits, having taken a leaf out of the book of that tremendous Northampton angler Alan Smith, who had done a lot of work along the same lines with Sywell fish. I remember well the first occasion I ever used flavouring at TC. It was the last morning of a three day stint and, with about six hours left before I had to make tracks for home, I was on a blank. I had Andy Barker and John Cadd either side of me, about fifty yards away, and they were similarly biteless. Both my end rigs were feeders with maggot hookbaits, and I remembered some pineapple flavouring in my bag that I had originally bought for reservoir roaching. I decided to flavour the hookbait on one rod only, leaving the other plain for comparison. Within minutes of casting out the first flavoured offering, it was away and in a very short space of time I had landed five tench to 7lb 1oz, as well as losing a couple of other fish in the weed. Throughout this spell, the plain maggots remained untouched, and both John and Andy blanked.

During what remained of the 1982 summer, I used pineapple flavourings on every trip, catching every time, but never quite so dramatically as on that first occasion.

What the experience did do, however, was open my eyes to the possibilities of flavourings in overcoming bait shyness in the tench, and in the summer of 1983 I extended my repertoire into flavoured pastes. One of my earliest concoctions was to result in one of the most remarkable tench catches I have ever seen.

Terry Jones with first confirmed TC nine pounder.

*My biggest ever from TC,
7lb 13oz.*

Again, I have Alan Smith to thank in no small way. We had many discussions on tench baits on the banks of TC, and one I remember vividly was when Alan had said quite how positive the reaction of Sywell fish had been to both yellow feed and almond flavouring. Consequently, in July 1983, I arrived for a three day tench session with a ball of yellow almond paste in my rucksack.

During the first day, I fished one rod on flavoured maggots and the other on lobs, having introduced quite a few free offerings of my paste in the loose feed. Once again, there were anglers either side of me and by the second morning we were all tenchless. At mid-morning, one of my rods was changed to almond paste and I must admit that I was not prepared for the reaction of the tench. They went absolutely crazy for the new bait and for the rest of that day and most of the next it was non-stop action. I know that I landed over thirty good tench, losing a dozen others in the thick weed and missing several more indications. All in all, I must have had about fifty bites, most of them butt ringers. During this time, both my companions fishing maggots blanked and I had but one solitary bite on lob, which I missed.

As with the pineapple maggots, the first catch on the almond paste was the most dramatic and that gave a reliable clue. It seemed that something different saw the tench lose all their inhibitions at first, before quickly wising up. Of course, much of this is old hat now, but it was new and exciting at the time.

This thinking led me to change my baits regularly during this period, and it is a fact that the first catch to each variant was usually the best. Nothing was ever as dramatic as the almond, although maple cream ran it close. Another flavour, which gave me one good catch and then died completely was vanilla, a flavour that was also a reliable one to use on maggots.

During my years at TC, from 1977 to my last visit in 1986, I was sad to see the decline in the fishery, a decline that accelerated visibly after the publicity attached to our bream campaign in 1981. With the quality of the fishing, after those first few giant tench were caught in the seventies, it was inevitable that the TC secret would be blown. I feel slightly guilty that the publicity surrounding some of our earlier catches may have been a contributory factor to the decline of a once gorgeous water.

Down South

The Dorset Stour Throop Fishery

The Stour has the distinction of being the venue for the first five pound chub of my big fish career, which was taken on a summer holiday at the famous caravan park near Iford Bridge, at Christchurch, in 1962. Strangely, it was to be six years before my return in 1968 with members of the Coventry Specimen Group, when we began to make regular visits to Dorset, targeting the chub and barbel of the famous Throop fishery. Most trips saw good fish landed, without anything earth shattering, and by the early seventies, Trefor and I were starting to conduct some more intensive campaigns. By 1972, chub to just over five pounds and barbel to over seven were taken by one of us on most trips and then, in September 1972, I was to take a barbel which was by far and away the biggest either of us had ever seen at the time. It was to stay my personal best for fifteen years.

For a few weeks, we had been concentrating on the swims immediately above the by-pass bridge, which we had been told produced barbel of a higher average weight than the norm. On our previous trip, two weeks before, Trefor had taken one of our biggest to date, about eight and a half pounds, and we had high hopes of perhaps breaking the nine pound barrier. We were fishing side by side, with my being about thirty yards downstream of Trefor, presenting my bait in a deep gully in midstream over a large bed of streamer. As there were gravel shallows immediately downstream, I felt that my swim was a perfect choice, especially towards evening, when the light began to fade.

Trefor and I had been in position about two hours, steadily feeding our swims with cubes of luncheon meat, and presenting one inch cubes of the deadly 'pink perfection' on size 4 hooks to 8lb Maxima. Dusk was approaching, with both of us biteless, and then I felt the merest pluck on my finger. This was followed by a quick succession of tiny taps on the rod top and a sensation

First Throop barbel, 7lb from near School Bridge.

on my finger as if it were being sandpapered. I had previously ignored several isolated taps, obviously from dace, but this sensation was just somehow different. So I struck, and immediately realised the problem, or thought I did. The rod hooped over, and stayed there, unmoving. For another two minutes, everything was solid, and I became convinced that the streamer fronds had somehow caught the line, giving me the strange indications, but snagging me solid. I remember getting off my seat and shouting to Trefor that I was snagged, but I will never forget his reply. He shouted for me not to do anything rash, like pulling for a break. He was sure a barbel was on the end. Another minute passed, and then Trefor was proved gloriously correct, as the barbel suddenly stopped its cat and mouse tactics and shot downstream with great purpose.

The fight was totally different from that given by the smaller barbel I had so far been used to, in that it fought slow and with power, rather than sprinting around, and several more arm aching minutes passed before Trefor was able to scoop our prize ashore. By now, it was nearly dark.

We knelt side by side looking at the magnificent creature, and were both convinced it was our first double. It was obviously my personal best by a mile, and when Trefor eventually declared 9lb 12oz, I was in a state of total euphoria. Trefor and Mick Nicholls, who was fishing downstream and came up to witness the fish, have both said that the sight of the magnificent fish stirred them into the barbel obsession that now grips them, in Trefor's case to the exclusion of all others.

There is a strange fact about that barbel. Before I caught it, I had read in articles, by Dick Walker among others, of these rasping type barbel bites, but that was the first I had ever experienced. As I write, 28 years later, I am still waiting for my second! Most barbel bites to a downstream presentation give an unmistakable, solid thump.

Earlier, I mentioned an eight pounder taken by Trefor two weeks previously. There is quite an amusing anecdote connected to that fish. We were fishing the same swims, and this time it was Trefor who was in first, about an hour before dark. For some reason, we only had one landing net with us, placed between us, and Trefor shouted for my assistance. As I started to walk towards him, I was looking directly intro the most brilliant setting sun, and mistook a solid mass of surface weed, algae and scum in the margins for solid ground. I quite literally walked straight into the river, and disappeared. It was about seven feet deep right in the edge. As I came to the surface, coughing and spluttering, Trefor gave me a rollicking for pratting about when I was supposed to be attending to netting a fish for him. I was really touched that he was so concerned for my safety!

Eventually, after scrambling out and successfully landing Trefor's barbel for him, I squelched back to the car to try and rustle up some dry clothing. All I could find was an old jumper full of holes, a pair of lightweight rubber overtrousers and some tatty old carpet slippers. Later that evening, I sat with Trefor in a café still dressed the same way, and from the looks we got I am sure most people thought that Trefor was gay and I was his hippy boyfriend with a rubber fetish!

To this day, I have never beaten that nine pounder from Throop, but perhaps one of my most memorable barbel trips there was in September 1975, when I discovered just how good flood conditions are for barbel fishing. When I arrived at dawn on Saturday morning, the weather conditions were simply diabolical. We'd had a lot of rain in the Midlands, but on the south coast a monsoon was in full force, with torrential rain driven by storm force winds. I remember sitting in the car for half an hour waiting for it to ease, but it showed no signs of abating so I donned all my waterproof gear and ventured out into that inhospitable scene. The wind really was incredible, difficult to walk against, and broken branches and bits of foliage were hurtling across the countryside. It was reminiscent of tumbleweed in those old Western movies.

On my trips to Throop, I used to park in the little lane by the school, and one of the first swims you come to is the famous Barbel Bend. When I arrived there, I was pleased to see the river still in its banks, but only just. I knew the river had to be carrying eight feet of floodwater, and this seemed an ideal swim to fish in the circumstances. The only drawback was that I would be fishing into the teeth of the wind, with driving rain in my face. It's a strange thing about fishing in such shocking weather conditions. After a while, in a perverse kind of way, it can be quite enjoyable once you can't get any wetter. For an hour or so, I concentrated hard, my luncheon meat bait only inches from the near, high bank that characterised the swim. And then, at mid-morning, the rod slowly bent round. However it was no barbel, but a huge clump of weed drifting on the flood. After that first encounter, the drifting flotsam problem steadily worsened through the day until I was forced to clear my tackle every few minutes.

By mid-afternoon, after having tried several other swims and being hit by the same problem, I was back at Barbel Bend. All I could do was keep my rod tip level

The Dorset Stour in flood.

with the bank, the bait literally touching the bottom of the near bank, in an attempt to keep the line clear of debris at least for a decent interval. In this I was reasonably successful, and could manage perhaps ten minutes between casts before I was forced to wind in again. But it did serve its purpose. Just after repositioning my bait for the umpteenth time, the rod gave a sudden, vicious lunge, and eventually, after a really tiring scrap in the heavy water, which saw the net continually washed away by the strong flow, I managed to land a plump barbel of 7lb 10oz. Under the circumstances, I was over the moon with that fish and, as it was approaching dark, packed up there and then and made my way back to the car for a welcome respite from the elements. An hour later, I was enjoying hot fish and chips and a pint mug of steaming tea.

The next morning, back on the bank at Barbel Bend, I surveyed an incredible scene. Water was now in the fields, the river was a surging brown torrent full of floating trees, hedges, even a garden shed came swooping past. And the wind was now just awesome. It had been gale force the day before, now it must have been approaching hurricane force and, as the rain was still unremittingly heavy I would be in for another wild day's fishing. I have to admit that for a while I considered whether it was even worth starting, the conditions looked so impossible. But I thought, what the hell. I've driven 150 miles to fish and if I go home now I'm going to catch nothing. So if I fish, I can't do any worse. So, I fished.

As the day wore on, though, the decision to fish seemed more and more ridiculous. Sometimes, a bait hardly hit bottom before it was whisked away by drifting rubbish and I remember making three casts in three minutes about 100 yards above the School Bridge and thinking, this is crazy, I'll pack up and make tracks for home. And then the rod bent round again, but this time when I pulled, the 'weed' pulled back. Next second, the clutch screamed as something shot into mid-river, using the strong flow to maximum advantage. What a battle that was, made even more dramatic by picking up a raft of weed in the process, and when I eventually netted the fish, my arm was dropping off. Another barbel of 7lb 9oz had thoroughly vindicated my decision to fish despite the difficulties, and on the strength of that fish I decided to persevere until dark. An hour later, in the same swim, despite continually being forced to cast and retrieve, an unmistakable lunge heralded the arrival of a second good fish of 7lb 4oz.

The final two hours were spent in Barbel Bend, and at last the rain was easing although there was no diminution in wind speed. For some strange reason, those final hours also saw a dramatic easing of the drifting rubbish problem, and I managed probably the most relaxing fishing of the weekend. I was fishing efficiently at last, and when it was time to go I had landed a further two fish, of 7lb 7oz and 8lb 2oz, to round off a truly memorable session.

That afternoon, two fellow barbel anglers, as idiotic as me for fishing in those conditions, came close to losing their lives. In fact, I truly believe I saved one man's life. It happened like this.

The first fish I had from Barbel Bend that evening was the eight-pounder, and I fetched the angler from the swim upstream to do the honours with the camera. Photographs taken, we were standing chatting, and he stepped back right to the edge of the bank. Barbel Bend was steeply undercut at that point, that's why it was

The lovely Hampshire Avon.

Landing an Avon chub for Bob James.

such a good flood swim, but obviously quite dangerous in high water. I was just advising him not to stand so close to the river when the bank collapsed and he vanished into the torrent. Luckily, my landing net was right beside me, and I threw myself on my stomach with the handle in the water, which the chap fortunately managed to grab. By walking him downstream a little way, where the river shallowed a fraction, I was eventually able to haul him out, but it was a close call. If he'd have missed that handle on his first grab, I think he'd have been swept away. It was a chastening experience.

The second incident was, at the time, quite hilarious for one with a warped sense of humour, but in hindsight that angler was exceptionally lucky as well. Facing me on the opposite bank from Barbel Bend an angler was attempting to use his umbrella, as the strong wind was behind him. Even that was difficult, but he eventually hit on the bright idea of lashing the brolly pole to the leg of the chair he was sitting on, so that his weight kept it in position. It worked, after a fashion, but of course what he hadn't reckoned on was what would happen when his body weight was removed, if he stood up for instance. Eventually, what I feared could happen, did. He wound in to clear weed, and must have half stood up to reach the line. A sudden fierce gust of wind got under the brolly, lifted it and the chair and catapulted the whole lot into the river, angler with it. It would have made a classic 'You've Been Framed' sequence, but in the strong current could easily have led to a tragic conclusion. As it was, he eventually scrambled out, minus chair and brolly, and the last I saw of him was a sorry, sodden figure shuffling off downstream. To my shame, I sat there giggling like a schoolgirl for half an hour.

If I've never landed a massive barbel at Throop, I've certainly hooked one, on the last day of the season in 1974. By a strange quirk of fate, that occurred on the day I had earlier taken my best ever Throop chub of 5lb 6oz, from one of my favourite chub swims, Pig Island. After a terrific day's chubbing, I'd arrived at the tail of Pig Island about an hour before dark, when I had to be off the water. For perhaps forty minutes, I steadily fed the swim with mashed bread and fresh breadcrumbs and then, as dusk was settling over the Stour valley, the tip whipped round and I was in battle with my big chub. That night, I was fishing with a friend from work, Fred, and after taking some photographs for me, Fred wanted to fish a final ten minutes. So, on impulse, I decided on one last cast myself with a huge lump of cheese paste. I felt the change of bait may give me a chance of a final day barbel to put the icing on the cake. What sweet icing it would have been if I'd have managed to land the barbel that hammered my rod round only moments after the cast. I said at the time, and have not revised my estimate since, that barbel was close to 13lb, a massive fish in its day. It is no disrespect to Fred, who was quite inexperienced, but had Trefor been alongside me, that barbel would have been landed. I had brought it upstream without too much difficulty, and then it rolled almost under the rod top. Fred had the net in hand by now, but instead of scooping the fish out, delayed a fateful few seconds and the chance was lost. The fish righted itself and then surged across river towards a large boulder of clay that had toppled from the bank in earlier floods. On my chub tackle, I was unable to stop the fish in its tracks, and within a minute there was a horrible grating on the line as it fouled under that boulder. The end was inevitable. The next time the barbel made a dash, the line, totally snagged, simply parted, and I was left to reflect on what might have been.

As far as Throop chub are concerned, no one particular fish or catch of fish really stands out over any other, but that is not to say that the fishing was not exceptional. It was, and therein lies my problem. This book simply has not the room to accommodate stories of the dozens of fabulous chub trips to Throop that Trefor and I enjoyed in the seventies. We lost count of the four pounders, they were so numerous, and five pounders were by no means uncommon, although 5lb 8oz was about the ceiling weight in those days. Obviously, those are almost average fish today from the water. Throop was then, and still is, a truly fabulous fishery.

Longham

At the start of the 1986 season, I seemed as far away as ever from my dreamed of double figure barbel from the Wensum, and decided on a change of venue for the summer months. I had by now formed a close friendship with Stef Horak, who knew the southern rivers extensively, having lived in Hampshire for a few years. It was Stef who told me that I would realise my dream at Longham, on the Stour. Consequently, I made my first two day trip to the venue in July, taking an eight pounder plus enough eels to keep me in pike baits for the winter. That began an exhausting campaign into early October that saw me making the 300 mile round trip every week, sometimes just for one day's fishing, and although I caught plenty more barbel and a few good chub, the early eight pounder remained my best by quite a margin. I seemed to be catching sixes every week. I was taking my Wensum bad habits down south!

I drove home after a fruitless October session vowing that I would not return until conditions had improved. The river was very low and stale, we had just had the first frost and the temperature had dropped sharply. Conditions for barbel were far from ideal, in fact a sudden temperature drop in late autumn after warm summer conditions can often be the hardest conditions of the lot.

A telephone call from Stef just after I'd arrived home changed my plans completely. He'd booked time off work for the following week specially so he could come with me to Longham and so, rather than mess him about, I confirmed that I was up for it. I would have one last session before winter conditions proper set in.

If anything, conditions on the following Thursday were even worse than when I had left the week before. The water was lower than ever, a very sharp frost the night before had put a white blanket everywhere, and we caught exactly what I thought we would, next to nothing. Stef had a very small barbel, but even that, I felt, was a major achievement. That night, we retired to the pub and the beer flowed quite freely for a few hours as we discussed matters piscatorial. Soon, it was closing time and we made our way back to the quiet country lane where we were spending the night. Stef doesn't drive, and these were the days before I owned a camper van, so we were both sleeping in my Granada hatchback.

Sometime in the early hours, I woke up feeling decidedly unwell. You know the symptoms, all hot and sweating, everything spinning. Next moment, I was sprawled in the undergrowth, throwing up. It was probably half an hour before I felt safe to get back in the car, but that was quite long enough to know that a really hard frost was forming. Things were looking better and better!

Next morning, fishing was the last thing on my mind. Had I been alone, I would have gone home without a second thought, I felt that terrible. However, I felt a little guilty because of Stef's predicament. He relied on me for transport home, and had booked holiday specially for the trip, so I gritted my teeth and decided to make the best of it. All that passed my lips for breakfast was a pint of freezing cold water.

At that time, access to the best swims at Longham required a good mile walk, and as we crossed the fields the bitter cold air started to have a therapeutic effect in clearing my head a little. By the time we'd reached the swims, I felt almost back to normal, but was still convinced we were totally wasting our time as far as catching barbel was concerned. Stef, however, was the eternal optimist. As we stood looking in a swim that he had convinced me would hold my elusive first double, we simultaneously caught a fleeting glimpse of coral fins, and then the outline of a very big barbel, before it ghosted back under the streamer bed at the downstream extremity of the swim.

I bowed to Stef's knowledge of the river and the conditions, and he advised me to bait lightly, but accurately, with about a pint of hemp and half a pint of mixed maggots and casters. That done, I waited half an hour before lowering a feeder rig, incorporating a two foot tail presenting two casters on a size 12. Then I sat back to wait. To be honest, I was far from confident in the cold conditions, and although the barbel periodically flashed at the bottom of the five foot swim, ninety minutes passed without incident. I remember my attention wandering to Stef moving swims and then, without warning, the rod was nearly ripped from my grasp as something big shot through the streamer. After several yards of line had been taken, everything went ominously solid, and pulling from different angles made no difference whatever. I was completely snagged. It wasn't difficult to see the problem. In clear view, at the base of the streamer root alongside which my bait had been presented, the feeder still lay there, and it had obviously been forced up the main line by being trapped against the root as the barbel had taken line. I would have no chance of landing the fish with the feeder trapped where it was, and I also had no idea where the fish was. It could have gone off in any direction. I knew it was still attached because, over the minutes that followed, there was the occasional lunge, and another yard or so of line would be lost.

Drastic action was required in that one of us had to go in and free the offending feeder and disentangle the line. I pointed out to Stef that he was younger than me and as I had the important job of holding the rod, the honour of retrieving the situation would rest with him. Besides, the river looked bloody cold! Stripped to his underpants, skin a fascinating pale blue tint in the cold air, Stef gingerly entered the river, following my line to the streamer root. Stef knew that the swim was about five feet deep, but when he suddenly vanished and came up spluttering I congratulated him in discovering a hitherto unknown depression! Unable to get any wetter, Stef soon managed to lift the feeder, and carefully brought it to the surface together with half the streamer bed. The barbel gave another frantic lunge, and two more yards of line whipped from the spool. One strand at a time, Stef broke the tresses away and then, all of a sudden, it was free. Abruptly, the barbel must have felt the easing of pressure and set off on a ten yard run. The line in Stef's hand turned abruptly upstream and tightened dramatically round his throat, almost garrotting him. He had to duck under water again to free himself. Obviously, the barbel had initially shot downstream through the streamer, and, with the feeder jammed, had turned back upstream.

At long last, after about forty-five minutes of mayhem, I was in direct contact with the barbel, as Stef emerged from the river, teeth chattering. There were no more dramas, although I thought for one horrible moment the fish was foul hooked when the line caught round a pectoral. Eventually, exactly one hour after I first hooked it, a huge barbel rolled in the net. Stef, forgetting the cold for a moment, shook my hand vigorously. I had my double after years of trying. Soon, we had confirmed 10lb 9oz and my elation at that moment knew no bounds.

There was quite a comical ending to the episode. I was at the time playing around with a new video camera, and Stef agreed to take a little footage for me. With the barbel still safely in the sack, I was giving him some instruction in the use of the camera, by leaping about on the bank while he practised focusing, zooming and so on. Remember, he was still only in underpants, dripping wet, on a freezing cold morning. Just at that moment, a woman went past on the opposite bank, walking her dog. The look on her face was a picture. I cannot imagine what she thought we were up to!

The Hampshire Avon

Although I have fished the Avon on and off since the late sixties, I have never had what I would consider a big fish from the river. I have taken lots of good barbel, specially from the Royalty and the Severals, but never a double. As far as the chub are concerned, the most interesting fishing has been at Ibsley, where I was forced to revise my tactics totally from those I normally used on the Midland rivers.

I first fished Ibsley in the seventies, but it wasn't until the early nineties that I conducted a serious campaign there. I devoted the last three months of the 1991 season in trying to tempt either a big chub or one of the exceptional roach that inhabited the river at the time. My first session in January was frantic. Fishing the famous Gorley Corner on the Ringwood ticket, I had only made my first cast about two minutes before the rod whipped round and I found myself attached to something that seemed hell bent on reaching the sea in record time. For a while, I thought I'd hooked the daddy of all barbel until a fresh run cock salmon eventually surrendered. Just over 8lb that weighed, a very entertaining little diversion.

Perhaps ten minutes later, I latched into a nine pound barbel, closely followed by an eight pounder and then, after a short break, a good chub of exactly five pounds. All those fish had come in the first hour, on meat, and after a quiet spell, I switched to legered crust with mashed bread feed. The change soon earned dividends when three bites in quick succession yielded two chub of 4lb 14oz apiece and then a gorgeous roach of 2lb 2oz.

3lb roach for Mark Vials.
First Royalty barbel I ever saw, nine pounds to a young, slim Terry Eustace.

All that action came in a total spell of under three hours and gave me a totally false picture of the fishing at Ibsley in general and Gorley in particular, because I was never to catch fish there as easily again. In subsequent trips, the river reverted to the dour fishery that I had been warned about, where fish rarely picked up big baits until the last knockings, and even then one fish was all you could normally expect.

One angler who regularly fished there at that time was Mark Vials, who certainly had the venue sussed. Mark fished with matched feeder outfits and ultra light tackle, and caught more than his share. The first session I fished

The Boathouse swim on the Royalty.

alongside Mark I was privileged to weigh and photograph a roach for him weighing a colossal 3lb 1oz. What a pristine fish that was, I wish I'd have caught it. Mark's advice radically changed my approach to the fishing at Ibsley and I gradually reverted to the ultra fine approach too. One day I remember is when I was fishing with a 3lb hooklink to a size 14 baited with two maggots, and was blanking impressively. I changed down to 2lb line, a size 16 and single maggot, and in the next hour took chub of 4lb 7oz, 4lb 9oz, 4lb 13oz and 5lb 5oz. I have always argued that in general you do not need very fine gear for big chub, and I still believe that, but I have to admit that Gorley Corner was the exception. Whether it was because it was so popular I don't know, but there is no doubt that the use of big baits there was asking to blank.

I suppose my most enduring memory of the Hampshire Avon is the week-long session at the end of the 1987 season on the Severals, which resulted in my decision to purchase a camper van ready for the next season. I had actually travelled to Ringwood to fish both the main river and the Kings Stream for the big roach, sleeping in my car. I spent my first day roaching, and the weather was absolutely freezing, with sleet on and off all day driven by a gale force east wind. When I packed up at night, I was soaked and numb. Those of you who have slept in a car will know the problems of having got wet. There is no way of drying your gear, so I had to make the best of it. Once I was settled down in my sleeping bag, I was reasonably warm, but the discomfort was further magnified next morning. With the wind even stronger, and snow flurries hurtling through Hampshire, there was no way I could prepare hot food. It is dangerous to use a gas cooker inside a cramped saloon with the windows closed, and opening windows or doors created so much draft it was impossible to keep the cooker alight. So I had to make do with a cold breakfast and water to drink all day as I could not boil water for my flask. By the third morning of this existence, with the arctic conditions showing no signs of relenting, I was mentally and physically wrecked and was forced to curtail my trip. As I drove home, I said never again. A month later, I had equipped myself with my first VW camper, and have never looked back since.

On the Beach

The Summer of '81

On June 16th 1981, Trefor West and I embarked on a campaign that was destined to be the most fascinating either of us have ever been involved in. After four years of intense tench angling at TC pit in Oxfordshire, we had decided to switch our attention to the very big bream the water contained. During the previous season, we had witnessed a magnificent eleven pounder for a friend, and Trefor had pulled out of a very big fish that had taken a tench bait. Those two events at last had instilled in us a desire to catch specimen bream, a species which had never inspired us previously.

Having agreed upon the campaign, we decided to commence operations in the swim where Trefor had lost the fish. This was a swim I had initially opened up in 1979 after seeing big tench roll, and we had enjoyed some quite spectacular tench action there during 1980.

Trefor arrived at the water two days before the season's opening, to both secure the swim we wanted and do advance baiting. What he found, however, was that the swim was already occupied by two new faces at the water, Des Taylor and Pete McMurray. News of our catches the previous season had obviously spread, and they had already been in residence for a few days! Luckily, we had anticipated that possible contingency and so Trefor moved in to our second choice area, a prominent point which had deep, weed free water within forty yards of the bank. I joined him in the swim in the early evening of the 15th and, all preparations complete, we awaited the midnight hour with the pent up excitement that only anglers can appreciate. Our bream hunt had begun.

To fully appreciate the euphoria that our eventual success generated, it is necessary to be aware of the full extent of our commitment to the task we had set ourselves. From the outset, we had decided to fish at least four days and nights every week in the chosen swim, until either we succeeded or the first frosts curtailed our activities. Our occupations at the time allowed me the time to fish from Thursday night until Sunday morning and Trefor from Friday night until Monday morning.

When our campaign started, we were well aware that the pace of the fishing would be extremely slow. Most of the big bream that had been taken over the years had been out of the blue, one off captures. That first week of the season in 1981 merely confirmed our expectations because, apart from a small handful of very average tench to occasionally liven up proceedings, there were many long, biteless hours. Not a sign of a bream did Trefor or I witness in our swim, but there was a little bream history created in our first choice swim on opening night. Pete McMurray, fishing where I

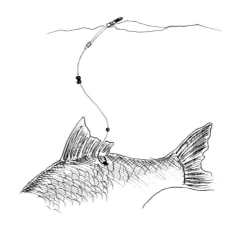

had taken a string of good tench a year earlier, increased the TC bream best to exactly 13lb in the early hours. What a magnificent fish that was, and one that fired our determination to fever pitch.

The next four weeks followed a similarly uneventful pattern, the occasional nice tench putting a bend in the rod, with a few sixes to 6lb 6oz. This period was the most difficult in which to maintain full concentration on the job in hand, as big tench went on a feeding binge in the shallows. Many sevens, an eight and the first authenticated TC nine pounder came out in that purple patch. Looking back on it now, Trefor and I were obviously a little blinkered in our approach at the time. We would have lost nothing in a short break after a big tench apiece, especially in light of the fact that, during this time, bream were observed spawning hundreds of yards from our swim. It was then that I witnessed one example of the modern malaise of "catch fish at all costs," in that an "angler" fished amongst those spawning bream with a float and a bait set at mid-water. It was obviously designed to foul hook and that is exactly what happened, with two double figure bream being landed, one hooked in the belly and one in the back. I wanted desperately to catch a double figure bream, but not that desperately.

And so we come to the night of Friday, 17th July 1981. By the time our preparatory work was completed, and a meal had been cooked and devoured, the sun was already setting deep orange in the western sky. The lake surface was mirror smooth, and over endless cups of tea Trefor and I talked, smoked, and waited. The atmosphere was heavy with expectation.

In the lengthening shadows, nothing moved to disturb the tranquillity until, with a suddenness that made us both jump, the quiet was broken by a loud shrill from an Optonic. One of my bobbins leapt up a few inches and then just as suddenly dropped to its original position. Seconds later, one of Trefor's bobbins did the same and we knew immediately that, at long last, there were bream in the swim. That type of line bite is a typical indicator of the presence of the broad flanks of our quarry.

For two hours, this activity continued unabated, during which time we lost count of the movements on our indicators. I had never before had to exercise such restraint. Striking at liners was the quickest way of spooking big bream, and we had to wait until feeding began in earnest, when we should get proper bites. For what seemed an eternity, we sat on our hands fifteen feet behind the rods, waiting for that first positive indication.

It came at a little before midnight. At last, on one of Trefor's rods, the indicator rose slowly and smoothly to the butt, and held. A sweeping strike, and immediately we knew that this was no tench. It was far too heavy, slow and ponderous. I remember Trefor being far from convinced that he had a bream on the end, in fact, he said that his lobworm bait had been taken by an average pike and he expected to be bitten off at any moment.

It was only when I switched on my torch, as the fish came in to the margins, that we realised that it was indeed a big bream. Moments later, I slipped the net under the fish and it was safely lifted ashore. There are certain angling moments to which it is impossible to do full justice with merely the written word. That was one of them, as Trefor and I knelt side by side admiring that magnificent bream, obviously a double, and the first fulfilment of our quest. After confirming a weight of 10lb 10oz and carefully consigning the fish to the gigantic keep net acquired specially for the purpose, Trefor and I shook hands in triumph.

Incredibly, only minutes later, Trefor was on his feet again, playing another heavy fish. I have to say that the fight was extremely poor considering the size of the fish, and it is as well that it was because, at an early stage in the contest, the bream fouled a second line. As the fish was slowly pumped towards the bank, line was disappearing off the second reel at an alarming rate. Not only that, where the two lines crossed in the margins was the focal point for an almighty birds nest that was soon jammed in Trefor's tip ring. With the bream still well out of netting range, it was clear that no more line could be won or given in the conventional manner and drastic action had to be taken, and quickly. Stripping in as much of the loose second line as possible, I wrapped it securely round my arm for retrieval later, before biting through it, to prevent further line from the second reel adding to the general chaos. I then instructed Trefor to walk back up the bank slowly, so that I could grab the reel line and hand line the fish into the net. One sudden kick from such a big fish would, of course, almost certainly have pulled the hook out, and so it was heart in the mouth stuff as the fish slowly approached the net cord. Thankfully, however, the fish behaved itself and we were soon weighing a fabulous fish of 12lb 10oz. What an incredible twenty minutes it had been.

That twelve pounder signalled the abrupt end of the activity that night and shortly afterwards I was on my way home. That must be one of the most frustrating moments of my angling career as, the following morning, I had to attend a vitally important sales meeting. Leaving a swim full of feeding bream was galling in the extreme and as I drove home in the early hours my mind was buzzing with it all. I was not at all surprised when Trefor had another superb fish of 10lb 8oz the following night and I was able to rejoin him on the Sunday evening. But it was too late, the bream were gone. We were not to find them again until September.

As the weeks slipped by, there was no further sign of bream. August was particularly gruelling, with flat calm, hot and oppressive days followed by chilly, misty nights. Although the two nights Trefor had caught were flat calm, they had been preceded by days where there was a good chop on the water. We both agreed that we needed the return of blustery conditions to stir things up a bit.

If conditions had not been good for bream in that period, the tench and perch certainly found them to their liking and most trips saw me take good tench without ever latching into a very big one. The real giants were still confined to the shallows, but I had one morning in particular when I caught three six pounders from

Trefor with a 10lb 8oz TC bream.

First success, 10lb 10oz and 12lb 10oz.

successive casts. Another problem was the increasing attention of perch, especially at dawn, and they weren't all small ones. Several fish to just over two pounds were a bonus, but obviously detrimental to the possibility of dawn feeding bream.

Trefor took our fourth bream in the first weekend in September, and for the first time I wondered whether I was actually destined to catch one. Over the previous three days and nights I had fished hard in a complete flat calm, with not a single bleep from an alarm. The nights were very cold and foggy and threatened the first frosts, but despite that, Trefor took over from me as usual and managed just a single bite, in the early hours of Sunday morning. At dawn, Trefor photographed another great bream of 10lb 5oz. My time, however, was running out. The first frost could not be far off, and the fishing would then get slower, if that were possible.

Early the following week, the weather changed at last, with a sustained low pressure system moving in from the west and moderate to strong winds, which were forecast to stay with us for several days. I knew that I had my best chance for weeks and Thursday morning again found me setting up camp for three days and nights. A brisk south-westerly meant that conditions were about perfect and as I sat in the shelter of my bivvy at dusk, a steaming mug of tea in my hand, I was in a high state of anticipation.

In the gathering dusk, the heavy swell rapidly dropped to a gentle ripple as the wind eased and for a couple of hours it was quite a pleasant evening, with one small tench coming to net. At about 11.00pm, however, there was an ominous increase in wind strength and then the heavens opened to a torrential deluge. It was time to batten down the hatches and for three hours that storm raged, with the rain so heavy it was difficult to see the bobbins.

The creaking and groaning from the bivvy and the howling wind made sleep but fitful at best and I remember glancing at my watch at about 1.00am. A cup of tea was indicated and just as I was climbing out of the sleeping bag there was a sudden scream from an Optonic. Within seconds the reel handle on my left hand rod was spinning crazily and I shot out of the bivvy to set the hook into something that was departing the scene at a real rate of knots. Big tench, I thought, as I was soaked in seconds. For half a minute that conviction remained, but then I was sadly disillusioned as an irate tufted duck crashed out of the water, and shot to my right, taking my other two lines with it. Things got no better as I brought the duck to the bank. I was happy to see that my hook was only lightly lodged in its bill but just as I was about to capture it, the bird set off down the bank like an Olympic sprinter. My despairing grab only resulted in my sprawling face down in the mud. I would like you to create a mental picture of the scene. It is the middle of the night, hammering down with rain, and with a wind so strong it is difficult to stand against. I am soaked to the skin, plastered in mud, as is my sleeping bag, which I have somehow dragged outside with me. All three Optonics are screaming at once as a demented tufted duck dashes around in a frenzy, knitting the lines into a mud encrusted tangle that has to be seen to be believed. All in all, total bloody chaos!

By the time I had successfully released the duck, I was totally demoralised and, in the dark and heavy rain, could not face the state of devastation my tackle had become. It would have to wait until morning. As I lay down in my wet gear in an attempt to get some sleep, I went through my entire repertoire of profanity, even inventing a few new words especially for the occasion.

The next day dawned bright and breezy, and within about an hour I was sorted out, there were three baits in position, my wet bedding and clothes were drying in the warm morning sun and I was enjoying the first cup of tea of the day.

I was soon to receive surprising consolation for the previous night's trauma. After landing three small perch on maggots, I decided on impulse to put out a longer cast using a big lobworm as bait, in the hope that a big perch might be on the fringes. At least I got that right, because the bait hadn't been out more than a few minutes before line was fizzing through the rod rings. Not for the first time, I was impressed with the fighting abilities of a big gravel pit perch. When it was eventually landed I knew it was the biggest I'd taken from the water. 3lb 1oz it weighed, the only three pound perch I know to have been taken from TC since my association with the water began.

During Friday afternoon, the wind veered round so that it was blowing strongly inshore, and I was becoming more and more convinced that something special was on the cards. So strong was my intuition that I stayed awake nearly all that night, but nothing transpired. That feeling remained unabated throughout Saturday. During the daylight hours a very strong wind kept a heavy swell on the surface, but, in early evening, the clouds parted, the water was bathed in the rays of the setting sun and the wind dramatically dropped. By dusk, the water was glassy smooth and the conditions were eerily reminiscent of that special night in July. That evening, I just could not relax.

My strange intuition was justified. By about 8.00pm, line bites had started on all three rods and I was nearly screaming in my impatience for something positive to develop. I knew my best chance had arrived, after four gruelling months of unfulfilled effort. At 9.00pm, my long vigil came to an end. Agonisingly slowly, the right hand bobbin began a slow crawl to the butt ring. My hand hovered over the rod, resisting the almost overpowering impulse to strike. It was a tortured few moments when the bobbin stopped some nine inches from the butt, but then it recommenced its slow ascent until all slack line had gone. Now was the moment of truth, and it is hard to describe my emotion as my strike was met by the satisfying thump of a big fish. The slow, heavy and sluggish fight told me that I had at last hooked a big bream, and I prayed that nothing would go wrong. About a minute into the contest, the fish was on the surface some thirty yards out and the moonlight gave me a clear view of a huge silvery shape gliding over the marginal weed fringe. Moments later, one of the most hard won specimen fish of my career was safely in the net.

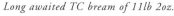

Long awaited TC bream of 11lb 2oz.

As long as I live, I shall never forget that evening. I remember trembling so much that it was several minutes before I could keep my hands steady enough to weigh the fish, when I was able to confirm 11lb 2oz. With the bream safely retained until morning, the euphoria suddenly took over and I remember letting out a loud shout of victory before doing an ungainly war dance round the bivvy! Perhaps that was the source of the rumours in the local paper

the following week about a witches coven being discovered in Oxfordshire!

I recommended fishing, and as with Trefor's first catch, the activity continued unabated until a second fish put in an appearance, a much smaller sample of 7lbs. Shortly after landing that, the sky clouded over, the wind picked up again and the swim died.

The last fish of that bream campaign was taken the following weekend, only days before the first frosts, when Trefor added an 11lb 4oz fish to the list, a fitting finale. Trefor and I are both agreed that, of all the memorable angling adventures we have shared, that TC bream campaign was one of the most stimulating and rewarding of our entire careers.

An Incredible Night

No history of TC would be complete without a description of one of the most remarkable nights in the history of specimen hunting. During the 1983 close season, I had made several trips to the water, looking for a feature to fish for bream away from the normal and now very popular swims. The feature would be preferably weed-free, as I was having misgivings about the efficiency of dragging bream swims. After hours of plumbing, I found what I was looking for. Towards the bottom of the left hand bank was a swim with two distinct features, a close range small gravel plateau to the left of the swim and a longer range and more substantial bar to the right.

I spent the first week of the season catching tench from that swim, but did pull out of one fish that could have been a bream. More tench came to net the following week, and I saw my first bream roll. Things were looking good, but then my luck deserted me as a young lad fished the swim the middle of the following week, had one bite and landed a bream just over ten pounds. I did not grudge him that fish for an instant but it alerted other anglers on the water to the location of a possible new bream swim. Thereafter, the swim was always occupied. Sometimes I got there first, but whenever I fished the swim the bream went on hunger strike. I could catch the tench all right, several seven pounders coming to net, but not a bream bite could I get. Alan Smith, on the other hand, enjoyed a purple patch in the swim, taking several big bream culminating in a new British record of 13lb 12oz. I was definitely jinxed that summer. Three times Alan and I agreed to fish the swim together, and on those occasions Alan never caught a bream either!.

I had been steadily fishing the swim since June 16th, but in September a new factor entered the equation in the shape of my old mate Phil Smith. Phil had been very ill and was on sick leave for several weeks. Not surprisingly, he decided to fish the swim and, when Alan Wilson arrived, also planning to fish there, Phil invited Alan to fish the swim with him. The stage was now set for one of the most incredible weeks of TC bream history.

12lb 4oz fish, July 1984.

To appreciate the quite remarkable events of the next few days, it is important to realise that Alan and Phil were literally fishing side by side, Alan to the left of the swim and Phil to the right. They both had baits on the same feature and that fact makes the action that followed even more extraordinary.

At 10.30am on the first morning, the sky went as black as night for over an hour as a torrential thunderstorm hit Oxfordshire. At the height of the storm TC yielded one of its very rare daytime bream, a personal best 12lb 14oz to Phil. That night, another huge fish found Phil's lobworm irresistible and a bream of 12lb 8oz folded into the net. Alan remained biteless.

The dark hours of the following night were hectic, with Phil taking no fewer than four more big bream, including three doubles, and a string of good tench. It was action non-stop while Alan, fishing the same bar with baits only a few yards away, never had a single indication. It was bizarre.

I arrived on the water early on the third morning and was delighted to take some video of Phil's fabulous bream quartet. After the fish had been safely returned, I shared a cup of tea with Alan and Phil before moving in to the swim to Alan's left. From there I could place baits on another feature that had yielded big bream, the close range plateau I had found and from where Cliff Dean had landed a thirteen pounder a few weeks previously. In late afternoon, Alan Smith also arrived, moving in to a swim some forty yards to Phil's right. As darkness slowly closed around us, little did we realise that angling history was about to be made.

That night was one of those sultry affairs when you are expecting something to happen at any moment. After the blustery and stormy week, the night was still, very black and eerily quiet. A light and persistent drizzle accentuated the darkness. The silence was unbroken until sometime around 11.30pm when I suddenly became aware of a rustling in the undergrowth as someone walked up to my bivvy. Out of the night, Phil appeared at the doorway, holding a large carrier bag with a big black tail draped over it. I'll never forget his words. "Alan's cracked it," he said, "he's got a thirteen eight!" Sure enough, when I witnessed the fish, the scales confirmed 13lb 8oz, Alan's first double figure bream. What a first!

Obviously, there was considerable excitement on the bank at this event and we all shared a cup of tea by Alan's bivvy before retiring once again to our respective pitches. At about that time, Phil and Alan Wilson, now seriously short of bait, wound in their rods and went off worming.

The next thing I remember is being woken with a start at about 2.00am by excited shouts, and as I was coming round I had an action replay, with Phil again appearing at my doorway with another black tail hanging out of the bag. Incredibly, Alan had done it again, with an even bigger bream. Not only that, it was a potential new record, and we all carefully witnessed the weighing, confirming 13lb 13oz. What a mind-boggling brace of fish!

Two more big fish were to come to net in quick succession a couple of hours later, a 12lb 13oz fish to Phil and incredibly, yet another thirteen pounder to Alan, 13lb 2oz to be exact. By this time, we were all slightly numb at the events that were unfolding. With no one was this more true than Alan Wilson. He looked in a state of shock.

Back at my bivvy door minutes after witnessing Alan's third fish, I looked almost in disbelief as one of my bobbins suddenly rose to the butt ring. A bite at last, but the story had no happy ending. Only a few minutes into the encounter, a good bream found a thick clump of submerged weed and that was that.

As daylight dawned and brought me back to consciousness, I suddenly became aware of the shrill of an Optonic from Alan's swim. I arrived just as he was sliding the net under another bream. Almost flippantly, I said, "It's probably another thirteen." Incredibly, it was exactly that, 13lb 6oz to be precise, and as Alan slipped it into his mammoth keepnet he was in a kind of trance. None of us spoke. It was almost surreal.

Later that morning, I had the great pleasure of capturing that remarkable catch on video, and from the footage we were able to confirm the outstanding bream potential of TC at the time. The catch did not include two known thirteen pounders, a 13lb 4oz two tone fish that Andy Barker had taken and Alan Smith's 13lb 12oz record, meaning that TC must have held at least six fish over 13lb in 1983, quite a staggering statistic.

Although I blanked on that momentous night, I feel extremely privileged to have shared in what must rank as one of the most remarkable occasions in specimen hunting history.

A Final Fish

My last, and biggest, TC bream came in July 1984. I had settled into the swim which had seen the epic catch the season before, and spent the best part of that blistering hot day paddling around on my inflatable, confirming that the weed growth was very late that season. In the early morning, I had taken several tench to 5lb 6oz and several perch on lobs, as well as witnessing a tench of 9lb 1oz, but after about 10am, everywhere was dead under the scorching sun.

I managed a few hours sleep in mid afternoon, and when I set about preparing my groundbait in early evening, a light breeze was blowing inshore, making conditions absolutely ideal. I was experimenting with flavoured groundbait and the feed that night consisted of a baby bath full of brown breadcrumbs sweetened and flavoured with caramel. To this were added four pints of casters and flake samples that had also been caramel flavoured.

My baits were cast out about two hours before dark, one rod being baited with a large lobworm and the other with flavoured flake/caster cocktail. The caramel flavouring was being used for the first time, so it was very gratifying that bites came

Final fish of the campaign, 11lb 4oz.

to the cocktail bait regularly from dusk until about 1.00am. In all, six tench to 6lb 9oz were landed, and I settled into my sleeping bag at about 2.00am in contented mood. Barely had I closed my eyes when I heard an Optonic and looking out of the bivvy door I could see that the bobbin on the lobworm rod was just dropping back after registering a sharp line bite. Bream were about!

Now fully alert, I made a fresh cup of tea and sat outside in the cool night air to await events. Intermittently, liners rattled the bobbin as I waited patiently for a definite indication. At last, about 3.30am, the bobbin began a slow crawl to the butt and then the reel began to backwind. My sweeping strike was met with the satisfying resistance of a big fish and shortly afterwards I was weighing my personal best of 12lb 4oz, my first double since 1981 despite countless hours of effort.

Just over a season later, my association with TC ended. Many of the newcomers to the water did not show the respect to either the fish or the environment that I feel we have a right to expect from anglers. Litter became an increasing problem, and many fish were treated badly, being crammed into inadequate keepnets, and there were many fatalities. To my certain knowledge, over twenty double figure fish perished that season, including four of the known thirteen pounders. Sadly, TC was never the same again.

A Dream Fulfilled

August 1985

I have always maintained that the major turning point in my budding angling career was receiving a copy of Stillwater Angling as a birthday present. I have never been quite as enthralled by a book since, and the chapter on catching big fish by design told me the direction I wanted my fishing to go, and the chapters on Redmire told me why. I read the Redmire chapters over and over again, I never tired of them.

The descriptions of the Redmire fishing contained some of Dick Walker's most classic writing. Who can forget that memorable passage, immortalised by Bernard Cribbins in his narrative over Passion for Angling, as Bob and Chris paddle out on a Redmire dawn?

"The sun rose deep orange, its rays making the lake steam. Nothing moved. I was lost in a quiet world of green, and grey, and gold." Wonderful stuff indeed, and inspirational to countless young anglers like myself.

Although many dreams centred around fishing Redmire, never in the wildest of them did I believe it would come true. And then in 1985, during the brief period of control over Redmire by Clive Diedrich of Richworth, the dream actually did come true. Clive had a free week in August, and Dave Plummer and I had Redmire to ourselves. The days before our trip seemed to drag on forever, but soon I was crossing the cattle grid, leaving the world behind and entering paradise. I coasted down the hill, through the little gate to the parking area by the Evening Pitch, and, moments later, stood in awe looking out over the water that had filled my boyhood dreams.

A few minutes later, I was on the dam and for a moment, I had Redmire to myself. Dave would be a further hour, allowing me blissful solitude to drink in the atmosphere, which this beautiful pool exuded from every pore. I was struck by the silence and that wonderful aroma of damp decay you associate with old, tree enclosed estate lakes. And as I stood, and stared, an armour-plated mirror carp, 30lb if it was an ounce, glided nonchalantly from under the famous old punt, secured to the dam rail. It turned as if to say welcome, and then disappeared into the depths. It was almost too much to take in.

With the sun beating down, I was in no hurry to start fishing or even empty the car. For the moment, it was sufficient just being there, and I donned waders and

commenced a slow circumnavigation of the lake. I had brought with me that brilliant book Redmire Pool, by Len Arbery and Kevin Clifford, and with it was able to identify the famous old swims as I came to them. I knew, however, which swim I would be starting in. For thirty years I had dreamed of fishing the Willow Pitch. The dream was now but hours away.

In late afternoon, Dave had joined me, and after he too had paid due reverence, we shared two leisurely beers before getting down, at last, to the serious business of preparing to fish. It had already been decided that Dave would start in the Evening Pitch, and so I ferried my gear across the dam while he put his own camp in order. By early evening, we were set and around 6pm, I cast into Redmire for the first time.

When I had first settled into the swim, the weather was already deteriorating. The evening had been gorgeous, blue sky, warm with not a breath of wind, but now it was ominously overcast, with ever strengthening fine drizzle making things quite uncomfortable. Scarcely one hour later, the sky had turned black. Gradually the wind picked up force and, about 8pm, the full force of the storm erupted around us. For the rest of the evening and night, I lay on my bedchair listening to the howling wind and torrential rain, hoping, even on my first night at this jewel of carp waters, that I would not get a run just yet! I was to find out the following

Rods on parade in the Willow Pitch.

week that that very first night in the Willow Pitch was the date of Richard Walker's death. It was fitting that such a sombre date in angling history should be marked by Redmire in angry mood.

As far as the actual fishing was concerned, that first week was an anti-climax in a way, although I wouldn't have missed a second of it. On the second morning, I missed a steaming run in the Willow, which I initially put down to one of the big mirrors, but on reflection and in light of subsequent events, was probably a small common. For the rest of the week, I covered a few swims, both with particles and blue cheese boilies, taking a few of the small commons with which Redmire was overrun at the time. These were from about 3lb to 8lb and although they were beautiful little battlers, they were not what we were after. Dave, too, had several, and as we began packing up at the end of our stay, I was sorry I hadn't had the opportunity to see one of the famous old residents. All the mug shots were there in Redmire Pool. I wanted to see one on the bank.

I was packed up and in the process of ferrying my gear back to the car when Dave gave a shout. His rods had been left until last, and he had struck into what

Dave Plummer with Raspberry.

he thought was yet another 7lb common when his rod hooped over and a big fish ploughed away. At last! I do not think Dave was any more excited than I was. It really didn't matter that week who caught the fish. Soon, the battle was won and we lifted ashore a lovely carp of just over 22lb. Try as I might, I could not find its picture in Redmire Pool!

Minutes later, Dave was in again and this time it was to be one of the most famous residents that had come calling, if not the most famous. Soon we were gazing at the lovely flanks of Raspberry, now exactly 23lb, and considerably older than either of us. Neither Dave nor I wanted to leave, but leave we had to, and in the pouring rain we silently packed the cars. As I finally drove up the hill, I momentarily glanced backwards. Would I ever fish here again, I wondered? I had to fish here again!

October 1985

The first week of October 1985 was quite simply one of the most wonderful weeks of my entire life. I had Redmire Pool to myself for six whole days. Could I possibly have imagined such a dream as a boy? The week had been planned as a joint venture for me and Andy Barker, but Andy had been forced to cry off at the last moment and this most famous of waters was all mine. As I stood in the Stumps Swim on the first afternoon, it was a heady moment.

I had decided to start in the Stumps. Despite a good look round, I had seen nothing moving and no signs of fish apart from masses of bubbles, which I now know were from small eels. On my first trip, I had been fooled into thinking they were carp. The Stumps Swim gave me a good access to different parts of the lake, allowing a left angled cast towards the Evening Pitch and the dam, a less acute cast towards In-Willow and a right angled cast towards the islands by the shallows.

Because of the eel problem, I had decided to base my loose feed around tiger nuts, fishing one rod on tigers and two on pop ups over the bed of bait. I was using Richworth's Tutti Frutti, but it was the tiger nuts that were first to go, less than an hour into my first evening. Moments later, I was sadly contemplating a limp line. I had struck into an undoubtedly big fish, felt its power momentarily, and then the hook had come away. In truth, I pull out of very few fish, but that one hurt like hell. I knew I had just lost a Redmire monster.

There was no time to brood over what might have been. I was in the process of rebaiting, when my middle rod was away, rattling in the rests. Something had picked up the boilie and was kiting right with it, fast. As I struck the hook home, a big fish swirled at the surface and I could see that in that short space of time it had nearly made the gap between the little islands on the far margins. It had to be stopped, and quickly, or it would be among those dangerous brambles. And then it would be goodnight, sweetheart!

Applying maximum sidestrain, I heaved to the right as hard as I could and in that I was successful, making the fish veer off course. At that, he did an abrupt about turn, and shot back up the lake in a straight line, heading for the dam. At first, I had a problem keeping in contact, because of the amount of slack this new manoeuvre had suddenly created, and when I eventually regained full contact I was pleased to find the carp still in the middle of the lake, away from the dangerous marginal snags. From that moment on, the battle was plain sailing and only a few minutes more elapsed before I was able to net an ambition I had been nurturing for many years, a 20lb common carp. When I confirmed 20lb 12oz, I punched the air in delight. After sacking the fish carefully, I made a celebratory cup of tea. What a welcome Redmire had given me. I wondered what the rest of the week had in store.

But the action was far from over that evening, because from just on dusk to around midnight, the Optonics screamed out another four times. The first run was unaccountably missed, but the other runs produced three more commons, one quite small fish and two other crackers of 16lb 10oz and 18lb 14oz. By the time the action was finally over, I was badly in need of sleep and curled up contentedly in my sleeping bag, to dream of even more carp.

In actual fact, that first evening flattered to deceive, because there then followed three completely blank days and nights, two of them in the Stumps, and one in the Evening Pitch, to which I had moved at the end of the third day. But the blanking hardly mattered. For three glorious days, a beautifully filtered autumn sun had overlaid Redmire with a myriad golden hues. I was entertained by the swarms of blue tits pinching tiger nuts from my bait box, and then holding them down firmly with one foot while punching a hole in them with their beaks. For four days, I'd heard no traffic, spoken to no one and just had the fish and birds for company. Who really needs to catch carp when surrounded by such serenity?

But, catching carp is what I was there for, and I was pleased that my all too short Redmire holiday ended on Friday with another cluster of fish. They were not big, but three other commons, biggest 14lb, ensured that I finished on a high.

As the song says, regrets, I have a few. My third and last week on Redmire was ruined by very strange occurrences, as you will read elsewhere in this book, and I left the water early, never to return. And I would dearly loved to have landed just one of the water's famous old mirrors. Sadly, one of these was cruising around the surface for the whole of the week just described, obviously in distress, and I thought it only a matter of time. I was told later, a very big mirror had been found dead a couple of weeks after my trip, almost certainly the fish I had been watching.

So there you have it. I certainly never set the carp world on fire with my catches from Redmire, but my first 20lb common was pleasing. But the experience of such a wonderful water will never leave me. I still often watch the video film I made at the time, as I wandered from swim to swim, and my mind drifts back to 1985, when I was privileged to spend two wonderful weeks there.

Ghosts & Goblins

A Cherwell Night

In thirty five years of angling, I have lost count of the number of nights I have spent on the bank, most of them totally alone, but it must now run into thousands. In all that time, I have had very few startling experiences, and all but two could be attributed to wild life. I have had a fox screaming in my bivvy in the early hours, a water vole jumping on my head, a horse ripping my sleeping bag off me and so on. Those two, however, I have never been able to explain satisfactorily to myself, and I would like to share them with you. To those readers who have read the stories before I apologise.

In the summer of 1984, I was, for the first time, seriously fishing for Cherwell barbel and one of the first swims I fished was actually located on an island in the river, which could only be reached by wading across a sidestream. At normal level, I could just about make the crossing in thigh waders. The point of the island featured an easily climbed tree, shading a substantial undercut, a favourite haunt of barbel, chub and bream.

It wasn't a big island, perhaps fifteen yards wide and thirty long, but it was very heavily overgrown with bracken, brambles, alders and willows. On the evening in question, I had decided to fish until about midnight, and sat on a completely still, warm and breathless, and very clear night. There was a good moon, every star in the sky was visible, and I was very relaxed as I concentrated on the beta light on the rod top. Total silence reigned.

Quite suddenly, the peace was broken by loud footsteps that sounded only a few yards away, cracking twigs and distinct heavy breathing sounds. It was as though a fully laden angler was struggling up to me after a long walk, and the noises were certainly far too loud to have been caused by small animals. A grown man or large animal would have been needed to create the disturbance I could plainly hear. I fully expected Alastair Nicholson, who was

The barbel swim at the point of "Haunted Island".

fishing the area in the mid-eighties, to come through the undergrowth at any moment. I actually called out, "Is that you, Alastair?" but did find it strange that I had heard no sounds of his crossing the sidestream.

There was no answer, and although the footsteps stopped for a while, the laboured panting noises continued unabated. I was not disturbed at that time, just puzzled, and I picked up my large torch to search for a possible explanation in the undergrowth. I was still half expecting a friend to leap out at me at any moment to lend the final touches to my prematurely greying hair! I searched that copse from end to end without finding a single living creature. I even crossed the stream into the open field beyond to see whether cattle had been let into the field, but that too was deserted. Satisfied that I was totally alone, I re-crossed the stream, returned to my tackle, and sat down again. I turned off the torch and listened for a moment. Complete silence had returned, and for a second or two I half convinced myself that I had imagined the whole thing. It really was very odd.

I barely had time to recast my bait before the next manifestations occurred. Once again, the loud footsteps and heavy breathing were unmistakable, now so loud that they seemed right behind me. The sharp cracking of twigs prompted me once again to grab my torch and search the undergrowth, now quite apprehensive. Before long, I again stood at the edge of the sidestream, having again confirmed that I was alone. Once more the noises had stopped suddenly, but I was quite clammy and for the first time realised how cold it had become. Fishing had now lost its appeal as I made my way back to my tackle, but I remember telling myself to calm down and try to think of a logical explanation for the weird events. In that I was unsuccessful. Nothing made any sense.

Seated on my tackle box again, I poured a cup of tea to warm my hands before starting to pack my gear. I never did drink that tea. Seconds after pouring it, there was a terrific crash in the undergrowth right alongside me, the foliage shook and I openly admit to now being scared. Although I again searched the thicket, totally without enthusiasm, I have to say, and certainly with more than a little trepidation, I again uncovered no explanation. This time, however, the noises did not stop. They were all around me, horrible wheezing, moaning sounds, almost like those

My 7lb 12oz tench taken in 1979.

Bob James lands a big Avon roach.

5lb 5oz Ibsley chub.

12lb 4oz fish, July 1984.

Fishing the shallow sidestream by the "Haunted Island" on the Cherwell.

Famous Redmire landmark.

My first 20lb common, from Redmire.

associated with a severe asthma attack. Also, for the first time, I became suddenly aware of the dense, clammy, swirling mist that had suddenly enveloped my little island. For a nerve wracking few minutes, with the noises everywhere around me and the visibility decreasing rapidly, I packed my gear and then literally ran through the thicket, jumped into the sidestream, getting two waders full of water in the process. I stumbled my way to the open field as fast as possible.

As I stood on the grass recovering my composure, I realised that I had only been minutes away from my nerve breaking completely, and I took many deep breaths to calm myself down. It was then that something struck me as being very weird, almost supernatural. The island was now cloaked in a very dense fog, while all around the night was as clear, warm and benign as it had always been. Nowhere else was there the slightest sign of mist. That defied logic.

That night, I am convinced that extraordinary forces were at work for which I have no explanation and towards the end of the experience I was as frightened as I have ever been in my lifetime. I truly believe that I was in the presence of evil on that summer night.

Although I did return to that island a few times afterwards, and caught a few barbel, nothing would persuade me to fish it again after dark. I never have.

A 7lb barbel from "Haunted Island" on the Cherwell.

The Redmire Mystery

In 1985, I was to realise boyhood dreams when I first walked the hallowed banks of Redmire Pool. My first two trips, in August and October, were full of nothing but pleasant memories of that beautiful water, not least of which is my first ever twenty pound common carp.

My third week, however, in the autumn of 1986, was memorable for very different reasons. I had arrived at mid-morning on the Monday, with five days on my own to look forward to. The intention had been to fish with Andy Barker, but he had been forced to back out at the last minute because of business pressures.

The first thing I noticed, as I pulled through the little gate into the parking area, were swirls just out from the bank, and as I stood in the Evening Pitch, one of the big mirrors obligingly rolled about thirty yards out. In the next few moments, several mud clouds rose as well as great mats of bubbles, and it was obvious there was intense activity in the swim. At least there was no need for indecision in choice of pitch and about half an hour later the Evening Pitch had been established as my temporary home.

As morning gave way to afternoon, there was that heaviness in the air that warns of an impending storm. The warmth and intense humidity, as well as complete absence of wind, made great beads of sweat stand out on my brow. As the hours passed, the sky grew more and more ominous and threatening, being almost as black as night by around 4pm, when the now light breeze suddenly picked up force. In the distance, the roaring of the gale could plainly be heard and, moments later, the storm erupted in full fury overhead. Within seconds, it was impossible to see through the solid sheets of rain cascading down. There then followed about fourteen hours of the most torrential and thunderous downpour I have ever experienced, the wind by about midnight reaching hurricane force. That night was cold, wet misery.

Next morning, although the rain was still heavy, the worst of the storm had passed and I looked around Redmire at the most astonishing sight. Everywhere was a glutinous red morass, a sea of liquid mud, and I could see where Redmire acquired its name. The water was of the most vivid crimson, so much mud had been washed through by the feeder stream. So swollen had that stream become by the torrents of water, that the sluice at the dam was unable to cope with the sheer volume of the flood and a red deluge poured over the dam itself. It was an awe-inspiring sight.

By about midday, the rain had stopped, it was totally calm once again, and I had restored some semblance of order to the muddy chaos my camp had become. By early afternoon, the previous night's trauma was a distant memory, as I sat behind three freshly positioned baits, eating a hot meal, and soaking up the warm afternoon sun.

As dusk approached, it was exceptionally warm and close, once again windless, the kind of night when you are expecting something to happen at any moment. Although autumn, so oppressive was it that I only fished in a jumper. Even after dark, the temperature stayed very high.

Despite my expectations of carp action, everything remained still and unmoving and it was perhaps around midnight when I decided to bury myself in the sleeping bag. As is my habit, the bag was not zipped, just thrown over me, and from its comfort I could see the betalights on my bobbins, as they glowed through the open bivvy doorway. I was soon asleep on that muggy, dark and still night.

It must have been around 3am when I awoke with a real start, and realised that the bivvy was shaking from side to side very violently, although there was not a

breath of wind. The shaking still continued as I shot out of my shelter, fully expecting to see a fox, badger or the like with a mouthful of bivvy, but there was nothing there. The shaking stopped abruptly. It was puzzling, but after I had checked up and down with my torch, I went back into the camp.

Now fully awake, I decided to have a brew up before getting my head down, and then I realised something else that was very strange. Inside my bivvy, everything I touched, and the air itself, was icy cold, whereas outside the night was as warm and humid as ever. At the time, I blamed condensation, but even then it was unnaturally chilly.

Having made my tea, I wandered down the bank with it to the Stumps swim, realising yet again the now incredible temperature difference between the outer world and the interior of my shelter. Nevertheless, tea finished, I climbed back into my sleeping bag and closed my eyes again. I put the cold down to some freak atmospheric condition.

In the next hour, I was awoken three times by what felt like someone blowing hard on my face with freezing cold breath, the third time being so startled that I shot bolt upright on my bedchair. This was now getting quite unnerving, further sleep being impossible. Then I noticed two things simultaneously. First, the inside of my bivvy was now partly frosted, like the inside of a refrigerator. Second, I could not see my tackle outside, it was as though someone had dropped a black curtain over the doorway. As I tried to make sense of that particular phenomenon, the black shadow moved to the side, revealing my bobbins again, before re-crossing the doorway, temporarily blocking the world out for a second time. I am sure you will believe me when I say that I was now distinctly uneasy. After a few more minutes with no further activity, I gingerly emerged from the bivvy, sleeping bag under my arm, and rapidly made my way to the car, parked only a short distance away. Once there, I locked myself in and made myself as comfortable as possible in the passenger seat for the remainder of the dark hours.

Although I tried to make sense of it all the next morning, I knew that the shaking, the intense cold and the threatening shadow had been only too real, and also knew that further fishing was impossible. I am a logical man, not normally nervous and certainly not scared of the dark, but that experience had badly shaken me. That week, I left Redmire two days early with no regrets.

It was several months after that experience that I was to learn, from Len and Tony Arbery, that the Evening Pitch had a reputation for strange occurrences. Len told me of the night he had experienced the same intense cold in his bivvy, and had woken the next morning to find articles inside frosted, even in high summer.

The most frightening occurrence was recounted by my good friend, Bob Karn. This was also covered in the weekly angling press. Bob was fishing the Stumps swim, there were an angler and his son sharing the Evening Pitch and, over the dam, a fourth angler fishing the Willow Pitch. Bob himself told me of a sudden feeling of unease in the middle of the night and the black curtain effect that had so disturbed me. Nothing else untoward occurred in his swim but a little later, he was suddenly awoken by screaming from the Evening Pitch. He ran down the bank, and I believe the angler in the Willows ran across the dam as well, to find out what was happening, and they found the two anglers in the Evening Pitch cowered in the back of their bivvy. Bob says they were obviously in a state of shock, and related a story of a hideous apparition with green, staring eyes starting to enter the bivvy, before it disappeared.

When I first read that account, and Bob had related it again to me first hand, my mind went back immediately to that strange night in 1986, when I had occupied the same swim. If I had seen that same hideous spectre, it would definitely have been a case of breaking out the brown trousers!

Perch - Then and Now

Like many anglers, I have long held a soft spot for perch, they are, after all, one of the first, and easiest, fish we catch as kids. However, I think it is true to say that most anglers do not take that early interest into their adult fishing lives, small perch then being a curse that take and gorge baits meant for worthier quarry. In my case, however, a lucky  accident led to my catching a specimen perch at a formative period in my angling career, and the sight of that hugely impressive fish led to a deep love of the species that persists today. That first big fish was from a small stream, the Claydon Brook, where many of my biggest chub were also caught, and over the years that followed I fished many thousands of hours for big perch and developed an understanding of the species. But I can only get interested in big perch from smaller rivers. For some reason, still water perch do little for me, although, on average, the chances of real monsters always seemed higher from large pits and reservoirs.

That first specimen was taken in 1962, and for the next nine years I was to pursue them intently, until my heart was broken with the onset of the terrible perch disease in the early seventies. The wipe out on the Ouse and its tributaries was nearly total, and it would be many years before they became a viable target for the big fish man again. After that, I did very little perching for a long while, other than the occasional morning trip to my local Leam, which saw fish taken to just under three pounds.

It was in the early nineties when my love affair was re-kindled. The Ouse perch were back with a vengeance, three pounders again showing, and when a friend of mine reported a fish over four pounds in a Buckingham & District Club match, I was well and truly hooked for a second time. My big perch career can therefore be said to be in two distinct halves, you could say pre-disease and post-disease eras. Let me tell you first about the early years.

The Early Years

Some moments in an angling career seem to be permanently highlighted in our memories, particularly when an incident occurs which proves to be really special. Just such a moment arrived on a very hot July morning on the Claydon Brook in 1962. I was into my roach fishing at the time, and had been laying on with stewed wheat in the middle of dense cabbages since early morning, taking several good roach and one chub. As the sun had become fiercer, the bites had gradually dried up and I was enjoying sun bathing, not expecting any more action from the roach until evening.

The swim was one of my favourites. On the far bank, dense blackthorns overhung the margin, creating a dark run, a favourite haunt of big chub. The roach were also to be found under those trees early and late, but as the sun came up, good fish could be caught right under the lily pads in mid-river, where the cabbages were really dense. The shade they afforded meant the roach often fed much later than they otherwise would have done.

At the upstream edge of the trees, under the far bank, quite a thick mat of surface algae and scum had formed, following weeks of warm, dry conditions. That surface raft had become quite extensive, perhaps eight yards long, and two yards wide, from the far bank to a mid-river rush bed. Under that scum there must have been conditions of permanent semi darkness.

As I lolled in the sun that morning, my attention wandered several times to that raft, and I contemplated crossing the river and dropping a chub bait underneath. I was on the point of winding in to make the move, when a commotion under the scum caught my attention. As I looked round, I could see a hole appearing in the greenery, and an ever widening vortex. And then there was a second upheaval, and this time a shower of minnows left the water. Close on their tails was a large, prickly dorsal.

Up to that time, I had caught lots of perch from the river, with nothing over a pound, and to be honest they had been a pain, taking the maggots intended for 2lb roach. But the fish I had just seen was in a different league altogether, and I crossed that river in double quick time. Only about twenty yards upstream, gravel shallows allowed a crossing in waders at summer level.

For a while, I contemplated how to fish the swim, and eventually decided to stick with my float gear. Carefully poking a small hole in the middle of the algae with my net handle, I quickly followed this with the float, shotted to be self cocking, and baited with a large lobworm fished well overdepth. I wanted to be certain to be laying on without having to retrieve the tackle for depth adjustments. Within a minute or so, the hole had re-closed, leaving my bright red float tip protruding from a sea of greenery. It was a fascinating sight, but not as fascinating as that tip suddenly vanishing, which it did suddenly, without warning.

As I struck, there was a violent thrashing under the scum, and again a big, impressive dorsal broke surface, before its owner took off intro the mid-river rushes. Luckily, it never found a snag and eventually I was able to net an absolutely magnificent perch, the biggest by a mile that I had ever seen. I was soon confirming 2lb 10oz, which exactly doubled my previous best I had fluked from a canal as a child.

That afternoon, there were to be two more fish from that raft, both about one and a half pounds, before I contrived to prick and lose a fish. That put paid to sport, a scenario that has been repeated countless times. Losing a big perch in a swim often kills sport.

What brought about that initial catch of good perch was quickly found to be one of the most reliable set of circumstances, and many good catches of fish came from such scum swims. Normally light sensitive fish were happy to feed on and off all day in the gloom.

For two years, that first big perch remained my best, but in those years I learned an awful lot about small stream perch fishing, summer and winter. I learned which swims they would be in, just by looking at the strength of the flow. I learned that the most reliable time was the crack of dawn, and that at this time of day the first perch caught was usually the biggest. I learned that the big fish prowled the gravel shallows in the hour before dawn, picking off minnows while they were half asleep, and it was fishing in this way in the summer of 1964 that produced a fish to beat 2lb 10oz.

Well before daylight, on a calm warm morning, I sat low and quiet by the shallows, waiting and watching. I had freelining gear with me, with just a single SSG pinched about a foot from the hook. Just in that half light that precedes dawn, the activity started, first from chub making sorties through the fry, and then the unmistakable arrowing of the erect dorsals of big perch. Quickly lip hooking a minnow, it was swung out to land ahead of the nearest dorsal. One second later, line was pulled from my fingers as a perch rocketed away with its breakfast. I remember the perch dashing across the shallows to the far bank rushes with me following, whereupon I stumbled and sat down heavily in mid river. A wet back end and two boots full was acceptable once I had confirmed 2lb 14oz.

Only a month later, I was to take my dream, a three pounder. The very first swim I had found the big perch in had proved to be one of the most reliable, specially in the winter. In the summer, when there was no surface algae, it was an early morning affair, laying on lobs as close to the mid-river rushes as possible. Only occasionally did the bottom bait not score, when I reverted to trotting off bottom, but I had never caught a really big fish this way. On this particular morning, I had taken two fish over two pounds in weight on bottom baits and then the bites dried up. Before moving on, I decided to try trotting for ten minutes and pushed the float up a foot. On the second trot down, a good fish whacked the float away,

Son Chris with 2lb 6oz fish.

and a few minutes later I was weighing an absolutely tremendous perch of 3lb 6oz.

Two more three pounders were to follow in December, the second of which was destined to remain my personal best for over 35 years! The sequence of events was like this.

During the winter months, when the river rose and the flow increased, the perch moved out of their normal summer quarters and migrated to a much quieter backwater. Normally, this was totally stagnant and overgrown in summer, but in the winter this used to feature a gentle flow. This was achieved by the simple expedient of an overflow weir. Once the main river had risen about two feet, surplus water trickled over the overflow to give the backwater some life. The onset of this current turned the perch and big roach on, and I had found two areas, by the simple expedient of wading the river in trunks, where there were substantial depressions in the river bed, in both cases associated with cabbage patches. You could only know about those holes by wading or very careful plumbing, and I had a distinct advantage over other anglers in the winter, when I knew exactly where to place my baits.

The first of my three pounders was taken on a mild December morning when the river was perfect, about a foot up and coloured and I was able to hold my bait in position comfortably in mid-river in the largest of the depressions. It needed the float to be set a good two feet overdepth to fish properly, but once the tackle was balanced, it gave efficient bite registration, yielding a perch well over a pound, a small roach and a clonking perch of 3lb 2oz.

On the strength of that fish, I was back in the same swim the following week, but this time the conditions had certainly taken a turn for the worse. Although the river was roughly the same height, the colour was far deeper and the current much

Lovely brace of three pounders.

faster. It was also very much colder. There had been a frost the previous night, and all morning I fished in freezing drizzle. After trying, I reluctantly came to the conclusion that laying on was not viable, unless I used excessive lead. Nevertheless, the depression still offered the best chance, and I opted to leger the swim. With me, this is always the last option with perch, they detest resistance so much. It is not so critical with modern, ultra soft quivertips, but I had nothing comparable those days. All I could do to alleviate the resistance a taking perch was bound to feel was hold a yard of slack line in my left hand, to be released as soon as I felt an indication. I also pointed the rod directly at the bait, to avoid rod top pressure.

I had the confidence boosters I needed fairly early in the session when two average perch put in an appearance, and my giving immediate slack certainly prolonged the bite enough to give a firm hookhold.

As the morning wore on, the conditions steadily became more unpleasant. The rain had turned from drizzle into a steady downpour, which was progressively turning to sleet as the temperature dropped noticeably. My fingers were numb with cold, and I was contemplating packing up early when there was an unmistakable jab on the rod, to be followed by a steady draw of slack line through my left hand. As the line cut upstream, I set the hook into a big fish I initially thought must be a good chub, but I was soon to see the most monstrous perch roll. I have to say the fight was disappointing, perhaps as well with my having almost no feeling in my fingers.

An adrenaline rush is said to keep out the cold, and all of a sudden the weather was forgotten as I stared in disbelief at the magnificent perch that emerged from my landing net. It was perfect in every stripe, weighing 3lb 14oz, and I happily packed my gear there and then. One of my bitterest regrets is having no photographs of that fish. I remember my mother had bought me a new camera a few weeks previously. I even remember the camera make, Baldinette. Just after Christmas, I had taken all 36 shots on the very first film I put through it, and it transpired that the film wind mechanism was faulty. All 36 exposures had been made on the same frame!

As far as I was able to ascertain at the time, my 3lb 14oz fish was the biggest to come from the brook, but, although I never landed or heard of a four pounder, I certainly saw two. The first of these incidents occurred in August 1962, only a month after I had landed that first big one of 2lb 10oz.

I was once again laying on in mid-river cabbages for roach, alternating wheat and maggots, and once again mid-morning and a bright sun had seen sport come to a full stop. About 10.30am, my mate, Dave, came racing up the bank to borrow my landing net. Another friend, Ken, had latched into a double figure pike in the mill pool about four hundred yards away, and there was no way their pathetic little net was going to cope. Reluctantly I agreed, with instructions to bring it back in short order, as you never knew when a big fish would come along. How prophetic those words turned out to be. Barely two minutes had elapsed, when my float suddenly shot up in the water, lay flat and then zoomed away under the pads. As I struck, a tremendous vortex formed as the rod hooped right over. I had obviously connected with something pretty useful. By dint of kid glove playing and a lot of good fortune, I managed to steer that fish from the mid-river snags into the clear water under the rod top, and then I glimpsed the fish for the first time, an absolutely colossal perch.

All my yelling, screaming and cursing was to no avail, Dave could not hear me, and there I was with the fish of my dreams swimming backwards and forwards on 2lb line and a 16 hook. I could see the hook hold was precarious in the extreme and I had to attempt to land it before it gave way. Eventually, I had the fish in the margins, quite placid, and then I knelt down, with the rod in my left hand maintaining a tight line, and scooped the fish into my right. The problem was that I was totally unbalanced, and as I tried to steady myself, the fish flipped out of my hand, the tiny hook pulled out, and that was that. For the few minutes following that gut wrenching occurrence, Dave's ears must have been burning.

How big was that perch? I would state categorically that it was certainly at least four and a half pounds. It was huge, with great humped shoulders. It was perhaps well for my peace of mind that I didn't realise at the time that it would be a further 37 years before I would hook another perch as big.

In 1968, not long after I had formed the Coventry Specimen Group, I had formed a close friendship with the late Peter Rayment, at the time Secretary of the Birmingham Specimen Group. Peter had expressed interest in my perch fishing, as I was catching a string of good fish plus the occasional three pounder in the late sixties. He had begged a trip with me, and we arrived before dawn in September, and made our way to the swim where I had taken my first ever big fish. Over the years, this swim had remained the most consistent.

As it became light, I pointed out the swim features to Pete, explaining that he had to cast his float tackle to lay on lobworm as close to the far bank rushes as he could. I then left him to it, guaranteeing him a perch to beat his then best of 2lb if

Catch of fish in the first twenty minutes of daylight.

he fished as I told him. I wandered upstream to fish other swims I had been meaning to investigate.

The conditions for perch that morning can only be described as perfect, warm, damp and overcast, with no wind, and I had a steady procession of perch, although nothing big. Pete, on the other hand, had not had a bite by mid-morning as I sat with him to share a coffee. I couldn't believe it, I had never blanked in the swim. The only thing I could see wrong, if anything, was that the bait was too far into the clear water for my liking. The float was perhaps a yard from those rushes, whereas I liked it touching them, if possible. I suggested Pete recast to see if it made any difference, which he dutifully did immediately. I remember him laughing because that cast was perfect, landing smack on the edge of the reeds. He said it was the best cast he'd made all morning, possibly because I was watching. With me, it's the other way round. If I have another angler watching, you can generally guarantee a cock up!

Anyway, whether the recast was responsible or whether it was just coincidence we shall never know, but a minute after the float had settled, it shot away into the foliage, Pete's rod was right over and the rushes swayed apart as something big and powerful forced its way through them. Whatever it was then stuck solid. Telling Pete not to panic and to maintain a tight line, I gingerly waded out to those offending rushes, getting soaked to the waist in the process, and gradually unhitched the line from the stems. When I came to the individual stem where the fish was lodged, I tugged it gently, the root came away and the fish was free. Seconds later, it rolled almost alongside me, a perch that was truly gigantic.

It was then that I made a bad mistake. I told Pete it was a huge perch, certainly well over four pounds, and he eased the pressure, trying to be too careful. Had he maintained or increased pressure at that moment, the perch would have been in the clear. As it was, it was able to right itself, shoot a further three yards into even denser foliage, whereupon Pete tried to stop it, breaking the line in the process. I really did think Pete was going to cry at that moment, and I knew how he felt. I had been just as gutted six years earlier.

Pete Rayment never got over losing that big perch. I remember sitting with him at a NASA conference, many years later and not long before his untimely death, talking over old times. It was then that he admitted to me that the loss of that fish, the only time he'd ever contacted a perch anywhere near that size, had been the lowest point of his angling career. Pete was a lovely bloke, a good fried, and I would love to be able to re-run that sequence of events, but this time present him with the fish of his dreams, safely in the bottom of a landing net.

Big Perch of the Nineties

As I said at the opening of this chapter, the marvellous perching on the Ouse came to a shuddering halt in the early seventies due to the ravages of the perch disease, and, although I still maintained a keen interest in small stream perching, taking many good fish from the local Leam and Cherwell, I never managed a three pounder from either, although I came close.

Elsewhere in this book, I have made reference to the renaissance that occurred with big Ouse chub in the late eighties, but the perch were slower to respond. I had several trips in that period, catching two pounders easily enough, but nothing to get really excited about, until a Buckingham & District Club match turned up a perch of 4lb 7oz. The significance of that fish was not lost on me, as it was the biggest authenticated fish I knew of from the Ouse and its tributaries. My love affair with the upper Ouse system was re-kindled.

The first big perch of this new era came about almost by accident. In 1993, I was a leading feature writer for a new magazine, Practical Coarse Fishing, and the editor, Luke Felton, and I had identified monthly projects to keep the magazine content fresh and variable. I would write about various fishing trips, giving me the opportunity to describe the day itself, but also go into technique, watercraft, and so on. One such project was early season perch on small rivers, and I had purposely selected an area of the Upper Ouse that was reliable for bites, although my biggest fish from there had been just over two pounds.

When I arrived at the intended swim, I could see that the previous winter's storms had done their work well. Where there had been a far bank willow, under the trailing branches of which had been a reliable perch hideaway, there was now a mass of fallen timber virtually blocking the stream. Around the upstream branches a fair accumulation of scum had built up, stretching almost to the rushes on the near bank. Where the fallen tree was actually lying I knew to be the deepest area, so I initially felt that the perch may have moved out. But I thought it at least worth a try for ten minutes, before moving on. How glad I am that I did, because the bite was literally instant. I had lowered my quill float close to the scum by the near bank rushes, and it did not have time even to cock. Within one second of touching the water, it was rocketing across the stream as though jet propelled, and, once I had felt the power of the fish responsible, I knew it was considerably bigger than the modest perch I had been expecting. That fish fought tremendously hard, several times taking line against the clutch, but eventually a scarlet finned, bristling thing of beauty sagged into the waiting net. That perch was short, hog backed and pristine, and at 3lb 5oz, my biggest since the halcyon days of the sixties. I was overjoyed. I had the material for my feature, in spades, as bridge aficionados would have it.

In the early morning dew of September 1998, it was still barely light as I lowered the gear at a swim I hadn't fished for the best part of thirty years. It was in a narrow section of river, well wooded, the willows on each bank having formed almost a full canopy over the stream, and entailing a full two miles walk to get to. That is why, although the season had been underway a full three months, the undergrowth was still head high, wildly overgrown. It had obviously seen no attentions from anglers for weeks. Once I was in position, my little bit of bank a clear oasis in a jungle wilderness, it was as if the rest of the world had ceased to exist. Before casting in, I let the peaceful seclusion wash over me for a few minutes. I am far from being anti social, but being on my own in the country, with kingfishers and field mice for company, and far enough from roads so the only sound is coming from gurgling shallows, is as near to paradise on Earth for me as it is possible to get.

The flow was very gentle, about seven feet deep, and therefore ideal for my favourite method of laying on with large lobs. Accordingly, I leisurely assembled my customary perch float rig, comprising a Drennan 3AAA waggler, fished as a slider, using a single SSG about 18" up the line and a single AAA six inches from the hook. The float was attached to one of Peter Drennan's silicon float attachments, and rested on the SSG for casting, being stopped at seven and a half feet by a power gum stop knot. The initially short distance from float to bait allows the terminal rig to be propelled much further under overhanging branches or tighter against rush beds than otherwise would be the case, and big perch love to be close to cover. The small shot just rests on the river bed, for early warning of a bite. In the old days, I didn't bother with that, using just one large shot and the float well overdepth, fished at half cock. The trouble now is the signal crayfish. The early attentions of these nuisances often sees minute lifts of the float, which the little shot helps to exaggerate, allowing me to wind in very slowly, hopefully dragging the cray out of the swim before it has had chance to filch the bait.

It was barely light enough to see the float, nestling against the outer edge of the algae around the draping near bank willow branches, when it had tilted and shot under the foliage. That first perch, about a pound, was followed almost immediately by a much worthier adversary, a perch that battled its way to the net with great gusto. When the scales eventually confirmed 3lb 2oz, I was delighted. It had been five years since my last three pounder, and a very pleasing start to a planned Autumn

Martin Bowler perching in a flood.

campaign, with a first four pounder the target. I hoped it wouldn't be another five before the next. Actually, it was going to be less than 24 hours.

The next morning, I stood on the bank of a different stretch, again just as dawn was breaking. I had never before fished the stretch, but on a previous reconnaissance had selected a few swims I wished to try at first light. The first was a cracking looking swim where a far bank willow overhung the river, with algae thickly draped around the trailing branches, a perfect set up for summer perch. I fished as I had the previous morning, and the only word that describes the first hour's action is frantic. I landed no less than nineteen perch, all quality fish from 8oz upwards, with the best four going 1lb 14oz, 2lb 2oz, 2lb 13oz and 3lb 3oz.

During that action packed period, not one crayfish bite was experienced, and it was obvious that there were so many good perch in residence that the signals were wisely keeping their heads down. In contrast, as soon as the perch activity ceased, which it did very abruptly, the crays invaded the swim. After a frustrating hour, I moved out in disgust, but before doing so deposited the best part of two pints of red maggots into the swim. The thinking here was that the maggots, hopefully, would draw fry and small silver fish into the area, and the big perch would follow.

When I eventually made my next cast into the swim, a good two hours later, perhaps the most significant factor was that the float never moved for ten minutes. It may sound perverse, but that is now a good sign on the Upper Ouse in summer. If signal crayfish are leaving your bait alone, it often means there is a big enough predator around to worry them, especially chub and big perch. The longer the float remained unmolested, the more confident I became, and this was fully justified when the float suddenly lifted and then vanished. The loose line zipping across the surface told me no crayfish was responsible and I struck into a good fish moving at speed. After a terrific scrap, I landed a super perch that turned out to be my biggest for nearly thirty years, taking the needle to 3lb 7oz. Shortly afterwards, I was on my

way home, with memories of two days brilliant perch fishing eating the miles effortlessly.

Elsewhere in this book, you will read the story of a magnificent 7lb chub taken by my friend Paul Fickling, which he caught from a swim I had prebaited and which I intended to move back into, had he not arrived in the meantime. In actual fact, there was a lot of déjà vue about that incident, because, earlier that season, Paul had done exactly the same thing to me with a big perch. I was fishing one of the stretches that had produced a crop of four pounders, and the first swim I fished was opposite a dwarf willow on the far bank. The edge of those branches, just past mid-river, had produced several good perch without me ever taking a big one.

This particular morning was the same, with a couple of half pound fish early on and then nothing. After two biteless hours, I decided on a move. I would go and fish a substantial raft two hundred yards downstream for a while, returning to the original swim for the evening session. However, when I arrived back at the swim around teatime, I found Paul well ensconced. He had been there about half an hour and had taken two modest fish already. I moved fifty yards above him. For a peaceful hour, not much occurred, for either of us, and then I heard a shout from Paul. He had a big fish, and could I bring my camera. When I arrived, Paul was lifting a cracking perch from his landing net. My immediate guess was 4lb, but I was an ounce out. At 3lb 15oz it was Paul's first perch over two pounds, let alone three. It would also have been my personal best, and I mentally cursed myself for moving out of the swim. Nevertheless, at that moment, I knew that my time would come.

My close season plans in 1999 included a more determined effort than ever to crack the 4lb barrier for perch from a small stream while there was still time. I say that because the species had certainly reached a peak in the 1998/99 season, with a significant number of four pounders having been taken from the Upper Ouse system. I knew, from the thirty years or more that I had fished the river, that big perch are very cyclic. They are not long lived fish, and a four pounder is obviously reaching the end of its natural span. I was expecting the number of four pounders to steadily decline over the coming years. In July 1999, therefore, I felt that my chances of an exceptional perch were still good, but that the longer I went without reaching my goal, the more difficult it would be.

Never did I dream or could I have hoped that my very first perch trip of the new season would yield not only the fish of a lifetime, but a perch that proved to be the

Another clonking great perch!

Fishing near-bank lilies.

Trefor unhooks a good chub in sub-zero conditions.

Playing a big Leam chub.

5lb 5oz chub from the Leam.

Summer chubbing.

Re-capture 6 days later at 10lb 12oz from the Cherwell.

biggest authenticated from any river. July 22nd, 1999, rates as one of the most incredible days of my angling life.

The session started modestly enough, in fact, had I not been so sweaty after a long walk to the swim on a very hot and humid early morning, I may well have moved to a different swim after only a few minutes. You see, after only fifteen minutes fishing, under the draping branches of a far bank willow, I had already taken ten small perch, before the signal crayfish had moved in. I had always found that, if small perch were active in a swim at the crack of dawn, there was rarely a big one there. It was only because I was so sweaty that I decided to stay put for another half hour or so to cool off. I told myself I must be getting old.

During that time, however, I was absolutely plagued by signals, and reluctantly came to the conclusion that I had to move on. That was disappointing, because the swim was a banker for me. I had taken three pounders there before, and felt that if anywhere could produce my dream perch, that swim could. It is a classic. The willow harbours a raft perhaps eight yards from front to back. All my perch from that swim had come from the upstream end, manoeuvring my float against the flotsam. I had often tried baits behind the raft, where it is shallower, but had never had any response other than from signals.

That morning, I do not know what made me try behind the raft, unless it was pure instinct. All I know is that one moment the float was settling beneath the branches, and the next it had whistled away. Seconds after setting the hook, I was playing a very heavy fish that I was convinced had to be a chub. In fact, so powerful did it feel that I thought I may even have latched into a double figure pike or big tench, both of which occasionally take lobs intended for perch. As it felt far too big for a perch, I was actually quite relaxed, and just wondered what bonus fish would pop its head out. I was, therefore, mentally unprepared for the fish that rolled under my rod top a couple of minutes later, a perch of quite staggering proportions. That first sighting was sufficient to convince me that I was doing battle with a perch that could make angling history. I knew this wasn't just four pounds, this was truly awesome.

The next few minutes were agonising. The fish fought hard, making several excursions under the tree branches, often taking line off me, and I was dreading the line suddenly falling slack. If it had, I think I'd have burnt my rods. But it didn't, and soon an absolute Goliath of a perch slid over the net cord. At that moment, I was as excited as a small kid on Christmas Eve.

I will never forget lifting that perch out of the net on to my weigh sling. I was trembling in anticipation, because I knew that here was a fish that could conceivably rock the British record. My first weighing was a total shambles because,

My magnificent five pounder.

in my state of uncontrolled euphoria, I forgot to zero the Avons. I recorded 5lb 4oz, and when I found that the scales were out I actually put the fish into a keep sack for a few minutes to calm down over a cup of tea. A few moments later, now in control, the scales were carefully zeroed, and the perch weighed again. This exercise was repeated twice more, and all three weighings confirmed exactly 5lb, to the dot. I tell you, that fact just wouldn't sink in. I kept repeating to myself, "A five pound perch, bloody hell, a FIVE pound perch!"

Getting some photographs was a game in itself. I have a good circle of friends, all of whom have come out to photograph very special fish for me at one time or another. So the mobile phone was brought into play, and I telephoned at least six people, all of whom were not answering. I, therefore, had to fall back on self portraiture. I am very adept at this, having experience over many years, but was a little nervous with a fish quite so incredible. Nevertheless, I had no choice and slowly set up my tripod and cable release. Then came the next problem. For some reason I have never been able to fathom, the cable release simply would not fire the shutter that morning, although it has since worked perfectly. Obviously, in my hyper state, I must have done something wrong, although I have no idea what.

Anyway, I was now in a quandary, and suddenly two other anglers came into view, introducing themselves as Pete and Steve. It is amusing to look back on because, when they asked me what I had caught, I came out with a right load of gibberish. I could hardly string two coherent words together until, after stopping and taking a deep breath, I said "I've had a five pound perch." You know those cartoons where one of the characters jaw drops, hits the floor and then rebounds, that's how those lads looked that morning when I showed them the fish. They were now as blown away as I was, perhaps explaining why the photographs they took that morning were nearly a disaster, with only one slide of any use. Still, I was extremely grateful, and had a record of one of my most momentous experiences in angling.

The following week, it occurred to me that I still hadn't taken a four pounder, but I suppose the next session was entirely predictable. Hardly surprisingly, I was back in the same swim at dawn, but this time there were no giants, just a

Signal crayfish claw coughed up by my five pounder.

succession of tiny perch and the ever present swarm of signal crays. Eventually, after fishing six swims and taking well over forty perch, I connected with a good fish of 3lb 4oz. This was 11.00am, later than I normally expect a good perch on a sunny summer morning.

After a pleasant few hours chasing chub on natural baits, I was back in the perch swim in early evening, but again there was no sign of a decent fish. After an hour being plagued by tiny perch and signals, I moved down stream fifty yards to a dense rush bed, where I flicked the float across river to settle against the far bank foliage.

As is often the case with big perch, the bite was instant, the float shooting under as soon as it had cocked. The water boiled as a big fish took off through the rushes, and for around five minutes a heart in the mouth tussle was played out in the dense foliage, before my net eventually closed around another monster perch. At first, I thought it was my five pounder again as there were distinct similarities in the stripe pattern. However, an old scar above its vent confirmed it was indeed different. When I weighed the fish at 4lb 10oz I permitted myself a wry smile. After thirty years of struggle for a four pounder, what odds would there have been on repeating the feat just seven days later.

At the time of writing, July 2000, it would seem that a lot of my fears are perhaps coming true. There are still big perch to be caught, but there were far fewer 4 pounders caught in 1999 than in 1998, and this season to date I have heard of only one. However, I remain positive. Next week, I may hook my five pounder again, with a year's added growth. Now that is a mouth watering prospect.

Big Chub in our Blood

Elsewhere in this book you will read about
fabulous chubbing I have enjoyed over the years
from the Great Ouse and Dorset Stour, without a
doubt my two favourite rivers. But no history of my big
fish exploits could possibly be complete without taking a
look at three other lovely rivers that have given me many big chub over the years,
the Cherwell, Wensum and my home river, the Warwickshire Leam.

It would be totally impossible to give anything but a brief overview of the
highlights of my chub fishing on these venues, there are simply so many memories,
so many big fish. I could, literally, write a book on each. All I can do, therefore, is
select a handful of special memories, highlights of over thirty years of my life. Let's
start with the Oxfordshire Cherwell.

The Cherwell

Sadly, the present day Cherwell is but a shadow of its former glory, at least as far
as its chub are concerned. Hopefully, like the Great Ouse before it, the problem is
temporary and we will soon be seeing reports of many big chub once again. But
from the early seventies, when I was reluctantly forced to move away from my
beloved Claydon Brook, to the late eighties, when the Upper Ouse again
commanded my attention, the River Cherwell was the focus of my chub fishing.
Between us, Trefor and I accounted for a colossal number of big chub in that time,
and it is no lie to say that we lost count of the number of four pounders. Five
pounders, however, were a different story. Chub anglers coming into the game in
the last year or so can be forgiven for thinking that five pounders are ten a penny,
but, believe me, they needed work to find in the seventies and eighties. There had
been a noticeable decline nationally in reports of big chub in just a few short years,
and six pounders became almost unheard of until the chubbing renaissance that
started in the late eighties and seems to have been accelerating ever since.

It is not unreasonable to say that Trefor and I learned our chubbing trade on the
Cherwell. We developed the art of natural bait fishing, especially with slugs and

crayfish, into a lethal method, often taking upwards of a dozen fish a day each. We perfected the skills of preferential baiting, induced bite techniques, upstream legering and surface fishing. Years of observation, trial and error and total dedication to our craft gave us the information to formulate techniques for fishing flood rafts, and how temperature, colour and flow variations affected the presentation required in crease swims. In short, we became so adept at what we did that we enjoyed catches of chub that others could never emulate. That Cherwell apprenticeship was an invaluable part of my development.

Slug - one of the best of all chub baits.

Space dictates that I can only relate two stories from those days, both involving strange instincts. The first concerns a most special chub that was not even my biggest. Just before the season ended in March 1983, I arrived at a very isolated stretch of the river at dawn in very sombre mood. The previous day, tears had flowed freely at the funeral of my father, the most wonderful man I have ever known. That had climaxed a week of heartbreak, which had started with my having to identify him on a mortician's slab, as Dad had died suddenly in the street. With all the formalities over, I just needed to be left alone. I needed solitude, and that is why, with my wife's blessing, I slowly wandered upstream to a stretch of river I had brought Dad to many years before, an overgrown spinney that hardly saw an angler from one season to the next. He had often spoken of that lovely, secluded spot, especially the number of kingfishers that lived there, his favourite bird.

To reach the spinney, I had to walk past a big pool on a right angle bend in the river, a pool that looked good but had never given me a bite. Trefor had also fared very badly there as well, it was just one of those swims where appearances were very deceptive. I had no intention whatever of fishing the pool, and yet, as I drew adjacent to it, I lowered my gear to the ground. There was a most overwhelming urge to fish one particular spot, despite upwards of twenty blanks I had endured in exactly the same place. It made no sense and yet I didn't fight it. I just went with the flow, the day wasn't about actually catching fish in any event.

Almost mechanically, I assembled the gear in a kind of daze, impaled a piece of breadcrust on the hook and lobbed it onto the little crease in mid-river. This was

Personal best from the Cherwell - 5lb 14oz.

followed by three handfuls of squeezed crumb, and then I put the rod on a rest. As I sat there in the early morning mist, quiet and alone, my grief was so intense, it could almost be tasted. Dad and I had been so close; I was lonely, and I was hurting.

I couldn't tell you how many minutes had passed when I suddenly jolted back to reality, to see the rod pulling round vigorously, sliding forward in the rest as it did so. Soon, the pulsating scrap of a muscular chub jolted me from my sad reverie and I was on my feet countering its attempt to bury me in the far bank rushes. It was never again to come close to snagging me, but fought like a thing possessed for a good few minutes before I was at last able to slide the net under it.

The fish was no monster by any means, but 5lb 5oz in 1983 was a very creditable capture and as I knelt looking at that short, deep immaculate specimen, I told myself that Dad had arranged it. Silly and sentimental of course, but the thought helped me, and thereafter I was able to move on. That morning, just as I slipped the fish back, I said out loud, "Thanks, Dad."

There's a strange fact about that pool. I'd had twenty blanks before that day, and I had at least another twenty blanks after it. The big chub that helped me over my grief that morning came from the only bite I ever had there.

Instincts that are strange but true played a major part in the capture of my biggest ever Cherwell chub, a fish that is the only known specimen fish I have deliberately targeted. Two winters before my capture, I had witnessed the fish at 6lb 4oz, the only genuine "six" I was ever to see from the river.

Trefor lands a Cherwell chub on crayfish.

The stretch that had produced that chub was one of the slower sections of the river, with a higher average size than normal, but with no apparent features and being of uniform flow it was very difficult to read. The previous day, I had fished hard for nothing and with it being bitterly cold, I felt it likely that a streamier stretch would be more productive. It would be easier to read, and I would be kept warmer being more mobile.

Before dawn, I had nearly arrived at this new destination when I suddenly pulled into a lay by, turned the car round and headed back towards the slow stretch I had fished the previous day. It wasn't even a conscious decision. Something just told me I had to go back. When I arrived at the river bridge, and saw, in the dawn light, the hard frost, ice margins and white, cobweb encrusted trees, I felt I had made a serious error. What had I been thinking of? But as I stood there, I suddenly knew I had to move downstream, on the far bank that I never fished. As I slowly walked the bank, I stopped dead at a line of pollarded willows. I knew my journey was over, I had to fish right there.

I can tell you that conscious thought would never have seen me settle in that particular spot. It was no different to a hundred yards up or downstream, same depth, same flow, nothing to particularly commend it whatever. To cap it all, there were two swans cavorting right in front of me, and I like to avoid those things like the plague. Nevertheless, I set the rod up, introduced some mashed bread despite the swans, and then swung out a large piece of crust to mid-river. Once it had settled, it must have been directly under the birds.

I stared intently at the quivertip, because I knew I was going to catch. Yes, I know that is easy to say after the event, but it is true none the less. Sure enough, barely two minutes had elapsed before the tip slammed round and I was playing the leviathan that had taken my scales to over six pounds two years previously, only a good two hundred yards away. The chub fought well on the very light rod I was using that day, and my heart was in my mouth for most of the fight because the fish had rolled at the surface only seconds after being hooked. I knew it was a monster; I was sure it was the "six".

When I eventually swung my prize over the marginal rushes, my elation knew no bounds. It had been twenty years since my last six-pounder. However, despite three re-zeroing and re-weighing sessions, the scales stubbornly refused to play ball, and I had to settle for 5lb 14oz. Believe it or not, my first reaction was one of disappointment, I had become so psyched up at the thought of a six pound chub after such a long time. But it took but a few moments to get things back in perspective. It was, after all, my biggest Cherwell chub by a considerable margin. I have never since had one bigger.

The Wensum

The River Wensum near Norwich had never figured in our thinking until my good friend Dave Plummer moved to Norfolk from Rotherham in the early eighties. It took very little time for Dave to start extracting some serious fish from the river, both chub and barbel, and he wasted no time in inviting Trefor and me down to join him. It was in 1981 that we had our first session there, and in the six years that followed I was to take over twenty five-pound chub and numerous fours. It is true that most of those fish came at night on large baits intended for barbel, but my two biggest Wensum chub, both weighing 5lb 7oz, were taken quite deliberately. Just as the two Cherwell fish I discussed were both taken as a result of obeying instinct, my two biggest Wensum chub came as a result of inducing bites. The first of these came on my second winter on the river, in the last week of the season, and it was actually my very first Wensum "five."

During that final week, Trefor and I were staying with Dave and Linda, and in our first four days fishing, we had all caught numbers of good fish, with five pounders to both Trefor and Dave, but I was still in waiting. With two days of the season to go, Trefor and I were searching a relatively featureless stretch which we had a feeling might just throw up a bigger than average specimen. Although the banks were pleasantly overgrown with trees and bushes, there was little variation in the flow itself, other than a barely discernible crease in mid-river along a line of trees. I remember detecting this when I introduced some mashed bread/dry breadcrumb feed, to see a distinct demarcation between faster and marginally slower water in mid-river. That was obviously better than no feature at all, and my initial presentation was to present a bait on the edge of the faster water, selecting a link weight to achieve that objective. The conditions were good, the water temperature high for March, and I felt the fish would be feeding in the faster flows. We just had to find them.

Syndicate stretch of the Wensum.

On my first cast, once the bait had settled, I allowed it to lie static for about five minutes with no response, before lifting the rod top, dislodging the terminal rig, and allowing the bait to swing inshore, settling into steadier water. No sooner had it settled than the rod bucked in my hand, and a big fish shot downstream to an overhanging willow. I could immediately see that I had a problem, as the line had thrown a double loop around the screw in quivertip I was using at the time, and I could neither give nor retrieve line. Luckily, before the hook pulled out or the line went, the quiver gave up the ghost and snapped in two pieces, leaving me able to play the fish normally. Minutes later, Trefor was doing the honours with the camera, with me grinning in time honoured fashion. I remarked to Trefor then, as I have many times since, how the Wensum strain of chub have always looked longer and leaner for their weight than Ouse fish, which are very short and stocky.

In early 1985, I was on the renowned barbel syndicate stretch of the Wensum below Costessy weir for a two day barbel session, and on the Thursday did manage a couple of average barbel from a swim known as the Copse. I had also baited the bottom most swim on the stretch, just as the feeder stream entered, which had never produced me a barbel at that time, although it held plenty. The trouble was, the swim was always occupied by a big shoal of chub, both big and small, making selective fishing difficult.

On the Friday, I was back on the river, this time in the company of Dave Plummer and John Bailey, and John fished this bottom swim in the afternoon,

Trefor lands a Wensum biggie.

suffering numerous little taps and bumps from small chub to his barbel baits, much as I had suffered the previous night. In late afternoon, John moved swims and, about an hour later, I decided to move in and give it a go with very large chunks of meat, hopefully to deter the small chub. I must have been using cubes of meat with two-inch sides!

However, there is hardly a bait big enough to deter hungry chub and for half an hour or more the rod top was barely still. Twice it went round to tempt me into a strike but to no avail. I struck into fresh air. Then, just as the light was starting to recede, I had a particularly ferocious series of bumps, bangs and tweaks, and I became so frustrated I wound the bait quickly a couple of feet upstream. I actually said out loud, "If you want the meat, come and get it." The response was instant. When the rod went round this time, it just continued going, and I set my hook into a very big fish that gave a stimulating tussle in the mouth of the feeder stream and in and out of the fallen branches that littered it. But there were no mistakes, and I soon knelt, admiring the lines of an immaculate Wensum chub of 5lb 7oz. Shortly afterwards, John and Dave were photographing the fish for me, to the tune of much raucous accusation of blind luck.

Fifteen minutes later, I was back at the swim and the very first cast saw the resumption of the chub concerto on the rod top. Once again, I pulled the bait fiercely upstream, and once again the response was from a very big fish, slamming the rod round in very determined fashion. It was very much a case of déjà vue as I recorded a second five pounder, 5lb 2oz this time, and for the rest of that evening John continually remarked that a certain part of my anatomy was apparently crafted from a precious metal.

It was at the end of a chubbing session on the Wensum that one of my most embarrassing moments in angling occurred. The van was packed for the long drive back to Coventry, and I was caught short, as they say. This was in the days before I was equipped with a Portaloo, and so I edged my way backwards into the thicket of trees and bushes that bordered the river close to Costessy bridge. Feeling nicely secluded, down came the trousers, and as I inched even further backwards, to make sure I couldn't be seen, I suddenly felt myself falling, rolling over backwards down the steep slope that led to the river. Moments later, I lay in the mud in the open air in full view of passing traffic, trousers round my ankles, as if waiting for a nappy change. Of course, wasn't my timing immaculate? At that precise moment, a young woman crossed the bridge on horseback, and I could see she was mightily unimpressed. To say I was mortified would be a gross understatement!

The Leam

My first ever fishing trip at the age of 13 took me to the banks of the Warwickshire Leam, and I have fished it ever since. In the early days, the river was alive with chub but never produced a big one. It was very rare indeed for a four pounder to be reported and even a three pounder was a notable capture, and for this reason the members of the Coventry Specimen Group, myself included, had discounted the river for a specimen by the late sixties. For the next five years or so, although I fished the river occasionally, only taking one four pounder, my serious chubbing took place on the Cherwell and the Ouse.

My return to the Leam was totally accidental, when my son, then seven, was bending my ear to take him fishing. The Leam, full of two pound chub and plenty of bites, was obviously ideal.

In November 1975, therefore, I returned to the Leam, but what occurred was totally unexpected. For a start, I really struggled for bites, whereas only a few short years earlier, there had been a terrific head of fish attacking the baits. But, in the first three sessions, although I totalled only seven chub, five of them were over four pounds, to a top weight of 4lb 14oz, and the whole complexion of Leam chubbing had changed. Something exciting had happened to the river in the years since I had last fished it.

After I had let Trefor in on the secret, we went on to enjoy fabulous chubbing for several seasons in peace, no one else having sussed the potential, but by 1980 still hadn't recorded a five pounder, although we had both come an agonising ounce short. And then we arrived on a bitterly cold morning in February 1980 for yet another attempt.

As I trudged through the snow, sinking to my knees in places, I thought the chances were good. I have always caught well with

chub when there is lying snow. It's almost as if they know the river will soon be out of sorts when the snow and ice melts and the water deoxygenates. Soon, I arrived at a swim which had been annoying me for the best part of four years. It was an absolutely classic raft, with an overhanging alder creating a secluded haven, the lower branches being draped with flotsam. The swim was also on an inside bend, featuring a slight increase in depth. In other words, it was an ideal set up for a big chub. Yet, in those four years,

Crayfish, great chub bait, now illegal.

I'd never mustered a single bite there, and I'd probably fished it over thirty times.

That morning, however, it took barely three minutes for my crust bait to be taken, by an obviously heavy fish but one that didn't seem to want to go anywhere in a hurry. To start with, I thought it was a good bream which often give this type of spiritless performance, especially in cold water. However, it was a chub all right, a deep, chunky specimen of 5lb 3oz that really had no excuse whatever for not fighting. I reckon it was shocked that someone had the temerity to stick a hook in its top lip! I was, however, prepared to forego the pleasure of a hard scrap in this instance. Here before me was a chub that we could not have dreamed of even a few years previously. Five pounders from the Leam were simply unheard of, and I raced across the field to impart the exciting news to Trefor. The great thing about fishing with Trefor is that we have always been able to enjoy each other's success, without jealousy creeping in. And so it was that morning. He was as over the moon with this new milestone in our Leam chubbing as I was, and once more we raised our sights.

The next five pound plus fish I took, three years later, remains my biggest Leam fish to this day, and was a very interesting capture in many ways. Since 1980, more and more anglers had sussed where we were fishing, but, without exception, were faring very poorly. There was a very simple reason for this. The River Leam those days was literally full of rafts. On the big fish stretches, you could find a classic looking raft every twenty yards or so, and these obviously attracted chub anglers like jam attracts wasps. The trouble was, most of these swims were barren. I have never fished a river, before or since, where appearances could be so deceptive. Obviously, there were raft swims containing good chub, but for every one of these here were ten that rarely, if ever, produced a chub. Out of the hundreds of good chub that Trefor and I took from the Leam, less than 10% came from swims of this type; most came from simple glides or creases. Over the years, we had learned about our river, and knew the depths and variations in depths over many miles of bank.

The swim from which I caught my biggest Leam chub illustrates this point perfectly. Between two tremendous looking rafts, about forty yards apart, there was a simple, straightforward glide with nothing apparently to commend it, and visiting anglers invariably fished under the flotsam around both the upstream and downstream trees. In all my years on the river, I never saw anyone else other than Trefor fish that glide. Yet we knew it featured a far bank depression, around six feet deep, sloping up to about four and a half feet in mid-river, where the bottom composition turned abruptly from clay to gravel. The only surface clue to this underwater irregularity was a slight crease that started under the far bank and slowly tracked across into mid-river, before disappearing under the lower tree. The way to fish this swim was to hold a bait on the far bank crease, and then progressively bump it down and across.

In March 1983, I had gone an entire winter without taking a chub from that particular swim, and on my previous three trips had actually walked past it. Chub swims can be like that. I have known others be barren for two or three years, and then suddenly become colonised, and vice versa. So when I arrived for a day's chubbing just before the end of the season, I did not intend to fish the swim. In fact, it was one of those days when you just know the fish will be having it. Mild, calm conditions and a river about a foot up and nicely stained with a temperature in the high forties Fahrenheit promised a day to remember.

Lovely Ouse swim.

Trefor's first Leam five pounder.

As is my usual practice with mobile winter chub fishing, the first job was to walk the stretch and prebait the swims I intended fishing. That day, I was on my favourite crust and mashed bread feed, and I slowly meandered about half a mile from the car, depositing four or five large handfuls of mashed bread into ten areas I fancied. Trefor was doing exactly the same, but I had dropped him off at a different access point. We would meet up in the middle of the stretch to compare notes.

I came to the glide after a couple of hours, with a couple of four pounders under my belt, intending to walk another fifty yards to my third prepared pitch, and I stopped at the head of the run. As always, it looked inviting and, against my better judgement, I decided to give it half an hour while I had a sandwich and cup of coffee. For perhaps ten minutes, I did not bother casting out, but sat there in the pleasant early spring sunshine flicking in bits of flake from my sandwiches. Then, I leisurely baited with a chunk of crust and tossed it under the far bank where the fairly sharp current caught it and took it downstream a couple of yards before it settled on the crease. It didn't settle for long. Two or three minutes later, the tip dragged slowly round, almost like weed catching the line, but when I struck, the "weed" woke up. Suddenly, the clutch was whining as something powerful shot back under the far bank, into the faster water. For perhaps five minutes the chub bored along that far margin, but slowly and surely gave ground until I was playing him just under the surface in mid-river. It was then that I saw quite what a precarious hook hold I had. The size 6 Au Lion D'or was nicked in the extreme edge of the top lip and, as I could see this was an exceptional chub, my heart was in my mouth. I played that fish thereafter with kid gloves, and breathed an enormous sigh of relief when it at long last folded into the net mesh.

I really thought for a while I had achieved the impossible, a Leam six pounder, but although the fish certainly had the frame for it, the belly was empty. But it was still a mightily impressive specimen and, at 5lb 10oz, one of the biggest by a long way to have ever been caught from the river.

It was some time later before Trefor had the opportunity to witness and photograph the fish for me and his words became prophetic. "I hope I catch that fish one day," he said.

And that is exactly what he did, the following Christmas Eve, of all days, which led to an incident I have never allowed him to forget.

It was early evening on Christmas Eve, and I was at home with my wife and kids, as you do when you are a family man. But Trefor had other ideas. He was fishing, and just after dark had landed a chub he immediately recognised as my big one from the previous March. When I had caught the fish it was empty, but when Trefor had it, the chub was very lean, weighing only 5lb 2oz. Nevertheless, it was still a massively framed chub, and Trefor wanted his photographs. So he telephoned me.

One of a brace of Leam 'fives'.

I am always glad to go out and photograph fish for Trefor, as he is for me, but I had to say, when I answered the phone, "You do know what night this is, don't you mate?"

As he begged me to come out, promising it would only take about an hour, and the wife giving me one of those looks that screamed "Don't you dare!" I agreed to drive out and do the honours. I took my two daughters with me, placating Fran a little as it gave her a little peace in preparing for the Christmas festivities.

About three quarters of an hour later, having had to borrow a flash gun from a mutual friend because Trefor's wasn't working and my camera was being serviced, I found Trefor on the bank. Together, we admired that big chub for a minute or so, and then I composed the shots, being pleased to note that the flash gun was working perfectly. Everything set, I went to wind on the film on Tref's camera. It went half a turn, and then jammed. That was the end of the film, and when I asked Trefor for his spare film he very sheepishly admitted that he hadn't brought one with him.

So we never did get a shot of my big chub when Trefor had it, and as I said earlier, I have made sure he has never forgotten that crazy Christmas Eve.

In 1987, I was putting the finishing touches to one of my first books, My Way with Chub, and the editor asked me to provide a particular shot for the front cover, a good close up of me with a fat, well conditioned fish. None of the shots in my library quite fitted his requirements, so I had to go and try and catch one to order. And I had to do it quickly. We were approaching deadline.

A fat fish of around four and a half pounds would be ideal, and so I targeted a stretch of the Leam near to Leamington Spa which is slow and featureless, but the chub all of good average size. Although I had never had a fish anywhere near five, I'd had a lot to 4lb 10oz, and felt confident that over a day I could muster a chub that would be suitable.

When I arrived just after dawn, with a nice, calm day in prospect, I had already decided my plan of campaign. I would refrain from actually fishing for at least four hours, spending the time steadily baiting a few swims and getting the fish really confident. In that way I hoped to achieve two things, first guarantee a bite or two and second target the biggest fish in each area. By baiting and leaving each swim for hours, I hoped the biggest chub in residence would assert feeding dominance. As it transpired, the ploy worked so well, it exceeded even my most optimistic dreams.

It was just before midday when I made my first cast, tight to the near bank along some wild blackberry bushes. Less than three minutes later the tip had whipped round and I was locked in combat with a strong adversary that rocketed backwards and forwards with great gusto for a while, before bowing to the inevitable. As soon as I lifted the fish ashore, I knew that I had achieved my objective, and how. This chub easily beat five pounds, in fact at 5lb 5oz it was my second biggest from the river. It was also truly immaculate and the editor's problems were over. After some very careful self-portrait work, and I had slipped the fish back, I went over the event again. Leam chub exceeding five pounds were

Leam in winter.

extremely rare creatures, and to catch one almost to order was pushing good fortune to the limit.

So what happened on the very next cast brought the day into the realms of fantasy. Again, the bite was immediate, after I had flicked the bait under a far bank alder, and again a big fish had scampered round with great alacrity before surrendering. 5lb 2oz this one weighed, to complete my one and only 5lb brace from the Leam. As far as I am aware, that is the only time that feat has been achieved on the river, and I drove home that night in a daze.

Come to daddy!

A Cherwell Discovery

My involvement with the barbel of the Oxfordshire Cherwell began as long ago as 1967, when I first fished the river in the company of Merv Wilkinson, just after I had started the Coventry Specimen Group. On one of my first trips, I was to spot a small barbel, about two pounds, in the company of a shoal of chub. Although I was never to spot another, that information was stored away in my memory bank and would not be called upon for another twenty years.

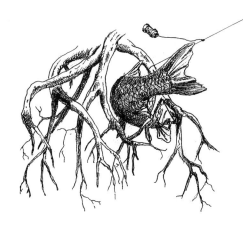

My interest was not fully aroused in the elusive barbel population until the summer of 1984, when a good head of fish was discovered in a short stretch which I had regularly chub fished. I put in many sessions for those barbel from 1984 to 1986, after which, as the area was rapidly becoming very well known, I became disenchanted with the element of racing for a few known swims. During that time, I caught a fair few barbel, to a shade under eight pounds, as well as losing a definite double in tree roots.

So popular had the area become in 1986 that I knew I had to find a new stretch, one that was lightly fished if possible. That is when the memory of that two pounder in the sixties came flooding back. My next venue had been decided and in early September 1987 I arrived on its banks for the first time in almost two decades.

Much had changed. My favourite chub swim under the high clay bank had gone, swept away by a winter flood or the dredger bucket. In fact, the banks were higher than I remembered in most places because of the dredging in the seventies, but enough years had passed for nature to have healed the worst of the scars.

One long stretch, a riot of head high bankside rush and sedge, was heavily overgrown with cabbages. As I paused to watch a couple of big chub in a small clearing, I distinctly caught a flash of orange alongside a small clump of mid-river rushes. I watched the spot intently and then I saw it, a barbel of about seven pounds slowly emerging from the foliage.

That was the only barbel I was to see on that preliminary excursion, but the following week I was back, tooled up with a gallon of hemp. Now there were three barbel in the little clearing, and although they were only about six pounds, it was very encouraging nonetheless. What those fish had told me was that there were probably sufficient barbel to make their pursuit worthwhile, although I hadn't yet found a big one. That was soon to change.

On my arrival, I had baited the swim with fifteen droppers of hemp and then left the barbel to feed in peace while I investigated other areas. Two hours later, having located only two other swims containing one very small barbel apiece, I was back in the prepared pitch. As I carefully peered through the head high foliage, I caught my breath in barely contained excitement. There were now five barbel feeding over the hemp, the two newcomers being much bigger fish, one possibly 8lb and the other a definite double. I had stumbled onto a gold mine, and a neglected one at that judging by the overgrown nature of the banks.

The rest of that day was total frustration. For hour after hour the barbel completely ignored my meat hook baits and when I left just after dark I'd had not a sign of a bite.

Success, however, came the following week. I'd theorised that the large hook bait had to be the problem and this time had baited initially with hemp, corn and casters. The same five barbel were soon in evidence, but they steadfastly refused both corn and caster hook baits. I tried them on small hooks, I tried them hair rigged and counterbalanced, but all to no avail. Once again, it was head-scratching time, and then it occurred to me that I might be missing the obvious. Perhaps I ought to be using a truly natural bait for these virgin fish. Accordingly, I fetched my bucket of lobs from the van and baited my size 4 Au Lion D'or with two of the biggest lobs I had.

Creeping down behind the rushes, I waited patiently until the barbel had made one of their temporary excursions out of the swim, and then silently lowered the worms to rest on the bed of hemp. That done, I backed away a few yards and sat behind the cover, my eyes glued to the quivertip. I didn't have long to wait. Although the hook bait was not visible from my sitting position I could see the gravel upstream of the bait, from where the barbel always seemed to enter the swim. After a couple of minutes, I caught sight of them returning and I can remember vividly how tensed up I was at that moment. Within seconds, the tip thumped round and that was the prelude to two hours fishing that saw me land four of the five fish present. The first three were average fish of between 5lb and 6lbs 10oz,but when I weighed the fourth I let out a whoop of joy that was probably heard in Oxford. 10lb 3oz it weighed, one of the most memorable fish of my career.

What a tremendous scrap that fish gave me, necessitating my joining it in the river to affect a successful netting. So hard did it fight that it took the best part of an hour to revive, being held upright in the streamy shallows until it suddenly shot off in a cloud of silt. I would have no trouble recognising it again. An unmistakable distorted pelvic fin with a double V would make it instantly recognisable.

When I returned the following week, it was with the intention of finding some new fish, but I went first of all to see if I could find my ten pounder and reassure myself that it had recovered from its ordeal. In that I was immediately successful, but the interesting thing was that there were now seven barbel present, all looking over seven pounds with two more that could have been nines. Certainly, the small fish I had caught the previous week were not present, which meant that at least four of those in front of me were new fish. As each week passed, this new stretch was becoming more exciting.

As I stood there in the autumn sunshine, watching those barbel drift leisurely over the gravel, I suddenly became aware of an eighth fish emerging slowly from the upstream cabbages, to join the ten pounder. Before my astonished gaze, here was a true leviathan, a fish that must weigh all of 13lb. What other surprises did this fabulous bit of river have for me.

Having found such an incredible barbel, the fates then conspired to play a cruel trick on me. After that day, when I couldn't get it to take a bait whatever I tried, the river was too coloured to find fish visually for two years. Only a few days later, heavy rain raised the level to that of winter and, although I still fished hard, only chub rewarded my efforts. The following season was equally frustrating. A combination of algal blooms and heavy rains meant that not once was I able to locate barbel visually for the entire season. Once again, I had to be content with chub and one average barbel from fishing blind.

The summer of 1989, however, was a scorcher, and in August I took my daughter Jacqui, for our first trip to the barbel stretch. I was pleased to see the river low and clear, but despite baiting several areas with hemp, really struggled to locate any barbel. I eventually managed to entice one barbel, of about 6lb, onto a clear gravel patch, but that was all. The rest of the fish were obviously keeping their heads down in the dense cabbages.

Even my attempts to catch that barbel failed miserably, and as Jacqui and I took a leisurely walk along the bank, watching chub taking floating crust, we stopped under the shade of a big willow.

The next few minutes are permanently etched in my memory. We were cooling off when something moved only inches from the near bank, right under my feet. There was a small clump of streamer there and whatever I had seen had been under that. I watched carefully and, sure enough, there it was again, a barbel tail. But what a tail. It was huge.

For the next ten minutes or so, we stood there quietly, watching the spot intently, and presently the fish obligingly backed slowly out from the cover, and did a tight little pirouette before resuming station under its streamer frond. I now knew that right under my feet was the monster of two years earlier.

Simon Lush with 11lb 14oz Cherwell fish.

The day had taken on a new urgency. This fish was now to be the target for dusk. But how was I to land it if I hooked it. Where we stood there was a tiny gap in a dense thirty-yard length of tangled alders and brambles, that hung well out from the high bank, at least four feet above water level. Dropping hemp and a hookbait where I had seen the fish would be no problem, but landing a big barbel would be difficult, if not impossible. Even with the landing net handle at full extension I could only just reach the surface of the water over the brambles. Still, the geography of the swim gave me no other choice, and so I commenced a three-hour baiting programme. Over that time, I gradually introduced three pints of hemp and a tin of corn. In early evening, Jacqui and I crept into position.

My corn hook bait can barely have come to rest when the tip thumped round and I found myself attached to an average chub. Although I mentally cursed the chub for disturbing the swim, the trouble I had landing it over the brambles convinced me that it would be an impossible task with a huge barbel. Before recasting, therefore, I stripped down to shorts and a T-shirt only, giving my watch and wallet to Jacqui for safe keeping. Almost certainly, I would have to take a flying leap over those brambles if I hooked the monster. I was really looking forward to that!

In the event, such acrobatics were unnecessary because when I did hook the barbel, about twenty minutes later, the fight was a very short lived affair. On feeling the hook, the fish shot upstream past me at high speed, giving me another good look at its enormous bulk, before turning abruptly back on itself and diving down once more into the tangle of bramble roots close to where I had hooked it. Momentarily there was an ominous grating on the line, a sudden sharp crack, and

The swim under the bushes that produced most of the big fish.

the limp line came fluttering back in the warm evening breeze. That evening, I was absolutely gutted, and knew that I would never rest until that great barbel reposed in my landing net.

The following week, I returned with a definite plan in mind, and went in the river with saw and secateurs. After about four hours graft I had created a small gap in those clogging brambles to fish through, without disturbing the cover where the barbel lay. I also formed, at the water line, a little step I could slide down on to while playing a barbel. That done, I cut some substantial willow branches, which I draped with cut brambles. These were to disguise my new swim on my departure.

All I caught from that swim that day were four nice chub, on corn, and it wasn't until the following week that I again saw barbel there. Disappointingly, however, there was no sign of the big one, the biggest present being about eight pounds. Having baited with hemp and corn, I wandered upriver and prepared several other areas as well. In one, a cabbage patch about ten yards upstream of the clearing where I had caught the ten pounder, I had a momentary glimpse of a big fish as it disappeared under an overhanging bush.

In mid-afternoon, that same fish reposed in my landing net, having accepted two grains of corn seconds after they had been introduced. Although I was pleased to get another Cherwell double, at 10lb 1oz, my pleasure was muted somewhat by the fact that it was a recapture. As soon as it had rolled into the net I had seen the

The barbel stretch in flood.

distinct double V on the pelvic fin, confirming the fish as my ten pounder of two years previously.

The second capture of that fish set off an interesting chain of events. Once again, it had fought very hard and I was in mid-river, nursing the fish back to strength, when I suddenly became aware that I was being watched. After all the time I had spent with the river to myself, or so I thought, I had been found at the worst possible moment, returning a double figure barbel. The angler recognised me, and in the conversation that followed, confided in me that an old friend, Simon Lush, had been fishing the same stretch of river at weekends, and had recently taken a barbel of just over twelve pounds.

This was fascinating. Possibly the twelve pounder was the fish I had lost. It was also interesting to discover that a very short fat barbel of 10lb 10oz, which certainly wasn't my ten pounder, had also been landed recently after being foul hooked. So there was a third double which, from the description, could be one of the fish I had estimated at nine pounds.

On my return home I telephoned Simon, both to congratulate him on a magnificent capture and correct any possible false impression that I was chasing his fishing. We were able to compare notes and agreed that, in future, we would keep each other informed of developments. It was only a few days later that I was to be back on the phone.

The bridge marking the upstream boundary of the barbel stretch.

The following Thursday is a major highlight in my angling memories. Only minutes after my arrival in mid-morning, I spotted four big fish in the cabbages. Two looked like nine pounders, one was my old friend with the distorted pelvic and the other was the monster I had lost several weeks before. Simon's twelve pounder, perhaps?

I had already determined that I would not be fishing for these fish prematurely, to allow confident feeding, nor would I be using corn, on which I had observed barbel spooking the previous week. The swim was fed, therefore, with maggots, casters and hemp on and off all day, while I actually fished elsewhere. I had decided not to position a hook bait in the hot spot until dusk.

At twilight, I carefully crept into position and lowered a bunch of sixteen casters on a size 6 to rest amongst the cabbages. Perhaps five minutes passed and then the rod top bounced. My hand tightened round the reel seat in readiness, just as the rod plunged towards the river. Seconds later, the clutch buzzed angrily as a huge fish shot upstream. In the half-light a tremendous dorsal and upper tail lobe broke surface as the fish powered towards the rushes. Praying that the fish would not come adrift, I slid into the margins off the high bank to keep my rod angle low. After a battle befitting the size of the fish, that mammoth barbel sagged into my net. When my scales steadied at 12lb 5oz, it was a moment of pure euphoria. What a magnificent barbel it was, perfect in every detail except for a raw looking scar at the root of its tail.

In the days that followed, Simon and I were able to confirm that his and my fish were indeed one and the same. We agreed that it looked an old fish, going back in condition. I don't think I was far out in my estimation of 13ls when I first found the fish in 1987.

Having taken the twelve pounder, I had it in my head that the only really big fish I hadn't taken was the 'short, fat one', the one that had been foul hooked. Simon was of like mind, that if any other really big barbel colonised this shallow stretch of river, we would have seen them. The following Friday night was, therefore, a valuable lesson in not prematurely pre-judging anything in big fish angling.

I had again spent the daylight hours in swim preparation with hemp, maggots and casters, and made my first cast, with a writhing bunch of maggots hookbait, when it was almost completely dark. It was a foul evening, with heavy, driving rain, which made an already black night stygian. Only the glowing beta light relieved the gloom. For about half an hour I sat unmoving, the line looped lazily over the index finger of my right hand, and the rain drumming on the hood of my Barbour.

All of a sudden, there was a little twitch like an electric shock, and then an urgent tightening of line across my finger, before the rod nearly shot off the rest. As I once more prepared to do battle with a monster Cherwell barbel, I again got off my seat and slid into the river.

Unlike the other big barbel I had taken, which had shot through the cabbages at speed, this one hugged the river-bed. It was like hooking the proverbial sandbag. For a few minutes, I stood half crouched in the margins, rod well bent, with the barbel disinclined to move, and for a while I thought I was snagged. At that moment, the gloom was thankfully lifted as the clouds parted and moonlight flooded the scene. I bent the rod more, and more, until I felt the handle flexing, and then I felt the fish yield, grudgingly. Seconds later, it was on the surface, trying to plough its way under the upstream draping hawthorns. In the fitful light of the moon, I could see the great length of the fish and knew at that moment that it was not the missing double, the 'short, fat one'. As it seemed to be too big for my ten pounder, I guessed that I was attached to the twelve pounder again, and idly speculated what it would weigh this time.

Once the fish was safely in the net, I scrambled on to the bank, retrieved my torch, and examined my prize. It was then that I noticed the absence of a scarred tail root, or distorted pelvic. So it was not, after all, one of my previous captures. In a state of mounting excitement, I went through the weighing procedure, to confirm 11lb 4oz. Here was a brand new fish, one that had thus far successfully evaded our observations. It was also instantly recognisable should it be caught again, in that it had very distinctive concave pelvic fins, totally different from the normal convex pattern. They looked just like large scallops, and that barbel became lovingly known to Simon and I as Scallop.

That capture actually fooled us into thinking there must be other, unknown doubles awaiting capture on the stretch, but in fact that proved not to be the case. In what remained of the '89/'90 season, Simon and I caught many more barbel, but all the big fish we took were re-captures, although neither of us had seen the 'short, fat one'. I had Scallop again at 10lb 12oz and we both landed the twelve pounder again, or Granny as she became affectionately known, after she was twice foul hooked in the pectoral. I think that both Simon and I knew that our time on the stretch was coming to an end when he had Granny at 11lb 14oz. She had once again come from the cabbages, and we made the decision to move her about 400 yards downstream.

As she slowly swam away in her new home, Simon and I walked leisurely back to our tackle, near the 'cabbages' swim. As we arrived at the high bank, we both looked over the rushes and there, entering the swim again, was Granny! At that moment, we knew we had to move on.

In the summer of 1990, I had not intended to go back to the stretch, but had another section of Cherwell in mind that received very little attention from specialist anglers. I would look at that in the Autumn, but the summer would be devoted to carp fishing. However, in the early hours of a Thursday in late June, my van was packed for another carp session, when the phone rang. It was Trefor West, bursting with the news that he had just taken his biggest ever Bristol Avon barbel of 12lb 12oz and could I go out and photograph it for him. That entailed the small matter of a 180 mile round trip!

Obviously, I was delighted to oblige, and my intended carp session was put on the back burner for a while. Within fifteen minutes of the call, I was on the road to the West Country.

After spending a few hours with Trefor, looking round what was to me a new stretch of river, and photographing that magnificent barbel, it was early afternoon before I was back home. Seeing that giant barbel had temporarily dulled my carp appetite, and I knew I had to have a barbel session instead. Immediately, I saw that as an omen, and knew I had to go back to the previous year's stretch of the Cherwell. I had never seen the mythical 'short, fat one'. I had an overpowering feeling that it was waiting for me.

As light was fading that evening, I was settling in to a new swim some thirty yards upstream of the cabbage patch where my twelve pounder had come from. To this day, I have no idea why I selected that swim, it just felt right somehow, and for the three hours prior to my first cast I had steadily fed with hemp and maggots.

Hook bait was a large bunch of maggots on a size 6, fished in conjunction with a 2oz feeder to give a bolt effect, and I sat back relaxing in the gathering darkness on a gorgeous summer night. The steady rain of earlier in the day had ceased long before dark, and there was an aromatic freshness in the head high reeds surrounding me.

My biggest Cherwell barbel at 12lb 5oz.

In the first hour that night, I took two average barbel of about seven pounds apiece, but then the swim went dead until well past midnight. All was quiet, there was not a breath of wind, and I sat there at peace with the world. My hand rested lightly on the rod butt, with the line over my index finger as normal, when the rod simply took off. Seconds later, I was on my feet, the clutch was screaming, and something big and powerful was heading for the willows adorning the opposite bank

What a memorable scrap that was. A dozen times the barbel tried for those roots, and a dozen times I thwarted it, with everything strained to the limit. Even then, it wasn't beaten, doggedly refusing to come off bottom as it plunged around in the margins under my rod top. Eventually, however, there could only be one winner and my torch beam soon picked out the awesome depth of the most magnificently conditioned barbel I'd ever seen. As soon as I had examined the fish properly, I knew that here was the legendary 'short, fat one'. It was indeed very short and deep, weighing a satisfying 11lb 3oz. Again, my instincts had not let me down, and mentally I thanked Trefor for the early hours' phone call that had resulted in my being barbel fishing in the first place.

It was now most definitely time to move on, and late August saw me preparing for my first two day session at the new stretch of the Cherwell. This area had never produced a big barbel, in fact very little was known about it.

One of my immediate problems with this new area was that it was generally too deep for visual observation, which had been such an important facet of the fishing over the previous few seasons. But, I felt I now knew enough about barbel behaviour to assess where was most likely to hold them. I was also supremely confident in the hemp/maggot approach, and decided to bait six swims intently on the first day, ready for commuting between all the areas after dark. If there were barbel in any of the swims, I knew the approach would eventually catch one of them.

My last Cherwell barbel, 11lb 7oz.

I took my time selecting the six swims, with the help of a plumbing rod, and by midday I was confident that I had picked out the prime feeding areas in the three hundred yards of bank on which I would be concentrating. My favourite was a steady run alongside marginal rushes, where the deepest water was almost under my feet. At the downstream extremity of this run a dwarf willow draped its branches in the water, making the swim an absolute classic. Surely, if the stretch contained barbel, they had to feed under there occasionally.

Never in my wildest dreams did I expect spectacular success on the first night in the first swim I fished, but that is exactly what happened. I moved into this glide at dusk, and only minutes later was cursing as I unhooked a pound perch that had done an excellent job of disturbing the swim. Common sense told me to move, and return when the swim had settled, but something stayed my hand. I would give it half an hour longer, and then move out if there were no action. How glad I am that I stayed put. Perhaps ten minutes after the perch, the rod slammed over and I was playing an obviously serious barbel. It seemed to like to fight on the surface, and although the fight was spectacular, with impressive vortices and surface commotion, I was never in any danger of losing it. Soon, I was admiring a sleek Cherwell barbel of 11lb 7oz, my second biggest ever.

I'm sure you will agree that I could be forgiven for believing that I'd stumbled on an untapped gold mine. If I could land a clonking great fish like that on my first night, what else lay in wait for me. I would keep this treasure trove strictly to myself. However, in the two seasons that followed, I was never to have another barbel bite on that stretch, despite another thirty odd sessions.

I cannot believe that, if there were barbel present, I would have blanked so consistently over two years of hard fishing. So where did that eleven pounder come from. The only answer I can come up with is that it was a travelling fish, temporarily a long way from home, that just happened to stumble across my baited swim on that fateful first night. Whatever the truth of the matter, it is one of the most puzzling episodes of my angling career.

The Cassien Monster

A particular fish may come to mind for many reasons. It may simply be the biggest, or the prettiest. It may have taken intense effort to catch, or given the hardest fight. It may have been specially hard to locate or been caught against tremendous odds. It must be extremely rare for one fish to satisfy all these criteria, but that is precisely the case with my personal best carp, a monstrous fish from Lake Cassien in the south of France.

Andy Barker and I had arrived in the spring of 1986 to be greeted with far from spring-like weather. The previous weeks had been unseasonably cold with heavy rain. Anglers, however, are eternal optimists and despite receiving the glum news that very few fish were being caught, Andy and I looked round the water on our arrival full of enthusiasm. We even had the encouragement of the first sunny afternoon the region had seen in over a month.

It was slightly discouraging not to have seen evidence of carp after several hours of looking, so we decided to start on one of the gravel bars on the south arm, not far from Chez Pierre. We had ten days at our disposal and by spending the first couple in the vicinity of the restaurant we would be in a good position to glean any information that was going.

That afternoon, shattered after our long drive, we decided not to fish until first light next morning, after a good sleep. First, however, we pre-baited the area with over 2000 boilies. This prebaiting had a main purpose of attracting the large population of soft crayfish with which Cassien abounds and on which the carp feed heavily. Drawing on my years of chubbing with crays, I knew that there was no better attractor for them than rotten fish and so the boilies for prebaiting were heavily atomised with fish flavourings, the amount used being totally over the top for normal baits. The basic baits were those Richworth neutrals that were available at the time. Believe me, those baits were rank! We made the mistake of atomising them in the caravan we had hired for our trip and the van stank of fish for the duration of our stay. We had selected three hook baits, all Richworth, those being Tutti Frutti, Salmon Supreme and a trout pellet

A rod battery!

mixture called Trout and Salmon. Our thinking behind using Tutti Frutti over beds of freebies heavily fish flavoured, was that the hookbaits would be different and possibly taken preferentially.

The next morning set the scene for the rest of the trip, in that it was cloudy and cold, with a strong wind. Not long after we had our hookbaits in position, the rain started. It was as well for our peace of mind that we did not know at the time that the rain was to continue unabated for five days, during which the lake was to rise over four feet.

We fished that swim for two days without the slightest hint of a fish. For hour after hour the rain lashed down and with the wind blowing into our pitch it was cold, wet misery. When we packed up on the third morning all our gear was completely drenched and we were in a disconsolate mood. That night, with our gear drying in the caravan, we cheered ourselves up with a civilised meal in Cannes.

I remember that meal providing some light relief. Andy was learning French at the time and insisted on ordering his meal in French. It was obvious that there had been a distinct communication breakdown when Andy was brought a plateful of raw mince for his main course. Of course, Andy being Andy, he had to pretend that is what he ordered and struggled manfully to eat it while I savoured a delicious medium fillet steak in front of him!

Next morning, we recommenced operations in a fresh swim further up the south arm, again a purely arbitrary choice as we had not seen a sign of a carp. During the establishing of our camp the rain had been merely a fine drizzle but that was soon to change. Before all the rods had been cast out the rain was back with a vengeance, falling with storm force for hour after miserable hour. One by one, the Optonics were packing up and it was getting utterly depressing. On that day we could actually watch the water rising, a situation that continued steadily until two days later, when we packed up in disgust. Once again, everything was awash, and that night in the caravan, with every bit of gear we owned in

Andy with a lovely 42lb specimen.

pieces and drying in front of the fire, including every Optonic, Andy and I had plumbed the depths of despair. The trip had been many months in the planning, the anticipation growing to fever pitch at the date of our departure from home. Now, here we were, with cold torrential rain hammering on the van roof, almost a week into our trip without a sign of a carp

That evening, we talked for hours. So dispirited had we been when we got back to the van that we were on the brink of cutting our losses and going home early, particularly as the weather forecast gave no promise of a break in the monsoon like conditions. However, the influence of a few beers and a warm fire raised our spirits and we determined that the next morning, Saturday, we would make one last throw of the dice for the last four days. Rain or no rain, we would drive round the water in a last attempt to find carp, starting with the west arm, which we had not yet fished. That was to prove a historic decision.

I was awake early the next morning, and the first thing I noticed was the silence, the rain had stopped at last. There was even a patch of blue sky overhead. For several hours that morning, we searched the water, a lot more hopeful of sightings now that the wind had gone. Eventually, we stood on a promontory commanding the entrance to a narrow neck between the west arm proper and the spawning bay. At the same instant, we both spotted what we had been searching for so long. At eighty yards, a tremendous upheaval on the surface was followed by the sight of a huge golden tail, before the carp dived again. That was all we needed to see, and all the old enthusiasm welled back as we unloaded the gear.

The first thing I did was to get my float rod out. Half an hour's plumbing established the essential features of the swim. We were on the point of a spit of land. Directly in front of us, and to the right, the bay was quite narrow, being perhaps only seventy yards to the opposite, tree lined bank. To the left it widened out to perhaps 150 yards and here the opposite bank was a steep boulder strewn cliff. Further left still was the entrance to the bay and the main body of the west arm. Directly in front of us there was a wide gravel bar a uniform fifteen feet deep, gradually tailing off to the right to about 22ft. The fall away to deeper water to the left was steeper, going down to thirty feet fairly quickly. There was a deep channel under the far bank at the narrowest point. All in all, it looked a perfect place to intercept fish, as they moved in and out of the bay.

As the evening approached, carp began rolling regularly and at long last one of my Optonics burst into life, the first time an alarm had sounded in anger since our arrival a week earlier. Something had picked up three Tutti Frutti boilies on my right hand rod, presented on the peak of the bar. The line was a blur as it left the spool and as I dropped in the pick up the rod slammed over. Despite being set at almost its tightest drag, the clutch screamed and several yards of line disappeared. Andy reminded me of the snags with which the bed of Cassien is littered. We had already decided to play fish hard, bringing them off bottom as fast as possible to keep the line free of obstructions. For this reason we were using 18lb Sylcast straight through.

Flipping off the anti reverse and tightening the stern drag completely, I clamped on the fish, determined that I would only yield line grudgingly by backwinding if I was in imminent danger of being pointed. Holding the fish hard and heaving was the order of the day. Playing the fish on a properly set clutch, as I like to do, was a luxury I could not afford. Every foot of line yielded increased the carp's chances of finding a snag and breaking loose.

Ten minutes later, after a really arm aching scrap, a big carp wallowed in the mesh, and Andy and I gazed at something we had felt we would never see, a Cassien carp. 32lb 4oz it weighed, the fish that marked the beginning of the end of our nightmare.

It was the following lunchtime when one of my greatest angling moments occurred. We had just finished photographing a fish of 26lb with which Andy had broken his duck, when one of my indicators rose slowly, so slowly that I discounted carp and thought a bream was responsible. I was soon to discover my error, as my strike was the prelude to the most incredible battle I've ever had with a fish. Despite the clutch being set at its tightest, and the reel being clamped in my hand, a fish of unbelievable power tore line off the clutch. For a few seconds I was out of control and the scream from the clutch rose to a high pitched whine. An incredible bow wave headed straight for those boulders on the opposite bank and, knowing that only a few yards separated the fish from disaster, I clamped the rod butt in my groin,

My first Cherwell double, 10lb 3oz in 1987.

Dawn sun through a winter mist.

My 58lb Cassien monster.

This lovely fish of exactly 20lb was taken at dawn when it was -5 centigrade.

A gorgeous Thurne '30'.

22lb fish taken in the teeth of a gale.

clamped the reel face tightly with my hand, and leaned into the fish as hard as I could. The rod was nearly ripped from my hands and it took all my strength to avoid being pointed. I hung on grimly, the rod bending way past its test curve; I could feel the flexing under the reel seat.

For a few seconds all was stalemate and then, with a thunderous roar, an enormous fish surfaced and lashed the water. What an unforgettable sight that was!. Foiled in its first attempt to gain sanctuary, the carp now rocketed to my left, heading for more boulders about 150 yards away. The problem now was that I had so

My 58lb Cassien monster.

much line out that it was impossible to prevent the fish kiting. Applying the heaviest amount of sidestrain possible I only just managed to turn the fish, and with every sinew straining I hauled the carp out of the danger area, gaining a few precious yards in the process. With the fish now swimming towards me for the first time, I crammed on the pressure to keep it high in the water. About thirty yards out the carp rolled, a huge golden flank and bright yellow tail making me catch my breath. "Please don't let me lose this," I said out loud.

At that moment, Andy was a calming influence. "Just take your time and keep the fish in midwater and he's ours," he said, "he's well over forty."

Andy only needed one chance with the net and about twenty minutes after I'd first hooked it, a tremendous carp rolled into the landing net. With an almighty heave, Andy hoisted it ashore. Only then did we realise the fish's incredible thickness. Even before we weighed it, Andy reached over and shook my hand. We both knew that this fish was not just big, it was gigantic, but I still couldn't believe it when Andy declared exactly 58lb. Surely I was dreaming. Those few moments after the weighing are permanently etched in my memory, a magical moment in time.

In the final two days of our Cassien trip, four more fish were to grace our nets, two thirties, a forty and an incredible leviathan of 66lb 8oz to Andy. When I am able to fish no more, I will still see the magnificent proportions of those French monsters, glinting golden in the warm sunlight. Such memories are beyond price.

The trip ended on a note of hilarity. We had been using a special rig for Cassien, incorporating a sunken pike float above the terminal rig, between two beads, free to slide to a sliding stop knot several yards up the line. The object of this was to keep as much of the line between rod top and bait off bottom, because of the horrendous snags at the water. The danger was obviously one of  line bites, or lines being picked up by hooked fish, but after six of our seven carp we had experienced no problems. The seventh fish was the one that redressed the balance.

I remember that we were in a contented mood, having taken three carp apiece, and the beer was flowing freely in the warm afternoon sun of our final day. A French angler who'd become a good friend, and whose father fortuitously owned a vineyard, had brought several bottles of Beaujolais to help the party along, and it was quite a merry crew on the bank as dusk settled.

Not long after dark, Andy had a run on his left hand rod, and the fish promptly kited right at a great rate of knots, taking every other line with it. With six Optonics screaming at once, and the carp fighting out of its skin, the situation became more chaotic by the minute. How the fish was landed I'll never know, because of the unbelievable tangle of lines, but landed it was, the hook removed and weighed at 35lb. After sacking the carp, we retrieved the rest of the lines, and eventually stood behind one of the most impressive birds nests I have ever seen. There must have been over two hundred yards of line, with leads, beads and floats in abundance. In the torch light, with the alcohol having taken its effect, neither Andy or I was capable or willing to attempt to sort it out. Instead we broke into hysterical laughter, cut every line above the mayhem, and called it a day there and then.

Pike of the Midland Stillwaters

Gravel Pits

I became interested in the big pike of the Midland gravel pits in the late sixties, when I first fished with Merv Wilkinson in the early days of the Coventry Specimen Group, but it was to be no less than ten frustrating years later that I managed my first twenty pounder. During those years, my biggest fish remained stubbornly just over sixteen pounds, although I was fishing waters with Merv and Trefor West that held plenty of twenties. In fact, on one water, Black Horse, now part of the Linford complex, where Trefor and I invariably fished side by side, I netted and photographed no less than six twenties for Trefor. During that period, I actually had a few more pike than he did, but could I get a big one, could I hell! The biggest Black Horse fish I ever managed was about 15lb.

Nevertheless, I have exceedingly fond memories of Black Horse pit and when I think back to those days, one particular memory invariably comes to the fore. This involved a fish caught by Trefor in the most bizarre circumstances, against odds that must be astronomical. He and I were fishing a favourite feature together, a pronounced gravel bar with drop offs either side, and had each taken a low double by around lunchtime. Fishing on the opposite side of the bay, directly facing us, was Merv, some three hundred yards away. Presently, we saw him jump to his feet, run down to the rods, wait a few seconds and then strike. Even at that distance, we could see the rod bending and obviously he had a good pike on. But it wasn't to last long. A minute or so later, we saw him throw down his rod in disgust, wind in his other bait and come stalking round for a good moan about the one that got away.

Apparently, Merv had been playing the pike normally, and then his main line had just parted. As the line seemed perfect, it possibly had chafed on sharp gravel, but whatever the reason Merv was very unhappy not only about losing the fish but also

23lb reservoir pike.

leaving a trace in it. We had been chatting perhaps fifteen minutes, sharing a brew, when one of Trefor's drop off indicators fell away and line started peeling off steadily. His freelined mackerel tail had elicited some interest, obviously. After tightening down, he struck into the fish and then began the weirdest battle. Trefor remarked at the time that he seemed to have no control over the fish whatever, whenever he pulled one way the fish seemed to head off at an angle. He said it was a bit like backing a car round a corner with a trailer attached. If you want the trailer to go one way, you turn the steering wheel the other. So it was with this pike. To get it moving left, he pulled to the right.

Eventually, all was revealed. With the fish deep under the rod top, I crouched down with the net. Up came the swivel on the trace, closely followed by the trace with bait still attached, but no pike. Then I noticed that the point of one of the trebles had gone clean through the eye of another swivel. Moments later, a second trace appeared, and to this was attached a double figure pike. Merv immediately recognised the trace as his, and was delighted he was able to unhook the fish and carry on fishing with a clear conscience.

You tell me the odds against that happening. They must be incalculable.

Our favourite pit in the seventies was undoubtedly Hardwick, near Oxford, a water that had produced authenticated thirty pounders. This scenic water comprised two pits joined by a narrow causeway, and around the causeway were several reliable pike swims. You could drive along the spit of land between the pits and over a small bridge, parking close to the water's edge, and these swims were, naturally, popular. Later they were to become famous for huge chub to Peter Stone and others.

The only problem with Hardwick was the owner. At the time, he lived in a bungalow on a large island in the middle of the bigger pit, commuting backwards and forwards by boat, and he threw some wild parties on that island. We often fished late into the dark hours, sometimes all night, and the water would occasionally be rocking to the rhythm until dawn. He was totally unpredictable. Every time we went to Hardwick, he checked our tickets, which was fine, but as they were season permits issued by himself you would have thought he would have recognised us as members after the first couple of occasions. On one bizarre morning, an angler who had been a member for four years, and was well known to the owner, was made to drive home over sixty miles to collect his ticket because he had forgotten it. On another occasion, a young woman had driven round the pit for a look, and had stopped her car on the little bridge to feed the swans. The owner came up behind her car in his land rover and, although she was only a few yards away, proceeded to push her car straight into the lake out of his way. He was also given to naked jogging

Returning a good twenty.

around the lake at midnight, chattering to himself with a wild look in his eyes. On those occasions, you simply kept a low profile. If he stopped for a chat he could be as nice as pie one minute, ranting and raving the next.

That disconcerting behaviour apart, the fishing at Hardwick was always interesting and the first few years saw Trefor and I take many doubles, but nothing over sixteen pounds. But we kept our belief, because the water was producing twenty pounders regularly, and the occasional thirty. Had we known at the time how few individual big fish there actually were, we would probably have abandoned the water much earlier than we did. But I'm glad we didn't, because a memorable night in November 1978 bore witness to the capture of a specimen pike that had been a burning ambition for over a decade.

Once again, Trefor and I were fishing side by side, off the beach into the larger of the two lakes. Trefor was placing his baits opposite the mouth of the causeway, while I was a little further left, my baits being fished alongside a sunken tree about forty yards out. This feature had produced several doubles for me over the weeks, but nothing really exciting. As the pike were confirmed night feeders, we had settled down to fish at least the first three hours of dark, and right on cue, on dusk, Trefor had our first fish, a scrappy eleven pounder.

As the night wore on, one of the first frosts of the winter began to form and, under a bright moon, the temperature plummeted. It had been dark perhaps two hours when my left hand drop bobbin suddenly fell away and line began pouring from the open spool. I'll never forget that run. Most pike go away with freelined deadbaits steadily rather than in a mad dash, but that run was more like a carp. The line was literally a blur as it whistled from the spool, and the speed the pike was moving was confirmed immediately after I had set the hooks, when a big fish cleared the water in a spectacular leap, shaking its head viciously. In the minutes that followed, the pike repeatedly tail walked in an awesome demonstration of power, frantically trying to throw the hooks, twisting and turning in the air,

My first twenty - 20lb 4oz from Hardwick.

throwing water droplets far and wide that shimmered like a million silver sequins in the moonlight.

Trefor was at my elbow, net in hand, continually saying, "Don't lose it, it's definitely twenty." I have to say that did little to calm my nerves! But, there were no anxious moments, the pike was safely brought within range, and I have never known Trefor need more than one chance with the net. What a magnificent fish it was, unmarked, mean and lean, and spotted like a leopard,. My first guess was around nineteen pounds but Trefor was adamant it was twenty. Thankfully, he was right, and soon he was shaking my hand in congratulations at my first twenty pound pike. It was only just there at 20lb 4oz but at that moment I knew that my hoodoo had been broken at last. I honestly believe that Trefor was as pleased, if not more pleased, than I was. He was well aware how much I wanted that fish, and how, over the years, all the bigger fish seemed to fall to his rods. That is what true friendship is all about, and I have never forgotten the warmth of his congratulations that night.

Believe it or not, that is the only twenty pound pike I have ever taken from a gravel pit, although I have since gone on to take innumerable good doubles to 19lb 12oz from several pits. All my other twenties have come from the Midland reservoirs, which I shall tell you about shortly, but there is one more incident from Hardwick pit that is worth recounting.

Trefor and I had arrived at dawn on a bitingly cold February morning, with a bitter east wind blowing snow flurries in our faces. We had elected to fish the west bank in the teeth of the wind, where we had taken several good fish in previous weeks, the consolation being that this bank had good car access. This meant that we could actually fish from the comfort of the car, watching our bobbins in the warm. After casting out, Trefor had done his usual beach combing bit, looking along the margins for discarded tackle, and had uncovered a perfectly good travel alarm clock, still ticking. Quite what it was doing there is a mystery that is irrelevant to this story. "Right," he said "this will be useful. We will set the alarm for when we want the runs and that way we can relax the rest of the day. What time do you want the first run." After I had specified 10.15, he set the alarm and we retired to the car for a brew. We were, of course, both crazy!

A couple of hours passed pleasantly, and then we both jumped as the alarm went off at the appointed hour. No sooner had the bell stopped when one of my bobbins dropped off. As we scrambled out of the car we were both laughing, and after I had returned the fish, a plump ten pounder, I told Trefor it was now his turn to specify a time for his first fish. He said 12.30, the clock was set, and it was back to

Mick Nicholls with 21 pounder from Black Horse.

the kettle. For it to work once was remarkable enough, but we couldn't believe it when one of Trefor's rods was away as the alarm bell was still ringing at 12.30. Thirteen pounds that one weighed, and never for a second thinking that it could possibly happen again, I re-set the clock for 2.30. Amazingly, it did happen again. This time, the bell had sounded about a minute early, but exactly 2.30 by my watch I had our third pike, a seven pounder. There is only one drawback to that incredible day. It would have been wonderful to have had a novice angler with us. Can you imagine the tales that would have resulted about the awesome, even magical, angling prowess of Trefor West and Tony Miles?

Reservoir Piking

Since the mid-eighties, I have taken 44 pike over twenty pounds from three Midland reservoirs, Hollowell, Stanford and Boddington. Of these three, Boddington was for years one of the best pike waters I ever fished, with many twenties and numerous big doubles. They fed on the large shoals of good roach and bream the water held. In recent years, thanks to the enlightened (!) activities of British Waterways, all those wonderful fish have been removed and in their place grotesquely overstocked small carp abound. In angling terms, the BWB have conducted the modern equivalent of rape and pillage on numerous Midland's waters that were once fine mixed fisheries. But, I digress.

My big pike record is, in some ways, quite remarkable, because of the 46 fish I have taken over 20lb in total, 44 have been under 24lb. My personal best you will read about in the chapter on the Thurne, but my second biggest was taken from Boddington, on a day that was quite amusing. Boddington was fed by a small stream that flows under the main road in one corner of the water, adjacent to the entrance gate to the reservoir. There is some convenient hard standing there and, to fish the original stream bed, you can fish feet away from where the car stands. A few

The business end.

yards to the left of the stream is the entrance to the left hand bank and going down that bank the original stream bed is a progressively longer cast the further you walk, the stream angling right as it snakes across the reservoir. The original stream bed was a definite hot spot at the back end of the season and my favourite fishing position was immediately to the right of the culvert through which the stream entered, from where I could place a bait straight out in front of me, with one angled right at longer range to find the same feature. The only problem was that, if another angler entered from the left hand side of the stream culvert to go down the left hand bank, he could conceivably cast across you if he wasn't careful. It was a well known hotspot, so anglers fishing those two spots needed to agree where their baits would be placed.

On this particular winter morning, I arrived in my camper van anxious to secure the swim on the hard standing, where I could fish out of the van, because I had my young daughter Jacqui with me. As it was bitterly cold, and the Portaloo facility in the van was obviously important for a little girl, it was an ideal position. I was therefore disappointed to find, on my arrival, that there was another angler in the hot spot, which meant that I had to fish away from the van, which was not ideal under the circumstances. And then I discovered it was Darryl Wilkinson, Merv's son, who I knew well. I explained my dilemma to him, and he suggested I fish the left hand bank, but quite close to the culvert, where I could place baits in the hot spot. Generously, he offered to angle his baits slightly right so that we did not foul one another. Normally, I would not impose like that, but with Jacqui to think of, I was grateful and accepted Darryl's suggestion. We would only be yards from the van if Jacqui needed it, and still in full view of my indicators. In our brief chat before I set up, I asked Darryl how it had been going and he said that he had been really struggling. He'd had quite a few fish to low doubles, but could get nothing big. Everyone was reporting twenties, he said, but he couldn't get one.

As I proceeded down the left hand bank, he wound in his bait from the middle of the stream culvert, recast it out of my way, and I set up my gear. The first rod was baited with a mackerel head, and that was lobbed out underhand. The bait must have landed not far from where Darryl had just removed his own bait. Having set the indicator, I commenced setting up the other rod. About thirty seconds later, there was a single bleep and I looked up to see the drop bobbin hanging clear of the line. There was, however, no line being taken, it was simply lying slack, unmoving. Obviously, I thought, I had set the bobbin incorrectly, and clipped it back in place, before carrying on with the second rod. There was a second single bleep. Exactly the same scenario was repeated. Again, the line lay slack and unmoving and again I re-clipped the bobbin, but this time watched intently. Sure enough, thirty seconds later, the bobbin moved up a few inches, pulled off the line, but nothing else happened. So I picked up the rod, carefully wound down, and then felt good resistance. I struck, and then all hell let loose. There was an explosion of spray as a huge pike left the water, and then surged across the surface, taking both of Darryl's lines with it. Darryl had an excellent view of the fish's size as it rocketed across his swim, and what he shouted to me at that moment is totally unprintable. Something about having golden appendages.

The fish was fighting like a thing possessed and Jacqui was hopping from one foot to the other in excitement. Just like the Hardwick fish described earlier, this one wanted to fight on the surface and several heart stopping tail walks were successfully negotiated before I could get the fish near enough to net. As it sagged in the mesh, I knew it was easily my second biggest pike. Moments later, Darryl was beside me and together we confirmed a weight of 25lb 1oz. To say I felt guilty was an understatement. He had been waiting over a season for a fish to beat 14lb and now he had almost certainly pulled his bait out of the jaws of a 25lb fish to let me catch it. He must have been gutted, but, fair play to him, he was all smiles and full of congratulations. Inside he must have been seething. I know I would have been. Thankfully, he was soon to break his jinx and went on to take the big fish that his perseverance deserved.

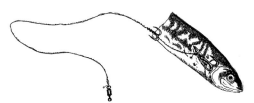

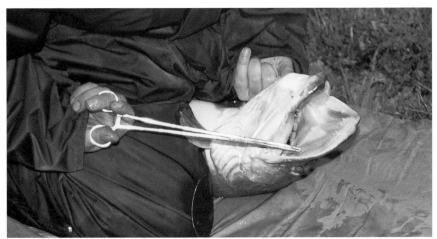

Unhooking a twenty.

Flavour Trials

Apart from that fish, none of my other twenty pound pike from the reservoirs mentioned make a particularly interesting story in themselves, although I obviously enjoyed catching each and every one of them. There is, however, an interesting story concerning the last three months of the 1995/96 season at Stanford, when I pike fished exclusively, conducting extensive flavour trials on deadbaits.

I love carrying out bait experiments under reasonably controlled conditions, and in January 1996 I made the decision to spend the last three months piking, testing out three flavours on deadbaits. They were eel oil, smelt oil and mackerel oil. As I could use three rods, a fair comparison could be obtained, so long as I used the same bait and alternated the rods so that each flavour was presented equally favourably. I knew there would inevitably be variables I could not contend with, such as unknown feeding start and stop times, but by rotating the rods every trip I hoped to even these anomalies out as much as possible. The bait I decided to use for the duration of the trial was half mackerel, a bait I have always had great faith in and that has produced me lots of fish. I also logged the results only for fish of ten pounds and above, as I was specifically looking for a flavour which produced the most big pike, if such a thing existed. I realise now that was probably a mistake, because logging every fish would have given more additional information, but the results were interesting nonetheless.

Where I felt the flavour trials were so important on a water like Stanford is that the reservoir is very subject to sub surface undertows, which obviously would carry oil trails far and wide. A simplistic viewpoint would be that the flavour producing the most pike would have been carried most efficiently by the current. Before fishing, my baits were pre-flavoured at home, and then sealed in individual sandwich bags, and frozen. After thawing, the flavours would be totally impregnated in the fish surface, but before casting I would give each bait a fresh painting with the appropriate oil to give an extra "flavour trail" effect.

I did have some pre-conceived notion of which flavour would be most effective. I was certain it would be mackerel oil, which I had used extensively at

Trefor with a Black Horse 22 pounder.

Boddington. With that expectation in the back of my mind, what the results actually showed were more than just interesting, and I pass them on now for what they are worth.

In the three months trial, I had a total of 45 pike over ten pounds, which included five twenties, top fish 22lb 14oz. Of those fish, no less than thirty came on baits soaked in eel oil, twelve on baits soaked in smelt oil and only five to mackerel flavoured baits. I know that the sample is far too small for really accurate statistical analysis, but I do believe that the difference between 30 fish to eel oil and 5 to mackerel oil is sufficiently large to be significant. Needless to say, I now fish eel oil soaked deadbaits with extreme confidence!

As I have mentioned elsewhere in this book, Stanford reservoir is a syndicated water with a publicity ban on catches, and in normal circumstances I would not have included this information. But, I am afraid, circumstances are not normal. As far as we can tell, 99% of Stanford pike are now dead, following the fish kill in 1999. As a viable pike fishery, Stanford is finished and this, together with the step by step deliberate destruction of fine mixed reservoir fisheries as mentioned earlier, has made the Midlands an increasingly bleak pike fishing desert, where, only a few short years ago, it was rich indeed. And that's more than sad, it's criminal.

Crucian Summers

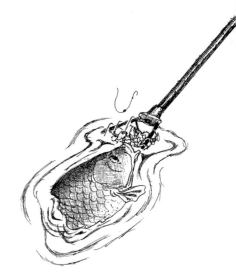

My first big crucian carp, including one of 3lb 3oz that is still my personal best to this day, were accidental captures, in that they were discovered in a session after tench.

They were taken from a Midlands' park lake called Fawsley, and friends and I took several nice fish one summer on paste baits. One friend, Ken, had an uncle who worked at an abattoir, and we experimented with blood soaked baits for a while. Disgusting, I know, and I wouldn't do it again, but those crucians loved it. We only had the one summer. The next season, they had disappeared as mysteriously as they had appeared and we never caught another. Shortly after, the little pool was netted, turned into a trout fishery, and that was that.

It was then many years before I went crucian fishing again, mainly because of the lack of a suitable water. And then I was told about Hawk Lake, which abuts Hawkstone Park golf course. Hawk Lake was very well known for the good head of big carp, especially some superb looking commons, but the crucian potential was not so widely known. However, the water was regularly producing two pounders, with several three's every season and one confirmed four-pounder. I had to have a look.

I acquired my Wem club ticket at the start of the 1988 season, and September saw me setting up for my first serious crucian session for over twenty years. I was to catch precisely nothing on that first trip, simply because I was unused to the delicacy of presentation necessary for these most shy biting of fish. I'm sure I had bites, but didn't see them, and determined that, on my second trip, I would be better equipped. I had given the presentation a lot of thought. My main line of 4lb would remain, but I would opt for a hooklink of only 2lb, to a size 14 hook baited with a single grain of corn. Maggots were discounted because of the large head of transparent little skimmer bream. What I thought most vital was a rig that would give positive bite indication the moment the bait was touched. The first session, I had been laying on in a way more suitable for roach, but obviously nowhere near sensitively enough for crucians. So, my game plan was to plumb the swim so accurately that the bottom shot on my float rig just, and only just, rested on the lake bed. The hook bait would be a mere one-inch away, and it would be impossible for any fish, however shy, to move that bait even a fraction without registering interest on the float.

For the after dark fishing, when I expected a lot of the action, I had equipped myself with a Drennan betalight float, taking just two AAA to cock. As even a bold crucian bite could move the float only a tiny amount, I felt that I may not see such a small movement at night. It would be masked by the bright light, unless of course a bolder bite took it away. To fish most effectively, I had to see the merest dip, so I shotted the float precisely so that

A scenic water indeed.

it rode with the betalight not flush with the surface, as normal, but one eighth of an inch above the surface. After dark, the view was of a streak of light with a quarter inch black band in the middle. In this way, a very slight dip would see this black band disappear, while a sudden widening of the band would be equally obvious if the float lifted. Because of the sensitivity required, I would be fishing no more than a rod length out, over marginal rushes.

By the time I was set up, it was early evening on my second session when I made my first cast. It was a lovely, humid, breathless day, the kind of day when you know something is going to happen. I stared at the red float tip just dimpling the surface for over an hour, and then thought my eyes were playing tricks on me. Was the float lifting ever so slowly? I struck just in case and, sure enough, an energetic crucian shot away. I had to play it carefully on the light gear, but a few minutes later I was unhooking the biggest crucian carp I'd seen in years. 2lb 10oz that first Hawk Lake fish weighed, a very good start indeed. It was also very gratifying to see that my delicate presentation had worked, even with such an incredibly circumspect bite.

It was a few hours later that my second crucian joined the party. It had been dark a while, and I watched fascinated as those two separate halves of light from the float merged into one. A firm strike, and pretty soon a fish of 2lb 7oz was joining his companion in my Queenford sack. I fished that betalight float a further two hours,

Part of a catch of ten 2lb+ fish, to 3lbs.

totally fascinated, and although all I caught before I eventually succumbed to a little sleep were bream to 3lb, the method was so entrancing that I couldn't remember when I'd enjoyed a session more.

The next day I recommenced operations at dawn, and I was to take crucians steadily throughout the day, racking up another eight fish, with seven of them between 2lb 1oz and 2lb 13oz and the eighth my second ever three pounder, being dead on the mark.

The biggest crucian I have ever hooked was lost at the net at Hawk Lake in the summer of 1993. I'd had a terrific session so far, taking four crucians between 2lb 9oz and 2lb 13oz, plus a couple of scrappy double figure commons on boilies at night. It was late on the second afternoon, and I'd had a hectic hour taking a string of small bream, tench and rudd. Then the swim went dead for ten minutes, before a huge sheet of tiny bubbles erupted around the float. It was just like tench froth.

I didn't have long to wait. For a change, I experienced a very positive bite, the float sailing away. As I struck, a good fish promptly rocketed thirty yards out and then gave me a very spirited resistance as I gradually worked it back towards me. At last the crucian was beaten and as it lay on its side as it approached the net I could see

that it was huge, possibly well over four pounds. It must have been literally inches from the net cord when the size 14 popped out and the fish slipped agonisingly into the depths. I could have cried. My personal best for the species had been set about thirty years previously. No one could say I hadn't been patient.

It certainly wasn't planned that way, but I haven't been back to Hawk Lake since.

One of Hawk's many good carp goes home.

An Awesome Bait

Until the early nineties, virtually all my carp fishing had been carried out with ready made frozen boilies, particularly the range available from Richworth. My results on Tutti Frutti at my local syndicate water had been as good as anyone's, and I had outcaught everyone on

the water in 1989 using Strawberry Yoghurt, including an opening night catch which had featured three twenties. I therefore saw no reason to change. Most of the other syndicate members were carp only anglers, and most had their own favourite home made recipes. I had been told often that my catch rate would improve if I moved on to home mades, but I was taking some convincing.

In the summer of 1992, I had planned an intensive carp campaign, having spent the previous summer in search of tench, and I arrived at the water on the afternoon of the 15th June with sufficient Strawberry Yoghurt boilies in a freezer box for four days. Immediately on arrival, I had observed swirls and tenting in and around a potomogeton bed thirty yards out from a swim known as the Point, and I moved my gear into that position. Two hours later, all preparations complete, I sat in the fading light with a fresh brew impatiently waiting for midnight.

The lake is very scenic, roughly rectangular, about twenty acres, and the Point swim located along one of the narrower ends, to a backdrop of gorgeous wild rhododendrons. From where I sat I had a good view of the rest of the lake, and by late evening most of the known swims were taken. Two new members, who I hadn't met before, were set up along the right hand bank from my position, perhaps a hundred yards away, fishing over dense marginal surface weed. Those two lads were to give me considerable food for thought over the next two weeks.

By 6.00am next morning, they had enjoyed at least a dozen runs between them and, although they had lost most of the fish in the weed by pulling out, had landed three carp to 25lb. I was just starting to wonder whether there were still any fish in front of me when I had a run at last, which produced a lean common of 16lb 2oz. That fish, however, flattered to deceive, because I was not to get another run in those first four days. Elsewhere, most of the other members struggled, but those two lads just kept getting run after run, frustratingly pulling out of the bulk of

The island point.

two lads just kept getting run after run, frustratingly pulling out of the bulk of them.

The following week followed an almost identical pattern. We were fishing the same swims again, and this time I only managed a 19-4 common on my boilies, although I did sneak out a couple of mid-doubles on margin fished peanuts. Once again, though, the lads must have had thirty runs between them, but had landed only a handful of fish.

In mid-afternoon of the third day, they both came round for a chat. I remember they wanted my advice on what they were doing wrong in pulling out of so many fish, as they were getting more and more frustrated. When I checked their tackle, it was obvious. They were both using size 8 Super Specialists, which, although an excellent hook when you have room to be gentle on fish, are eminently unsuitable when you need to stop a big fish or haul it through weed. Hooks of that general pattern, especially when chemically sharpened, simply cut out under pressure. I had discovered that to my cost many years previously in my barbel fishing and had, for many years, been advocating off set, beaked hooks for big fish work. I know that today carp anglers are using beaked patterns such as Raptors, but in the early nineties straight pointed, chemically sharpened hooks were in vogue. I always wondered why more anglers did not associate their high fish losses through hook pulls with the hook pattern. I saw them altering hair lengths, adding bits of silicon to the hook shank to make it offset, and other bits of nonsense, when a simple change of hook pattern would have cured the problem.

Anyway, I gave each of the lads half a dozen size 2 Au Lion D'or, which are equivalent to English size 4, a pattern I had never pulled out of a single fish in my

Three 2lb plus crucians.

2lb 12oz crucian.

My 3lb Hawk Lake crucian.

Beautiful mirror of 27lb 4oz.

Another 20 plus is returned.

22lb, and it fought nearly three hours!

The island channel.

angling career. I had lost fish in snags certainly, but hook pulls just did not happen. It was quite amusing to see the look of horror on their faces as they examined them, but, later that evening, they were back again, thanking me, and reporting a further six runs with all six fish successfully landed.

It was now their turn to help me, and I asked them what they were doing differently, in getting so many runs. Their answer was simple. They were using home made baits using a fish meal base mix, with bulk oil and a flavour. They did not elaborate on their actual recipe, but stressed that it was the base mix that was the key. Other waters, they said, had responded to fishmeal baits so dramatically that most other baits had become almost useless. As the season was now two weeks old, and they'd had around sixty runs between them to my two on ready mades, I could readily believe it.

Over the next few days, I did my homework and by midweek had obtained a bulk supply of Premier fishmeal base mix plus getting plenty of advice on oils and flavours. My recipe was 16oz base mix, 30ms of Crunt Oil, 7ml of Peach Melba flavour and six eggs. No, I've no idea what Crunt Oil is made from, I was just told it was good! Salmon oil I can understand, but I don't recollect ever seeing a crunt!

There was one more highly significant ingredient. During my discussions with carp fishing friends, they had told me that under no circumstances was I to put sweetener with a fishmeal. It was not recommended for any fishmeal recipe, they said. That seemed to me a good enough reason for adding sweetener to mine, and

26lb of solid muscle.

I included 10ml of Richworth concentrated sweetener from the off. At least I would be different.

My first 48 hour session with this new bait was memorable. Just after dawn on a lovely warm and overcast July morning, I once more set up camp in the Point swim. I had decided to fish two distinct areas, one to the point of a small island close to the potomogeton bed, and the other down a fairly narrow channel to my right, which actually encircles the small island. Two hundred 18mm baits were catapulted to each area.

At about 9.00am, I cast out, each terminal rig adorned with a four-bait stringer, and settled back to wait. As usual, on went the trusty kettle. An hour later, the rain started, and I do mean rain. For hour after hour it threw it down, and by mid-afternoon I was still biteless when, all of a sudden, an Optonic was screaming. By the time I landed the fish, a scrappy common of about 13lb, I was soaked. But I was also pleased to record my first carp to the new bait.

With no more runs as dusk approached, I agonised for ages about whether to introduce any more freebies, but eventually I settled on fifty more to each hook bait. Possibly the carp were taking time to switch on to the new food source, but when they did, it could be action all the way.

I remember sometime around midnight, being very drowsy as I listened to the torrential rain drumming on the brolly, when I was snapped to attention by my butt indicator dropping like a stone, and the rod shaking in the rests as line poured off the reel. The Optonic was squealing like a Banshee. Unusually, the fight was very poor. The carp in that water normally fought like tigers, but I soon found the reason, when I netted a big fish which had its eyes totally obscured by blanket weed. The fight started on the bank when I removed the weed and tried to weigh the carp. It went berserk, and I was thankful for the recently acquired unhooking mat in preventing the fish damaging itself. After a few minutes, it had calmed down, and I was able to record a satisfying 20lb 8oz.

After I had slipped the fish back, and before I'd had chance to rebait, my other rod was away on a blistering run. This fish fought like a demon, and although it took very little line off me after the initial rush, it stubbornly refused to yield, hugging the bottom. The Point swim features quite a deep trench under the near

bank, making it an excellent swim for
margin fishing. It also encourages hooked
fish to make one last dive before netting, and
this is what happened that night. Having
successfully brought the carp under the rod
top, it decided to go to ground and would
not budge. It must have been a good five
minutes of solid bullying before the carp
eventually gave up the unequal struggle, and
allowed itself to be brought up in the water
and netted. In my torch beam, I illuminated
an immaculate mirror of 23lb 6oz.

Sleek 16lb common.

After such a cracking brace of fish in
quick succession, I reasoned that the freebies had probably been mopped up and,
after recasting both rods, fired another fifty baits around each terminal rig. That
done, tired, drenched but happy, I sought the comfort of my shelter and broke out
the kettle for a celebratory mug of tea. It never had chance to come to the boil.
Only minutes after recasting, the right hand rod was away again. Initially, I
thought I was attached to an average fish only, as it came straight towards me with
minimal resistance. Once it was about twenty yards away, however, it woke up with
a vengeance, and then commenced one of the most protracted battles I've had with
any fish.

A dozen times that carp attempted to bury itself under the trailing foliage at the
point of the island, with my arm aching as I constantly applied maximum left hand
sidestrain. It was a battle of attrition. Each time I turned the fish from danger, it
would only be seconds before it was trying again.

Realising that it was losing that particular contest, the carp then changed tactics,
shooting across to my left where there were dense rushes under the near bank.
There again followed a good ten minutes of frantic heaving from both sides until,
at last, the carp circled deep in the trench under the rod top. Even then, with the
fish only feet from the net, it stubbornly refused to yield, ten times at least
approaching the net cord before making another strong lunge for freedom.

Yet again, the carp's nose approached the net cord, and at last I felt she was
mine. But there was to be a final act in this particular drama. With one last titanic
effort, the fish turned away and rocketed with terrific power to my right, heading
down the narrow channel that circled the island. That run was completely
irresistible and I was forced to give line. About thirty yards down the bank of the
channel, an overhanging willow made it impossible to follow a hooked fish further,

From this swim, my bait drove the carp wild in 15 minutes!

so it was imperative the fish was prevented from going past that point. Expecting the 12lb line to break at any moment, I clamped on the reel and gave it everything I had. For a few seconds an awful stalemate occurred, with the rod creaking under the reel seat, and then there was a thunderous crashing of water as the carp gave up, lashed the surface, and then shot under the trailing branches of the willow, and stuck fast.

Picking up my big net, I went crashing through the rushes until I stood alongside the willow, and then exerted as much pressure on the fish as I could, from a different angle of pull.

Within seconds, it was free, and shot into the middle of the channel where the war of attrition started again. Once more the carp rolled, its big mirror scales glinting in the moonlight, and for the first time I realised that the heavy rain had stopped during the battle.

All of a sudden, the fish surrendered, and, with my right arm numb from cramp, the folds of my big net at last closed round a worthy adversary. Before I even lifted the fish clear of the water, I dropped the rod on the rushes and collapsed in the bank for a breather. I was drenched with rain, soaked in sweat and absolutely knackered. I glanced at my watch, which read 3.40am. I knew I had put the kettle on at 2.40am, which meant that I must have been playing that fish for at least 55 minutes. Truly a memorable and exhilarating encounter.

The fish itself was a mirror in absolutely magnificent condition, long, lean and muscular, and weighing 25lb 10oz. Twenty minutes later, having fully recovered from the fight and a short self portrait photography session, the carp returned to her home and I, at last, enjoyed a welcome brew up and two hours of much needed sleep. Before retiring, however, out went another hundred baits.

By about 9.00am, having taken one more fish of 12lb 8oz at 6.00am, I was lying in the warm morning sun, the previous night's downpour a distant memory, and my wet clothes drying in the light breeze. I was sitting at peace with the world, tying up a few stringers, not really expecting any more action till evening. And then I was away again, the left hand rod shaking in the rests as another big carp departed the scene of the crime in haste. Incredibly, another protracted battle ensued, and when, half an hour later, another big fish sagged into the net, I knew that I had achieved a first in my carp angling career, four twenties in a session. This latest capture weighed in at exactly 23lb to complete an unforgettable quartet.

After that inspiring first session on my new bait, my confidence was sky high, and I was to get evidence the following week that I may have stumbled on to something really special. I remember arriving at the fishery at midday on Thursday to find every swim taken. It was a lovely day, blue sky, hot and sunny, but not conducive to catching carp until evening. I was struggling to find a pitch until Bob Frost, who was fishing an open swim off the field bank, suggested I fish next to him. He would be leaving at dusk, and by angling his rods to the right and mine to the left, we could talk carp fishing for a few hours but have our baits well apart. What happened in the next few hours was quite remarkable.

Bob had confirmed that the fishing was slow, in fact it was at full stop. No-one had taken a fish that day, and everything seemed dead under the hot sun. As we talked, and Bob made me a mug of tea, I introduced a hundred 18mm freebies, and then set about putting my camp together. I was in no rush to get hookbaits out, but less than fifteen minutes later Bob and I stood open mouthed as carp after carp rolled and crashed over my baits. The action was frenzied, a fish surfacing every few minutes. I remember Bob asking what the hell I had put in my baits. Obviously, the carp had switched on to feeding mode big time.

Not surprisingly, I wasted no more time in getting two baits in position, each one accompanied by six-bait stringers, plus another fifty freebies introduced by catapult. The first run came only ten minutes later, from a lovely linear mirror of 18lb 8oz, to be followed, shortly afterwards, by an inexplicably missed run to my other rod. Two mid-doubles followed in short order, and then something happened which was unique in my angling career. Using one of my

trusty Au Lion D'or hooks, I pulled out of a big fish at range. When I retrieved the terminal rig, I initially noticed nothing untoward but when I pulled out of a second fish on the same rod less than half an hour later, I knew that something was occurring. Sure enough, a more thorough examination revealed that the hook point was slightly damaged. I deserved to lose those fish through an avoidable oversight.

A second 18 pounder was landed in early evening, and then there was another disaster when I broke on the strike, again very unusual for me. I was using a back lead to avoid problems with Canada geese constantly fouling the lines, and the lead had caught a marginal root.

A further injection of freebies around 8.00pm stoked the action again, and a run of three fish in twenty minutes, of 17lb 6oz, 15lb 10oz and 19lb 8oz was followed by a four hour lull before I landed my biggest fish of the session so far. This was a lovely deep bodied mirror of 21lb 12oz at 1.00am.

Mercifully, the rest of the dark hours were quiet, and I managed a few hours sleep, before the feeding abandon recommenced at 6.00am with two runs simultaneously. I thought I was seeing things when both drop arms fell at precisely the same instant, and was initially convinced that one carp had taken both lines. However, I soon discovered differently, striking into the left-hand fish and then opening the bale arm while I dealt with the other. The fates were certainly with me that morning, for I was lucky enough to land both, a couple of pretty commons of 12lb 8oz and 13lb 12oz.

The remainder of the session was crazy. Periodically topping up the bait, I went on to take six more fish to 15lb, plus bigger carp of 16lb 10os, 18lb 4oz, 18lb 2oz, 19lb 7oz, 19lb 12oz, and a top fish a pot bellied common of 23lb 10oz. By early evening, I was knackered, out of bait, and studying the lightening flashes and intense blackness of an impending storm. The first heavy drops of rain were falling as I pulled out of the car park, and on the drive home I mentally re-lived the session. As far as I could ascertain, there had been four fish taken on the whole lake apart from the ones I'd taken. My bait was working well!

My next carp session was two weeks later, and I again arrived on a gorgeous

afternoon in bright sun. Business had badly delayed my start and when I arrived I think every syndicate member was present. There wasn't one swim vacant on the main body of the lake, and the only place I could fish was in the channel around the island, which

An hour into a protracted battle.

was solidly choked with surface duckweed. Standing by the small willow where I'd eventually landed the 25 pounder three weeks previously, I weighed up the options. Further down the channel, the water opened slightly into a bay some thirty yards across, before the sluice gate where the feeder stream leaves the water. Tight against the island and into the bay there were small clear areas dotted in the surface greenery. I felt that I should be in with a chance of fish if I could present a bait in these clear spots, and as it was all going through my mind, a big fish swirled a few feet from the overhanging undergrowth of the island. There then followed an exciting trail of bubbles rising through the scum as a fish came across the channel towards me, and then a large dorsal broke surface no more than thirty feet away. It had to be an omen, and I wasted no time in firing out a hundred of my sweet toffees, as I had mentally christened my sweetened fishmeal boilies, into each of two areas. The first was directly opposite me, where the fish had swirled, and the second was in the bay itself, at the bottom corner of the island.

By the time all preparations were complete, it was about 1.00pm, and I cast hookbaits to each position, attached to four-bait stringers, and settled down to wait.

That afternoon was baking hot, certainly into the nineties, and after ten minutes two members had come round for a chat, and we sat in the welcome shade of the small willow. They were able to confirm that very little had come out in the previous 36 hours, and I was just recounting the events of the previous week, when one of my Optonics sounded, on the rod cast to the bay. The bait had been in position about twenty minutes only.

It was obvious I had hooked a big fish from the off, judging by the sheer weight on the line, but the fight was disappointing. After quite a half hearted foray into the rushes on my own bank, which was easily countered, the carp allowed itself to be led quite docilely towards me and into the waiting net. The duration of the fight cannot have exceeded five minutes and yet here was obviously a new English personal best, an immaculate mirror of 27lb 4oz. Apparently, the fish was well known as one that rarely gave much of an account of itself, although it had little excuse as it was classically proportioned.

I was obviously delighted to have taken a new personal best, and from my first cast from a swim I had literally been forced to fish as I had no other choice. I was to find out later that my catching that fish so quickly, when others had been struggling for runs, had drawn some adverse comments. Rumours started about my putting out baits by the thousand, when I was doing no more baiting than anyone else, but it was a fact that I was catching fish when others weren't. The first seeds of discontent had been sown.

The rest of that afternoon and evening were uneventful, and just before dusk I went for broke and put in a further hundred baits. Midnight came and went on that beautifully breathless August night, and then, from 1.00am until just before dawn, I took four carp. There were no big fish, but carp of 12lb 8oz, 13lb 8oz, 16lb 4oz and 16lb 10oz provided a lot of excitement, and ensured an enjoyable breakfast.

By 7.00am, my eyes drooping, I put out a further fifty baits in each swim and lay back on my bedchair for some sleep. I must have gone out like a light, for the next thing I knew, it was 9.00am, I'm on my feet, semi conscious, with a rod in my hand well bent, and something big and powerful is trying to go round the back of the island. I was in serious trouble with this fish from the word go. Although the fish was not snagged, the intermediate line was caught on a trailing branch, and try as I might I could not get it to free itself. Several times I felt the carp run, taking line, and I would retrieve it again, but always we would come to the same point where I was exerting pressure on the tree branch rather than the fish. Eventually, the inevitable occurred, the hook hold failed and I was forced to pull for a break. An hour later, I was to lose a second big fish although this was a straight hook pull. When I retrieved the terminal rig I found a hook with the point turned right over and I am as convinced as I can be that the carp had been foul hooked.

By midday, it had become oppressively hot once again, and four of us were standing by the willow a few feet from my bedchair, the others bemoaning their lack of action. I remember glancing at my watch at 12.05pm, and just as I did so my longer range bait was away in a pulsating run. An impressive bow wave headed towards the sluice and as I struck the rod was slammed over by a fish moving at break neck speed. I had little choice but to yield line initially but as the carp appeared intent on vaulting the sluice gate and disappearing down the feeder stream, I exerted increasing pressure until the Armalite was creaking under the strain. The pressure on my right arm was tremendous as I engaged in a muscle wrenching tug of war.

The fat common of 23lb 10oz.

For a while, it was stalemate and then the carp gave ground, inch by grudging inch, until it suddenly gave up the struggle and shot across the bay to the right, diving headlong into the rushes on my bank, about thirty yards down the channel.

There then began a heave and haul encounter, with the carp being dragged through the rushes inch by inch. At any moment I expected to be inextricably snagged, or the hook to come adrift under the extreme pressure, but neither transpired. Slowly, the carp was being extricated from the undergrowth. When it eventually came free of the rushes, and moved to the centre of the bay, sulking on the bottom but away from immediate danger, I was able to ease the pressure on my arm for a moment. I glanced at my watch again. Twenty minutes had passed. With the carp now apparently under control, one of my companions picked up my big net. "It won't be long now," I stated confidently. It was perhaps well for my peace of mind that I didn't know how long.

As if in response to my comment, the carp suddenly woke from its temporary torpor and set off on another excursion to the sluice. In a series of short, powerful rushes thirty yards disappeared off the spool. Once again, with the fish perilously close to the gates, the fight descended into a tugging match, and I was only able to bring the fish back to the relative safety of the middle of the bay after many minutes of strength sapping sidestrain. Soon it was simply swimming round in small circles on the bottom, resisting all my attempts to bring it up in the water. One of my companions confirmed that an hour had now passed and we began speculating on the size of the fish and whether it was possibly foul hooked.

Incredibly, another half hour passed with the carp never more than fifteen yards from the rod top, and in all that time not once did it show the slightest sign of tiring. Great clouds of disturbed silt were rising all over the channel as the fish continued to bore powerfully along the bottom. This was becoming unreal.

At about this time, we managed our first look at the fish as it surfaced and commenced a powerful rush to my left, in an attempt to gain the main body of the lake. Two things were immediately apparent. First, although the fish was certainly a twenty pounder, it was no monster and secondly, it was fairly hooked. Nothing seemed to explain its quite exceptional performance.

This was now starting to annoy me. Never in my angling career had a fish dictated proceedings in this manner, and I now determined to give it absolutely maximum pressure, not to take no for an answer. It was time to stop messing about. I bent the rod more and more until the handle bent under the reel seat, which takes some doing with a 3lb Armalite. I bent that rod until my arm was trembling with the exertion. It would have been impossible for me to have put any greater pressure on that fish, and with the pull now being almost directly from above it seemed impossible for any fish to withstand it. But not only did the carp withstand it, it pulled back even harder and then shot off on another twenty yard run, this time trying to make the overhanging branches on the island. "This is bloody unreal," I shouted in frustration, as the watch now confirmed the passing of two hours.

Every muscle in my body was now aching and the pain in my right arm had risen to the level of torture. I started to wonder who would weaken first, me or the fish. Having forced the fish back from the brink of disaster under the island trees, the battle had again settled into a gruelling arm wrestling match. For what seemed an eternity, the carp was never more than five yards from the net, but stubbornly refused to come off bottom. I would strain every sinew to lift the carp and, with arm trembling, catch sight of the top few inches of my rig tubing. Then the fish would pull back and the tubing would disappear again.

The end, when it came, was quite sudden. Once again, I applied all my strength to lift my adversary, felt it yield, and then quite unexpectedly it came straight to the top, lay on its side and allowed the net to close round it. In relief, I dropped the rod, collapsed on the bank, and allowed my companions the job of completing the formalities. Incredibly, the duration of the fight was 2 hours 45 minutes, and I was extremely grateful to my companions for not only their assistance and encouragement during the scrap, but the fact that they were there to witness proceedings. Without witnesses, no one would have believed my version of events.

I was amazed to confirm that the carp, exactly 22lb, was fairly hooked in the bottom lip, and there was nothing to account for the staggering resistance it put up. Even when it was returned, after such a protracted scrap, it shot off in a cloud

Returning a 20lb mirror.

of silt as though jet propelled. Perhaps my sweetened fish meal boilies were the piscine equivalent of rocket fuel !

After that epic confrontation, I was mentally unprepared to fish again for a while, and it was perhaps an hour later when I recast both rods. Barely fifteen minutes later, I was weighing another terrific mirror of 20lb 8oz. This was quickly followed by a lovely streamlined common of 14lb 2oz in early evening, before all activity ceased at the onset of dusk.

I must admit I was half hoping for a night undisturbed by Optonics as I was badly in need of sleep. I was dead to the world by 11.00pm, and there I remained until some time around 3.00am, when my slumber was rudely curtailed by the howl of an alarm. I'll swear I was asleep on my feet for the first few minutes of the fight, everything was on auto pilot. But I must have done everything right, because there were no anxious moments in the twenty minute scrap, before the torch beam confirmed another twenty, 20lb 4oz to be exact, which was to prove the last fish of the session.

In the short time I was to have left at the syndicate water, I continued to make spectacular catches, taking another fourteen doubles and mirrors of 24lb 6oz and 23lb 14oz over two days the following week and another seven doubles plus big fish of 19lbs 10oz, 19lbs 14oz and 22lbs 10oz on a final overnighter in mid-August. In total, after putting my new bait together, in just twelve day's fishing in total, I'd amassed thirteen carp in excess of twenty pounds, plus another twenty nine doubles. No other syndicate member had come close to that total.

I am not taking any particular credit for stunning angling ability in catching those fish, though I did little wrong when I had my chances. I had stumbled fortuitously on a bait combination that proved irresistible at the time. Whether it was the sweetener I cannot be sure, but by early July most members were aware of the fishmeal base. For whatever reason, my bait was devastating for those few weeks.

Unfortunately, there are among anglers those who resent the success of others. Most of the members were brilliant lads but one or two began a campaign that was to result in my being expelled from the water in late August. I was simply catching too many carp. I know this has happened to others in the past and will happen to others in the future, but it does leave a very bitter taste. Although I was invited back into the syndicate the following season, and duly paid my fees, it didn't seem the same somehow and I never got round to fishing there again. The following year, I relinquished my membership with great sadness. I had fished a beautiful, scenic paradise for the best part of nine years, and that had been ruined by petty jealousy. Perhaps one day I can fish there again. I like to think so.

Moonlight Monsters

When Alan Wilson took his incredible quartet of thirteen pound bream in the Autumn of 1983, an experience I was lucky enough to share, it was the general consensus that such a catch of specimen bream would be impossible to better. Little did I realise that within a few short months I would be involved with a bream water where a thirteen pounder was a well below average specimen. That came about directly as a result of my growing friendship with Alastair Nicholson, who I had met for the first time in March 1984.

In the 1984 close season, Alastair was to show me round Deans Farm, where he had been taking some very big tench, and where Trefor and I were opening our campaign in June. During the journey on a sunny Sunday morning, we passed a daunting looking gravel pit and, quite casually, Alastair announced that he intended to break the bream record there, after the early season tenching at Deans. Naturally, such a comment was intriguing, and I pressed him for more details. Apparently, the water was named Queenford Lagoon, and the previous autumn an exceptionally big bream had been found dead, and had been found to weigh close to the British record. A record fish was one of Alastair's burning ambitions.

By July of that year, the name Alastair Nicholson had been imprinted indelibly in the annals of angling history, as his early conquest of the Queenford giants has become legendary. It has always been my belief that Alastair's

Queenford weed.

first bream from the water is one of the greatest feats of specimen hunting in my lifetime. He had to contend with endless blanks, his car being twice vandalised, and the constant fear of apprehension, as night fishing was not officially allowed. Eventually, however, Alastair's perseverance and dogged determination not to be beaten paid off, and a huge bream of 13lb 14oz was landed.

Obviously, it is very difficult to keep a fish of that size, two ounces above the official bream record, quiet for long, and within only a few days of the capture representations to the owners, ARC, led to their agreeing the formation of a limited night syndicate, led by well known and popular Bicester angler Joe Taylor. I was privileged to be one of the lucky few.

The events that transpired in what remained of the 1984 season left us all in no doubt as to what we were up against. Despite intensive angling, only three more bream were banked. Strangely, all three came to Alastair. His second Queenford fish was the one that really started the big fish world buzzing. Phil Smith has recounted the events to me many times. Apparently, at about midnight, Alastair suddenly appeared at Phil's bivvy door and almost casually announced that he had just caught a bream that he thought may beat the newly established record of 15lb 6oz, Tony Bromley's Cheshire mere fish. Phil agonised over the accuracy of the weighing for some time before he announced 15lb 6oz, the same weight as the Cheshire fish. Alastair had realised his dream, a British record. It is an amazing fact that the swim that produced that bream, thereafter known by the syndicate members as the fifteen-six swim, never produced another fish, although it was fished extensively.

Although my first season at Queenford was blank as far as bream were concerned, it was quite one of the most unforgettable experiences of my angling career. On my first visit, I had spent hours drifting around in my inflatable boat, and had confirmed the technical problems to be overcome to have any chance of success. There were two main problems. First, there was an incredible number of features, which would make the selecting of the right feature on any particular night an absolute lottery, and second the volume of weed was frightening. Over vast areas, weed stretched completely to the surface to form large mats.

The features in the pit were unusual in that the vast majority of them were extremely small, with dramatic depth differenes from the surrounding areas. There were many features only a few feet square and about five feet deep, where the bottom was clean gravel and totally devoid of weed, but surrounded completely by water twelve feet deep and solid with weed. One feature that produced bream was no more than two feet across at its apex about ninety yards from the bank. I defy a world champion caster to land a bait on that bar, at night, with a strong south westerly blowing!

Queenford did feature odd bigger features, one or two of which were within easy casting distance from the bank. One of those was known as Knowles Bar, on account of a huge fish taken by John Knowles in the late summer of 1985,a fish which shattered the bream record again, weighing 15lb 10oz. That fish was recognisable by an unmistakable blemish on one flank and, as the years passed, we all said that if that bream ever put in another appearance, it could well take the record again. It was not seen again until 1990, when the record stood at 16lb 6oz, and this time it was Derek Quirk who gently lifted the fish out of his landing net. To his utter dismay, Derek saw immediately that, not only was it indeed the record fish of five years previously but that it was also foul hooked. Without weighing the bream and obviously totally gutted, Derek slipped the fish back immediately. In that, I feel he made a mistake. I can well understand his not wishing to claim the fish, but it would have been a piece of important angling history to have the weight recorded for posterity. Peter Coates, who was with Derek on that eventful night, has said that the bream could well have beaten the 16lb 6oz mark.

To go back to my first trip in 1984, after I had drifted around for many hours, I had drawn up a shortlist of two areas. One was a fairly narrow bar off the attractively wooded north bank, while the other was a large, clear area off the south bank, uniformly twelve feet deep, and of a fine silt bottom. This was probably fifty yards along the bank from the 15-6 swim.

In the end, I decided upon the narrow bar, and spent the rest of the afternoon preparing my pitch. In the light of subsequent events, how I wish I had made the other choice!. By early evening, Phil Smith had arrived, and decided to fish the same bank as me, some hundred yards away, while Alastair Nicholson was, by a strange coincidence, setting up in my second choice swim.

As dusk lapsed into darkness everything fell silent, and Phil and I had the normal result for a Queenford session, a total blank!. But on the south bank, around midnight, one alarm had sounded. Alastair had taken his third Queenford giant, another incredible fish of 14lb 14oz. I will never forget witnessing that fish next morning. It was quite simply an awesome bream. Single handedly, Alastair was re-writing the script as far as big bream were concerned.

On the strength of that fish, taken as it had been in close proximity to the 15-6 record, Phil and I moved our gear to the south bank for the next two nights, both of us a respectful distance from Alastair. The events of that second night were virtually identical to the first, in that Phil and I again blanked, the only success going Alastair's way. I remember waking with a start to the sound of an alarm just before midnight, and was disappointed to find that it wasn't one of mine. I wandered down the bank to Alastair just in time to join him as he was landing the fish, another lump of 14lb 12oz.

A few hours later, we all again stood around Alastair during the photographic session and discussed events. Obviously, in Queenford Lagoon, we had found a water of quite staggering potential. So far, in a few short weeks, Alastair had taken four bream, all of which had beaten the previous record, three of them by a large margin.

Having failed to open my account in 1984, and being totally obsessed with carp in 1985, I commenced the 1986/87 season with renewed enthusiasm. From information gleaned from other syndicate members, and from my experiences of gravel pit bream at TC, it was becoming increasingly obvious that the bream liked to feed over areas that were naturally weed free rather than over swims that had been created by dragging. Several superb looking swims had been created by dragging the previous two seasons, and not one bream had resulted from these tactics. From summer 1986 onwards, none of us bothered with weed clearance, other than in shifting surface debris, preferring to search for the weed free areas at the start of each season. Thus it was that that season saw the bulk of the angling effort concentrated at the wooded north bank. Most of the swims there were weed free whereas the weed was bad elsewhere. In July 1986, I commenced a three day stint on a warm and sunny Wednesday afternoon. The swim consisted of a fairly small gravel bar only about forty yards out and, after a quiet Wednesday night, Thursday night saw the onset of line bites. My thoughts were back at TC pit that night, where liners almost always preceded the arrival of bream bites proper. It was not to be, however, and although I had about six real butt ringing liners, the next morning still saw me breamless.

The Friday night was one of those angling sessions that will live with me for ever. Phil Smith had arrived in late afternoon for a two week holiday and, as all the swims on the North bank were taken, was undecided where to fish. As several of the members apart from me had experienced liners I told Phil that it would be sensible to sit with me that night and take over my

First success, 13lb 2oz.

swim when I had to leave the following morning. This he did, and over endless cups of tea during the dark hours, both Phil and I were on the edge of our seats as line bite after line bite kept the Optonics ringing out. The number of indications I had that night was phenomenal, and although two or three looked for all the world like the real thing my strikes met with nothing but fresh air. As I packed up shortly after dawn to commence the long drive back to Coventry I was one very frustrated angler.

Despite comments I heard attributed to me afterwards, there was no one more delighted than I was when I learned the following week that Phil had taken fish from the swim. Apparently, he had undergone a similar ordeal on the Saturday night, but proper bites had eventually materialised on Sunday and resulted in a superb brace of fish topped by a 15lb 3oz specimen.

I remember saying to Phil at the time that I was not at all worried that he had taken fish from my swim as it was only a matter of time before I had my first Queenford bream. Little did I realise that it was to be the following week.

On Thursday afternoon I had settled into one of my favourite swims, a tiny little bar about thirty yards out from the north bank known as Flanders Bar, on account of the fact that Andy Flanders had taken the first fish from it. As soon as darkness had fallen, it was like reliving the previous week, as indications started on both rods. From then until about 2.00am, the bobbins were rarely still and I was expecting a proper bite at any moment. But it never happened, and by 3.00am it was all quiet and I was in my sleeping bag. Dawn came and went, and it had been light about an

My second Queenford fish of 14lb 3oz.

hour when a sudden jump of the bobbin to the butt signalled the arrival of one of Queenford's small perch. Minutes after recasting another small perch put in an appearance and I assessed that my chance of bream had gone.

Leisurely, I cooked myself a sumptuous breakfast of bacon, eggs, mushrooms and fried bread and had just started to tuck in when one of the bobbins jumped up an inch and then another inch, before dropping back to its original position. Another perch, obviously, and I ignored it. Minutes later, the bobbin dropped to the floor and then jerked its way back to its original position again. Again I ignored it and carried on eating. Eventually, it twitched its way to the butt ring and stayed there. Putting my half eaten breakfast to one side and cursing the perch for its poor timing I picked up the rod and struck. Instead of the feeble resistance I was expecting, the rod slammed over and something heavy powered across the swim. It was then it became obvious what had happened, or so I thought. A pike had picked up the worms, the bite had been typical. Not wanting my breakfast to go cold, I heaved on the "pike" for all I was worth, half hoping it would bite me off. I will never forget the feeling in the pit of my stomach when the fish rolled at the edge of the bushes and I caught a glimpse for the first time of a great expanse of bronze flank. I broke out in a cold sweat at the thought of the ham fisted manner in which I had played that fish. Luckily, I managed to keep my composure, and was soon punching the air in delight as my scales confirmed a new personal best of 13lb 2oz.

In June 1987, my second Queenford bream, and another personal best, was to be taken from the same swim. It was also my only bream that season. If only I had known, I could have saved a lot of blanks!

I had settled into the swim on Thursday afternoon, on a very wet and miserable day, when there was quite a stiff breeze blowing inshore. I was joined at teatime by Andy Flanders and we were the only two on the bank that night. Andy was fishing about fifty yards down the bank to my left. At the onset of dark, the steady rain had dropped to a fine drizzle and the wind disappeared. Despite the damp, it was an extremely muggy night and I sat outside my bivvy in waterproofs. It was one of those occasions when I knew I was going to catch. Liners started about midnight and I had about four in quick succession in a couple of minutes. And then, at ten past twelve, the line was a blur and the reel backwinding furiously as something took off with my lobworm at high speed.

For almost the entire duration of that fight I was convinced that I was attached to one of the pits few common carp, so powerful was the fish. It had kited strongly along the overgrown bush fringe to my left, and I had waded out as far as I dare into the steeply shelving margins. In my haste to get to the rod and silence the screaming Optonic I had left the landing net out of reach on the high bank about ten yards away. I was in a real quandary when the fish eventually found an immovable snag right under the near bank about ten yards to my left. Applying maximum side strain had no effect on the fish and I was shouting as loud as I could to wake Andy and get him to come and give me a hand. Andy slept on. I soon realised that I was getting nowhere like this and, even if the fish came free, I would have no way of landing it. Dropping the rod back on the rest, I quickly retrieved the landing net and then recommenced the battle. The rod bent more and more as I increased pressure. All of a sudden the rod straightened, and I started to wind in, thinking the line had parted. I was very disappointed for a couple of seconds and then there was a terrific thump on the rod top as the fish swam strongly off shore again. I had been very lucky. The underwater branch the fish had been snagged on had broken away, leading to the fish swimming towards me unfettered. Thereafter it was plain sailing, and a few minutes later Andy and I knelt side by side admiring my second Queenford bream of 14lb 3oz, a male as evidenced by the mass of tubercles on its head.

One of the most interesting seasons was 1988/89, for several reasons. Many of us had been discovering hitherto unsuspected swims further and further offshore, which had led to occasional bream being caught at distances of up to a hundred yards. The technical difficulty of such fishing at Queenford was immense and we developed a whole new technique for fishing at these ranges, which obviously included being forced to introduce hookbaits by boating them out. We all faced what I think was unfair criticism for this, always by people who had no conception of the problems we had to overcome. Because of the volumes of weed, such a length of line was often near the surface in many places, leading to false bites by birds, drifting weed and so on. Also, we were all plagued regularly by small perch, and there is nothing more galling than landing a small perch just on dark as you are settling down to wait for a bream, specially if the swim is ninety yards out, in the dark and in the teeth of a gale. Placing a hookbait accurately by rowing it out in a strong wind at night, when the swim is only feet across, is not as easy as it sounds and we have all got into some terrible pickles at times.

The 1988/89 season was also the year of the weed, tons of the stuff, which by a strange twist of fate left a hundred yard strip of water off the west bank virtually weed free while the rest of the water was choked. That season saw many previously unfishable features suddenly become accessible, and just such a swim Derek Quirk moved into in July 1988, having just endured several days of the statutory Queenford blank. As darkness fell on his first night in the new swim, little did Derek realise that he was about to make angling history, by surpassing Alan Wilson's seemingly unassailable TC achievement. A few hours later, he had banked bream of 15lb 8oz,15lb 9oz,14lb 6oz,14lb 6oz and 12lb 5oz.

Derek Quirk also brought to Queenford the echo sounder. Hitherto, we had all found new swims by the more painstaking methods of searching with long handled rakes and by sight for the shallow bars, but there is no doubt that the echo sounder revolutionised the swim identification process. I obtained my Humminbird shortly after Derek's epic catch, and it was to lead, indirectly, to the fish of my dreams in August 1988.

On my arrival that Thursday, I reflected that not a single bream had been caught for the previous fortnight. I also had in my mind a conversation I had with Phil Smith about prebaiting for the bream. Despite the fact that we had all been using quantities of hemp in our groundbait not a single landed bream showed any signs of having eaten it, although the carp sacks were often full of regurgitated corn and casters. The first decision then was to eliminate the hemp, in case it was acting as a deterrent rather than attractant. The second point we had discussed was that most of the bream that had been taken had come on the first night in a new swim, the second night usually being blank. Was that because, we wondered, it was human nature to bait up heavily after having taken bream, and was that actually acting as a deterrent also. I had decided therefore, that on this session I would both bait lightly on the first night, and, whatever the outcome, not bait at all for the second.

Before I decided on my pitch, I took out my echo sounder and searched all the swims on the west bank. Having the water to myself that afternoon I had the choice of them all. Although the echo sounder was not used to find fish but to find features, I was nevertheless excited when several very big traces crossed the screen over the highest point of Knowles' Bar. When I looked overboard, although I did not see the fish responsible I did see the vortex that had been created by a big fish. It need not have been a bream, of course, but at that moment I decided that this session would be in that swim. Strangely enough, although I had been a member of the syndicate since inception, this was to be the first time I had fished the swim.

That night, I baited with three tins of corn only, using double hook rigs carrying a corn/caster cocktail on one hook and lob on the other. Throughout the night, I was really keyed up, expecting something to happen. But nothing did, and when I was eventually cooking breakfast the next morning I remarked to myself that on my next trip I would leave at home unnecessary items like landing nets and batteries for the Optonics!

On Friday afternoon I was joined on the bank by Peter Coates and after a pleasant chat, Peter

Rowing baits out to the M1 bar.

moved in to the swim that had produced the large catch to Derek. That night, I stuck to my predetermined plan not to introduce any more free feed, but I was far from confident as darkness fell. For hour after hour, all was silence and at about 11.00pm, unable to keep my eyes open any longer, I slid down in my sleeping bag. At about 12.30am, I was awoken with a jolt by a screaming Optonic, and looking out of the bivvy door, I could clearly see my reel backwinding furiously in the moonlight. I was out of the camp like a shot and soon stood on the high bank with rod well bent as a powerful fish took a few yards of line on an irresistible first rush. After that initial headlong dash, the bream was turned quite easily and the fight

Alan Wilson baits the "14s" swim.

thereafter was very straightforward. Moments later, I was admiring a gigantic bream. 15lb 2oz it weighed, a new personal best, and one of the most dramatically two tone fish I have ever seen..

That night also saw another first at Queenford, in that two different swims produced bream on the same night, for I found out the following morning that Pete had also banked a magnificent 15lb 10oz specimen.

It was during that 1988 season that I first met one of my now dearest friends, Marsh Pratley. Marsh initially fished the water on the guest ticket and quickly became one of the most popular figures there. He also became totally obsessed with the water and his story is one of dedication to the point of heartbreak. It is a matter of record that Marsh fished the water for three whole years before eventually landing his first bream from the water, when he at last made a fabulous catch in the summer of 1991. Even that, of course, was tinged with sadness, following as it did the tragic drowning of our dear friend Andy Mundy a few weeks earlier.

In the 1988 and 1989 seasons, several more tremendous bream had been taken, including fish of 15lb 14oz to Phil Smith, Peter Coates and Mark Chivers, and the onset of the 1989 season saw another milestone reached, the first sixteen pounder to Derek Quirk. We all felt it just a matter of time before the record again came back to Queenford, and in the 1990 season the syndicate was joined by a man who was to come an agonising three ounces short of the record at 16lb 3oz, Andy Mundy. Andy had actually fished very hard for no reward at all the previous season on the guest ticket, and the first few trips in the summer of 1990 were equally fruitless. That was to change in July, thanks in no small measure to the selflessness and generosity of Marsh Pratley. Marsh had seen signs of bream activity in the shallows on his arrival and had set swim markers in the appropriate positions and already baited the swim when Andy arrived for a two day session. Andy was debating where to fish when Marsh magnanimously invited him to share the swim and fish to one side of the markers while he fished the other. The following morning, Marsh had recorded a blank and Andy had landed his first Queenford bream of 15lb 3oz. That first fish opened the floodgates for Andy and in the weeks that followed he had several more tremendous bream, topped off by that magnificent fish of 16lb 3oz.

As well as the bream, there were also good pike, tench and perch in the water. No one ever landed an exceptional tench, although there were several exciting night-time battles with twenty pound plus pike that picked up lobs intended for bream. As for the perch, many two pounders were taken, but the only three pounder was one that came to my rod in July 1990. I was fishing a swim off the main road south bank, at fairly long range, and just before dark had carefully rowed out my baits to the correct position. Minutes after setting the butt indicators, both baits had been taken with the result that I was soon out in the boat again, trying to play two fish simultaneously. A big percentage of Queenford fish had often needed to be landed by boat on account of the thick mats of weed with which the water abounded. On the night in question, both the fish turned out to be small perch. By the time I had released the fish, rebaited, and rowed fresh baits out, it was virtually pitch black. No sooner had I returned to the bank when the left hand rod was away again, and once more I had to take to the boat. Again, a small perch was landed and by the time I was again settled down behind my rods I was exhausted. It was also highly unusual, since although small perch were almost always a nuisance at dawn, they were rarely active at dusk.

Probably half an hour after dark, I was away again and this time when I struck I knew I had hooked something of a different class altogether. Strangely, this fish was successfully landed from the bank, despite the tremendous scrap it gave me, and I really had no idea what I had hooked until it came in close. The size of the perch made up for having to go out on my boat to rebait yet again, and I sacked an immaculate specimen of 3lb 2oz to await a photographic session the next morning.

The last bream I took from Queenford came a few weeks later, from the same swim I had caught the perch. I was fishing about forty yards from Derek Quirk, and on the Thursday night we stood talking for about three hours after dark with no sign of activity to either of us. Shortly after he had retired to his bivvy, I had a sudden drop back of my bobbin, probably about two inches. In the next minute, the bobbin crept back to where it had been in a series of minute little jumps. Hearing the intermittent bleeps Derek came down the bank to watch what was going on. For the next ten minutes or so, the bobbin gave imperceptible little jumps up or slight drops back without ever doing anything to warrant a strike, and yet it was obvious there was fish activity around the bait. I was having a job keeping control of my striking arm when, out of the blue, the positive movement I had been praying for occurred at last. Steadily, the bobbin dropped to the floor and the line fell completely slack. A sweeping strike set the hook into another of the Queenford leviathans which fought well without doing anything particularly alarming. Pretty soon, an immaculate bream was reposing in my weigh sling and Derek was announcing 14lb 4oz, my second biggest by an ounce.

The above account of my eight lovely years at Queenford of necessity has been sketchy, with obvious bias on the fish I took myself. It has covered many of the high spots of my memories as well as the appalling tragedy that took Andy Mundy's life. What no treatise on Queenford can hope to do is explain exactly what motivated us to endure countless blanks, what it was about the water that I can call success catching four bream in over seventy nights' fishing. It cannot start to describe the backbreaking task of six solid hours of clearing tons of surface weed and the frustration of sitting through nights when a sudden gale has blown so much weed over the lines as to make fishing totally impossible. There has been no mention of the absolute frustration of having the swim marker dragged away by drifting weed in a strong wind just after you have finished baiting, or of reaching screaming pitch when you have just rowed out to your swim a hundred yards away and carefully lowered your hook bait over the side only to find, when you return to shore, the hook bait firmly fastened to the anchor rope. There are probably a hundred and one other reasons why the fishing at Queenford has at times been nothing more than a pain in the backside. But I tell you, I have never been involved in any fishing campaign in the company of a greater bunch of guys. The syndicate from start to finish had a camaraderie that was almost unique, with a totally open news network that saw no information held back whatever from other members. We all enjoyed each other's fish. With a water as difficult as Queenford Lagoon, that was the only way to approach it. When I think of the hours and years I devoted to the water for just four of its bream I have to ask myself whether it was all worth it. I only have to think of the euphoria of landing one of those mammoth bronze slabs to have my answer. Queenford will always have an extra special place in my heart. It was a sad day indeed when we lost the water and it was turned into a water sports complex, with the delights of jet skis, quad bike racing and so on. Those magnificent bream are probably lost to angling forever.

I cannot close this chapter without describing an incident that tested my friendship with Marsh Pratley to its limit. It was 1990, at which time Marsh had gone over two years without a single bream bite.

We were fishing adjacent swims, probably a hundred yards apart, on the shallows, and during the night I had an incredibly fast run. It soon became apparent that a swan had become fouled in the line and for what seemed an eternity the bird lashed around about forty yards out. Suddenly, the line fell slack, and I reeled in a limp line minus a terminal rig.

As dawn broke the following morning, I became aware of a large white shape motionless alongside my swim marker. It was a swan with its head down, and I watched it for a good fifteen minutes, not detecting any signs of movement. It was obviously, I thought, badly hurt or dead, and I knew I had to go out and investigate.

Therein lay my problem. I have only one real phobia, that being birds flapping close to my face. I knew that, if the swan was injured and started to create a commotion on my arrival, I could conceivably panic. Over deep, weedy water, that would be very dangerous. I knew I had to get help and so I wandered down to Marsh, who was just coming round. Once again, his bobbins had not moved all night, recording yet another total blank. Typically of Marsh, he never hesitated to help me out of my dilemma. Not bothering to wind in, he came round to my pitch, and we both embarked in my boat to sort the swan out, with me rowing and Marsh in the prow to do the business.

Amazingly, when we were about six feet from the bird, it suddenly lifted its head, looked around as if to say, "Where am I?", and then swam off strongly. There was nothing wrong with the damn thing!!

By the time we had arrived back at the bank, twenty minutes had probably elapsed, and Marsh suggested I go with him to his pitch for a brew. As we arrived, Marsh's face was a picture. Both his bobbins were jammed in the butt rings, and one spool was half empty. In both cases there was no fish on the end, although both baits were gone, suggesting that the fish responsible had not been small perch, which gorged the hook if not struck in time. For the first time in two years, Marsh had experienced bream bites at Queenford, but instead of being behind his rods he had been busy helping me rescue a sleeping swan that didn't need rescuing! That morning, I felt it prudent to sneak back to my pitch without further comment!!!

Early Ouse Barbel

A Hard Won Double

At the start of the 1992 season, having by then fished eight intense years on the Cherwell for barbel, I was looking for pastures new. I also felt that, at that time, my 12lb 5oz Cherwell fish was perhaps near the limit for the river, and I now had thoughts of pushing for a thirteen pounder. The obvious choice was the middle reaches of the Great Ouse, some areas of which had certainly produced several thirteens and a rumoured fourteen pounder.

My first foray, in July 1992, was to a stretch not known specifically for extra big fish but which was rumoured to hold a fair head of barbel. My first priority was to catch a few Ouse barbel, of whatever size, learn about their habits, and move on to the more lightly inhabited stretches, where the bigger fish apparently lived, from 1993 onwards.

The first barbel I ever hooked on that stretch is still probably the biggest, to this day. I had settled into a lovely swim on the point of a little island, where a smooth mid-river flow over clean gravel screamed chub and barbel. At the upstream extremity of the swim, level with my sitting position, a large fallen tree ensured that the flow downstream of the branches was gentle, by throwing the heavier flows across to the far bank. The river featured a gravel depression about fifteen yards downstream, and this is where my hemp and corn prebait was concentrated for the evening and night session to come.

It was about half an hour before dark on a still, muggy evening and an extensive hatch of a nondescript brown moth had chub going mad at the surface, concentrated around the trailing branches opposite me. Every few seconds there would be a swirl and as some of these came from obviously serious chub, I decided to take advantage while light remained. I had some lobs with me, and decided to fish these floating by air injecting them. Quickly amending my terminal gear to fish freeline, I gave the last few feet of line a quick grease and cast a buoyant lobworm at the rear edge of the trailing branches. There was an immediate swirl, a heavy lunge, and pretty soon I was admiring a cracking chub only an ounce under five pounds.

Another bait went back to the same place, there was another immediate snatch, but this time what I hooked was most definitely not a chub! A very big barbel,

certainly well in excess of twelve pounds, shot upstream through the trailing branches, and as it did so I noticed one long, whippy branch come to the surface. During the minutes that followed, it became obvious that I was exerting no pressure on the fish whatever. The line was
firmly attached to the branch, and I was effectively playing the branch and not the fish. Eventually, the barbel was on the surface, tethered to the branch in mid-river, and I was becoming increasingly concerned for its welfare. As the river was about six feet deep at that point, flowing strongly, and it was now nearly dark, I was reluctant to go in after it. Luckily, with me in a frenzy of indecision, the fish solved the problem for me. As it made a last frantic surge, the line parted, and the barbel was free.

After losing that fish, I was convinced that it would be in my net in short order, now that it had been located. How wrong I was. Not unnaturally, my first few trips to the stretch after losing the big one were spent in and around the same area, but to no avail. Barbel bites actually became very few and far between, and when the rains came with a vengeance in September, I'd only managed a few average fish, to just over nine pounds.

Sods law was to dictate that my next encounter with a very big barbel should occur on a day when I was chubbing with a light quivertip rod. I had arrived at the river to find it high and cold. The temperature had been steadily dropping, and when I recorded only 40°F, I decided that chub offered a better chance of sport.

In mid-afternoon, I arrived at a lovely crease swim, forty yards upstream of where I had lost the big barbel in summer, but looking very different with two feet of extra water in the river. The downstream extremity of the run was a large, fallen willow, a well known chub swim. I had fished the swim often for barbel in the summer without a single bite.

I wasted no time in propelling a sugar cube-sized meat bait to rest under the trailing branches of the willow, but it wasn't destined to rest there long. Within minutes, the rod had hammered round and was soon buckling under a tremendous run from what was obviously a good barbel.

After absorbing the power of that initial surge, I actually started to gain some line and then I saw two things simultaneously. One was the tail of a very big barbel

10lb 14oz fish on spicy meat.

and the other a long, whip like trailing root. I remember saying out loud, "Oh no, not again!"

I was never to get the barbel upstream of that root. Whenever I gained the ascendancy, the fish would come so far and then I was powerless to bring it any further. After a short rest, downstream would go the fish again, and so on. Eventually, the inevitable happened and the line parted.

I really was gutted after that disappointment, but that was as nothing to how I felt ten minutes later after exactly the same thing had happened for a second time. I remember leaving the swim that night promising to be back the following week with a barbel rod and gear man enough for the job. In the event, I was unable to fish that swim again that winter. The land in that vicinity is cut by deep folds, and the extra four feet of floodwater that entered the river the following week effectively made my swim part of an island, and inaccessible for the rest of the season.

The third disaster with a very big barbel was to come in November, on a warm, oppressive night when there had to be at least eight feet of floodwater in the river. It had occurred to me that some of the summer swims could be excellent barbel feeding spots in high water. The river in one section features very high, wildly overgrown banks, and at intervals clearings through the jungle had been cut down to the river. Invariably, the sitting areas had been flattened out to take a seat box, and these would now be lovely peaceful havens for feeding fish. Landing hook baits on these flat areas had to be worth a try.

A swim I knew well looked a screamer. At normal height, a dwarf willow protrudes a few yards from the bank at the head of the run. With eight feet of floodwater on, a large slack had been created behind the tree. This, coupled with the flat, clear area on which to present the bait, should make the swim about perfect. There was only one thing I was mindful of. Where the flat sitting area had been created, the natural bank had been reinforced with vertical wooden stakes, the tops of which stood proud about a foot. I would have to get a hooked fish off bottom as quickly as possible, to minimise the risk of fouling those stakes.

A little before dark, I lowered a large piece of luncheon meat to rest on that step and sat back to wait. Perhaps ten minutes later, the rod top suddenly plunged over and I was once more in conflict with an extra big barbel. I never once felt in serious trouble with that fish. Although it fought hard, I was able to counter its every

move, and eventually it was under the
rod top, stubbornly refusing to come
off the bottom. And then I felt it snag
for a short while before suddenly
coming free, and remembered those
stakes.

Moments later, the fish was on the
surface and as I turned on my head
lamp to assist with the netting I had
my first good look at my adversary. It

Hard won double of 10lb 13oz.

was certainly a good double, possibly as much as twelve pounds. That was the last
time I was to see it. Just out of reach of the net, the fish dived once more and the
clutch shrieked as the barbel again found those stakes. For a second time, the
snagging was only momentary and I was able to heave the fish clear. The third time
that happened spelt disaster. I had once more hauled the fish from danger, and was
drawing it towards me with maximum pressure, sensing that the barbel was about
beaten. And then everything suddenly went slack. My words at that instant are
unprintable.

My first reaction was that I must have pulled out or straightened the hook. But
when I checked my terminal rig I could see that my 12lb Silkworm hooklink had
frayed through. When I thought about it, what had happened became obvious. As
the trace had rubbed against the wooden stakes, possibly small splinters had been
constantly picking at the braid, eventually weakening it enough to break. I was in
sombre mood as I replaced the broken trace with 8lb monofilament. That night, I
went on to land five barbel to 8lb 10oz, a terrific session normally but small
recompense for the monster I had lost.

The following summer, the water was low and clear and I again set about
searching for those elusive monsters. The old fallen willow drew me like a magnet,
and I spent hours in its branches, lowering droppers of hemp on the clean gravel
beneath, without ever catching sight of a single barbel. All I could see were hordes
of chub. My thoughts that perhaps the barbel stayed right under cover of the
foliage until after dark never received any encouragement either. Four complete
nights in the swim resulted in not a single bite other than from average chub. I was
forced to the conclusion that the swim is one solely for flood conditions.

From mid-July to mid-August, I moved around the stretch a fair bit, trying
different swims and approaches, and I learned a lot and had a lot of fun. During
that period, I caught a lot of good barbel, with several nine pounders, including a
lovely brace of 8lb 14oz and 9lb 5oz on boilies.

In late August, a sudden impulse told me to fish an area much further upstream than I had tried before, and a bright Thursday morning saw me investigating a new and very interesting area. It was a fascinating mix of overgrown, streamer filled gravelly shallows and deeper, more sedate stretches.

I had a problem that day determining where to fish, as everywhere looked promising, but eventually I decided that my first night would be spent on a long sweeping right hand bend, heavily rush lined on both banks. The main depth was hard against the reeds of the far bank, the upstream extremity of that run being where a dense bed of streamer ended and there was a sudden depth increase. There just had to be barbel in that far bank glide somewhere along its forty yards, and I baited every ten yards or so, only feet from the far rushes, with ten droppers of hemp. Each dropper contained finely diced luncheon meat which had been soaked in SBS Frankfurter Sausage flavour. I also baited the near bank rushes the same way, although it was the bank opposite that looked the business.

After the baiting, I investigated the near bank run in my chest waders, looking for any special feature, and did locate an interesting area where the gravel suddenly rose, the water going from waist deep to only about knee deep. A bait positioned at the onset of that rise had to be interesting, and I decided to tackle the swim with two rods. I would fish that near bank feature statically, placing meat on a bolt rig, fishing it in conjunction with a centrepin with the check engaged. That rod would take care of itself while I fished my normal searching method for the far bank glide.

There is an old saying that begins with the words, "The best laid plans.....," and after my first hour's fishing I realised that I was up against it for fishing across river. In the gathering dusk, I hadn't noticed that the river was starting to rise, although I fancied that the current was appreciably sharper than when I had first arrived. Obviously, the heavy overnight rain was now making its presence felt. The sharper flow and a rising summer river were in themselves no problem, but what was a problem was the rapidly increasing levels of drifting blanket weed and other flotsam that had broken loose upstream. After an hour of darkness had elapsed,

10lb 4oz, part of a large catch while testing Action Baits Oriental Dream.

and the longest I had kept a bait in position by the far reeds before it was swept away by weed was about three minutes, I realised that I had to abandon my carefully thought out strategy. By 11.00pm, I had reverted to one rod, fishing the near bank run, where floating weed was almost non-existent.

That night was one of tremendous frustration, because at least six times along the far bank fringes, barbel rolled noisily over my baited areas. After each roll, I wound in and tried a cast, but each time with the same result. Sometimes, the bait was swept away before it even settled. It was most galling, and the first light of dawn found me ready for sleep, having managed the grand total of two chub of around three pounds apiece.

Before retiring to the van, I marked the swim with a stick to check whether the river was rising or falling when I returned at around midday to recommence baiting operations. In the dawn half-light, I could see that the river had risen about nine inches overnight, and floating weed rafts were now easily visible as they broke away from the margins.

It was early afternoon before I again ventured down to the river for a reconnaissance, and what I found was not encouraging. The river was still rising, much more slowly, but floating debris was still in evidence. It didn't need much thinking about. That night, I had to fish areas tight to the near bank.

Once again, I went walkabout and eventually came to an area where there were very dense marginal rushes for about a hundred yards, the bank behind the rushes

Typical middle Ouse swims in mid-summer.

being very boggy. I had taken the precaution of wearing chest waders, and when I peered through the reeds in a few areas, I was knee deep in water. I was amazed how deep it was hard against the near bank. I had been expecting to find a couple of feet over gravel, but actually discovered about six feet.

A couple of yards out from the bank were several beds of onions and reedmace, intertwined with streamer and cabbages, and I started to get excited by the possibilities this narrow, near bank trench offered. The average angler would walk straight past this area, as it was so inconvenient to fish, but I knew I had discovered a definite hotspot. Barbel love deep, overgrown margins.

At intervals along the reeds, I cut the smallest hole possible, no more than sufficient to poke my rod top through, and baited each area with my usual ten droppers of hemp and finely diced meat. Fishing would be awkward, as there was no solid ground to place my chair anywhere near the river. Sitting right back so that my rod top was only level with the rushes still saw me almost knee deep in water and mud. Fishing these swims all night would be a messy business, but I had a feeling it could be worth it. At least I knew that my baited swims would be unlikely to be fished by any other anglers that arrived. With five spots well primed, I eventually lowered my first bait in the margins in early evening, and settled down for a long vigil that was to go to daybreak, and beyond. With about ten hours of darkness ahead of me, including the half light times of dusk and dawn, I calculated that I would remain in each swim about two hours. Events would dictate how rigidly I stuck to that plan.

Above: baiting Flanders Bar at Queenford.

Right: Alastair Nicholson with his 15lb 6oz record.

Final fish of 14lb 4oz.

Peter Coates with a massive 15lb 10oz fish.

Jacqui with my 14lb 4oz bream.

An absolutely immaculate specimen of 6lb 3oz.

Following my instincts led to this 6lb 10oz monster.

2lb 11oz personal best.

A 2lb roach that took a tench bait.

Another typical middle Ouse swim.

From commencement of fishing until about 10.30pm, all was very quiet, not a single indication having rewarded my patience in the first two swims. But in swim number three, I struck gold. My bait of Frankfurter Sausage flavoured meat had been in position about ten minutes, the night was now still, the beta light glowed brightly against the black backdrop of the dense rushes and the line lay at rest over my right index finger. Suddenly, in an instant, the bait was picked up and immediately dropped. I knew that because of the fractional increase and decrease in tension on the line, accompanied by an almost imperceptible nod on the rod top.

Now fully alert, I sat forward in my chair, knowing that something would happen at any moment. Thirty seconds elapsed, and there was that sudden increase in tension again. But this time it didn't relax. Instead, there was an urgent tug on my finger, and then the rod plunged over as a muscular opponent rocketed downstream through the marginal cabbages, making my tightly set clutch whine.

I knew that I could not let the fish have an inch more line than necessary in this overgrown little swim, and so I crammed on pressure to the limit. The first few seconds of the battle were crucial, as the barbel surged towards dense reedmace. My finger applied maximum pressure to the reel spool, and the rod went past its normal fighting arc, as the fish fought for those extra two yards that could have given it salvation. But I was equally determined to deny the barbel that opportunity and eventually the rod eased back as the fish yielded to the pressure and grudgingly gave ground.

From that moment, I was in total control of the situation, and although the fish had to be twice heaved out of the cabbages under my feet, the plants were not dense enough to cause any real headaches. Finally, after about five minutes of dour struggle, my headlamp picked out the shape of a magnificent barbel sliding over the net cord. In that instant of euphoria, I knew that my quest for the first double from this new river was over, and with that initial barrier breached, I could go on and catch others. Moments later, I confirmed a weight of 10lb 13oz.

All the previous year's disappointments, the long biteless hours, were now forgotten. My instinct to fish a new area had again proved reliable and the dark hours spent fishing a soggy morass had been vindicated. Although I say it myself, I deserved that fish.

Bait Experiments

Towards the end of my association with the Cherwell barbel, I was beginning to conduct experiments with so called 'designer' baits for barbel, the first I ever concocted being based on SBS Original 50/50 base mix and SBS Fruity base mix. At the time, I was working along the lines of a fruity bait for summer with meat in the colder months. I took these ideas to the Great Ouse in 1991 onwards. I'd settled on the SBS flavours Spicy Meat or Frankfurter Sausage with the 50/50 mix, adding liver powder to each, and Strawberry Jam or Blackcurrant with the Fruity base, adding a sweet flavour enhancer.

It is very interesting to note that my initial trials with fruity baits on the Ouse were extremely encouraging, but only in hot weather. Several multiple catches came on both strawberry and blackcurrant boilies in heat wave conditions, but results were invariably disappointing once high summer had passed. This first use of boilies on the Ouse in 1992 made me realise what an effective bait for a barbel a boilie is. Both of my Cherwell pastes caught well when mixed with eggs and boiled and, apart from the fact that they are no longer on SBS bases, these baits developed into Action Baits Mega Meat and Juicy Fruit mixes.

Another interesting development came about in 1994, after I had met my good friend Matthew Bodily a year earlier. Matthew had put together a barbel bait loosely based on Rod's Seafoodblend, and proceeded to take good catches of barbel on these boilies. In the three years that followed, we worked closely on refining this, as well as conducting experiments with a spice variant, using Rod's Ultra Spice flavour on Promix base. Action Baits Marine Harvest and Oriental Dream bases are the result of that work. The advantage I had after meeting Matt was that, as he fishes four or five nights a week, the amount of field testing that could be carried out by a good angler increased enormously. This is vitally important. If you have

Fishing eight feet of flood water.

devised your own bait, the one thing that can work against you is lack of confidence. I am perhaps over confident in my own ideas, possibly even arrogant, and working alone has never worried me. But I must admit that it is a great advantage if two or more friends can work together in establishing a bait.

As well as putting together new barbel baits, a lot of work was carried out in the early nineties in testing attractors to be used in enhancing meat baits, specially in high, coloured water. The first idea I tried was a simple powder coating. In the winters of 1992 to 1994 I fished hundreds of night hours with coated meats, the first coatings being readily available powders such as spices from any supermarket, such as Tikka, and then the more specialised products of Rod Hutchinson, such as Ultimate Spice and Crab Extract from his Nature's Gems range, as well as his powdered appetite stimulators Shellfish, Nectar and Savoury Liver. Action Baits range of dusting powders are a direct derivative of that work. Chub anglers may be interested to know that in the case of nectar powder, frenzied chub activity hardly gave the barbel a look in, which further confirmed findings Trefor and I had made in the 1980's about the efficiency of Nectar (wasp grub extract) as a chub attractor. In fact, the first two designer pastes I ever made for river work were aimed at chub in the 1980's, using Blue Cheese and Nectar flavours respectively on a 50/50 base mix.

Working on the assumption that the extra enhancement of the bait resulted from sustained flavour leakage downstream, I came to the rapid conclusion that it was preferable to section the meat, dust it and freeze the day before fishing. That way, the powder coating certainly took longer to wash off than if the meat were treated on the day. When I felt I needed a bait to be left where it was cast for a long time, or where I wanted the flavour to linger much longer, say for fishing in highly coloured water but in a steady flow, I combined the powder coating with a liquid enhancer, and the most successful combination I used involved wetting cubed meat with one of Rod's Sense Appeals, and then rolling it in the selected powder before freezing. Treated that way, the flavour lingered for hours.

At the same time that I was experimenting with coated meat baits, straightforward liquid flavourings were being employed, many sessions being fished with two rods, with different baits on each, for comparison purposes. The top two flavours were undoubtedly SBS Frankfurter Sausage and Rod's Ultra Spice, closely followed by Monster Crab. Frankfurter Sausage in particular was awesome, and when Trefor and I, in conjunction with Rod Hutchinson, launched our Action Baits range, the first flavour we required was a Frankfurter Sausage lookalike. The result was a flavour I quaintly named Sausage Sizzle and you can ask Trefor how many barbel he has since caught on that flavour. It runs into hundreds.

Perhaps one of the most memorable nights from those days is the first occasion I ever used Rod's Ultimate Spice powder on luncheon meat. I was fishing a stretch of the middle river with a good head of barbel, but where doubles were quite rare. Matthew and I had been joined by my good mate Graham Marsden, who was keen to sample Ouse barbel for the first time.

A couple of hours before dark, Graham and I were settled in adjacent swims, in a reliable area for barbel, but although we fished hard for a few hours, all that rewarded our efforts were a few average chub. Unfortunately for Graham, as the night wore on he started to feel really rough, and I remember going round to his swim just before midnight to find him lying flat on the bank, obviously in severe discomfort from stomach cramps. Apparently, he had been having these attacks for some while, and they were getting very worrying, but this was the most severe yet. He decided there and then that he would have to go home straight away, and get to the doctor next morning. Not long after, we said our goodbyes and Graham started the long haul back to Cheshire, only a few hours after he had arrived. I was sad to see him go, because I had an unshakeable conviction that there were barbel to be caught that night. Everything felt right.

Shortly after Graham's departure, Matthew and I made our way downstream to two new swims, one of which we had already mentioned to Graham as the swim he should fish next. Two weeks previously, Matthew had taken a rare double from it. In the event, I moved into the swim, Matthew trying another new area he fancied. On impulse, I decided to flavour the luncheon meat I was using with Ultimate Spice powder, sprinkling a more than generous amount on the sectioned meat. I didn't have long to wait. Ten minutes after my first cast, I had the first bite, and that heralded the start of one of the most frenzied nights activity I've ever had. From about 1.00am until just before dawn, I must have had over fifty savage pulls, landing several good chub before the bites became faster and faster.

But it's that first bite I remember most. I have often written about savage bites from barbel, but this one really was something else. Having cast in, I was relaxing in my chair, the rod butt resting on my knee as usual, with my hand round the reel seat, the line over my index finger. A quiet ten minutes passed and my eyes must have closed for a while because the next thing I remember is being dragged forward in my chair. The rod rest was now flat, and the rod itself bent into the most incredible arc as it tried to take off downstream. It was a good few minutes before I felt in any measure of control, and then there commenced a spectacular battle. It is not too often that very big barbel fight at speed, they are generally dour, relying on power. But this thing was possessed, shooting upstream and down at breakneck pace. I lost count of the number of times I was forced to concede up to ten yards of line on these headlong dashes, and it was a full twenty minutes before the fish was beaten. When it was eventually safely ensconced in the net, I could see what a truly immaculate fish it was. It was quite long for its weight of 10lb 14oz, sleek and all muscle, with an enormous tail, and it remains my biggest barbel from that particular stretch, as well as being one of the most memorable. When I later told Graham what I had caught, and that that was the swim we were going to put him in, it didn't make him feel any better!

After taking that barbel, and a subsequent clutch of chub, I became puzzled as to why I began missing apparently unmissable bites. It was only when I took a bite from a sandwich after rebaiting that I had a clue as to the cause. Within seconds, my lips were on fire! Obviously, I had dramatically overdone the coating of spice, so that the meat was now red hot. It must have been really frustrating for the chub. They really wanted that bait, but were continually forced to spit it out!

During my bait trials, it was very evident that treated meat is much less effective in normal river conditions, and this is where the designer pastes score. Matthew and I, working in concert, quickly discovered that low dosage baits, best for long term use, took time to establish, and if an instant response was required flavour levels had to be increased. The drawback with this, I felt, was that too high a flavour would render the bait bitter, and that overcoming such bitterness with sweeteners was the way forward. Initially, my trials along those lines were very encouraging, but success was short lived, reinforcing my current belief that higher flavour levels may be a valid move for those of you who just fish occasional sessions, but are counter productive if you are planning a serious assault on one water.

An excellent example of that concept occurred in the 1997/98 season, when Matthew and I carried out trials on the spice bait that was to be launched as Oriental Dream, which, it has to be said, is very close in make up to Rod's Ultra Spice. From the off, Matthew used the base mix as it came, with no additives whatever, while I added 2ml of Ultra Spice flavour and 5ml sweetener to each 16oz mix. The first session was fascinating, in that my version took a swim apart. After introducing two dozen 16mm freebies in mid-afternoon, fishing commenced at dusk, and continued through the dark hours. In that time, I took no fewer than eight barbel and nine chub, the best barbel being a cracker of 10lb 4oz and the best chub 4lb 14oz. Eight barbel from any swim on the Great Ouse is virtually unheard of. The following night, adopting the same tactics, I recorded a further four barbel and five chub, the biggest barbel a belter of 11lb 5oz. Significantly, as I was to discover later, there were no recaptures. During the same period, although Matthew caught both barbel and chub, he caught far fewer, and it was apparent that the more heavily flavoured bait had produced the goods.

In the weeks and months that followed, however, a fascinating dossier of information was compiled. First, I was never to take as many fish again, in fact my catches steadily tailed off, while Matthew's remained at a consistent level initially, and then gradually increased as the autumn and winter set in. By the winter, Matthew could cast virtually anywhere on the stretch with his bait and catch, while I was blanking more often than not. But most fascinating of all is the fact that Matthew began experiencing more and more recaptures, while I never had one.

There is an obvious conclusion to all this. It appears to me that the fish were highly attracted to my bait initially, by the smell, tested it by picking it up and were caught as a result. But they apparently did not like the taste, because they never picked another hook bait up. In Matthew's case, however, they obviously did like the taste, because they kept coming back for more, despite the trauma of being caught.

To try and prove a point, we carried out an experiment in 1998, by introducing a dozen of Matthew's baits and a dozen of mine in a shallow clear area over gravel close to the bank, which were left alone all night. If undisturbed, we knew that

barbel browsed there in the dark hours. The next morning, there were still ten of my baits in evidence, but all of Matthew's had disappeared. I need no further evidence that, for a long term bait, the base mix is vitally important, but any flavours must be of low dosage and as subtle as possible.

Roach Days & Nights

River Roach

Roach have always been one of my favourite species and when I first began fishing the Claydon Brook, tributary of the upper Great Ouse, in the early sixties, the big roach were the prime target.

The stream undoubtedly held huge fish, certainly close to three pounds from the evidence of my own eyes, but they were very circumspect in their behaviour and I never got close to a big one. In fact, I never managed a two pounder, although the river held plenty, my biggest remaining stubbornly at 1lb 15oz.

Until the late sixties, I fished for those roach a lot, either free lining single maggots or flake samples in rush clearings, or laying on with stewed wheat in tiny gaps in the lilies. I could generally put together a catch of half a dozen fish most days, but, as I said earlier, never hooked one of the real giants. And then we had the columnaris outbreak. For those of you too young to remember, roach fishing the length and breadth of the country was devastated. It was as serious for the species as the perch disease that was to come later, and although there were still roach to be caught, their numbers had dwindled so alarmingly that I lost interest and turned my attention to big chub.

As the years passed, and Trefor and I chased big chub on the Ouse, Cherwell, Dorset Stour, Hampshire Avon and Leam, we regularly caught good roach by accident on our big chub baits, without ever taking a two-pounder. To be truthful, we viewed these roach as a nuisance. And then, in the winter of 1980, a session on the Warwickshire Leam convinced me that the roach were again a very worthwhile target in their own right. That winter was characterised by lots of high, coloured water, and Trefor and I were persisting in trying to catch chub despite knowing that the conditions were against us. On one memorable day, I had taken with me a bucket of lobs, to try for a big perch if the chub were uncooperative, to find the river very high and dirty. Chubbing was a total waste of time and I wandered down the bank looking for a potential perch swim. I came to an island, perhaps eighty yards long, where the main push of the river went round to the right, leaving a steady, canalised section to the left. I thought that quiet section looked ideal. Conveniently, there was a small river bridge giving access to the island and although fishing off the island was supposedly private, I didn't worry about such niceties. If tackled, I would plead insanity!

Removing my short hooklink I had been using for crusting for chub, and replacing it with an 18" hooklink of 4lb mono armed with a size 8, I impaled a large lobworm and tossed it across stream to settle under a branch of a fallen willow. Seconds later, the light quivertip whipped round, but instead of seeing the big perch I was hoping for, a chunky roach came to net, a fish I quickly confirmed as 1lb 14oz, at the time my biggest ever from the Leam. That was just the start. In the next hour, I was to take another ten fish, smallest one pound six ounces, and it was tremendous sport. So much so that I stopped fishing for a while, and went and found Trefor, who was fishing about three-quarters of a mile away. Trefor was similarly struggling for chub and, when I told him what I'd found, he came along to join in the fun. Before we packed up for the night, we had another six fish each, again of very high average size.

For the next two years, that little island became a regular venue whenever we found the river too coloured for chub, and we took some superb catches there. One session I will never forget is when I went to find the river flowing very mucky with melting snow water, possibly the worst conditions you can find. The temperature was only 37°F and conditions were dire, but for some reason the big roach turned on. Perhaps it was because the water had been frozen over for a week. In two hours around lunchtime, I had a dozen bites to full sized lobs, and the catch of roach that resulted is one of the most remarkable I've ever had. Those twelve fish weighed a total of 21lb, and there wasn't a two-pounder amongst them. The smallest was 1lb 10oz, the biggest a brace of 1lb 15oz, and that dozen mint conditioned roach made a glorious sight in the winter sunshine.

In September 1981, I was to take my first ever 2lb roach from that little backwater, and the fact it was my home river made it even more special. I had arrived to find the river a rich brown colour after the first autumn flood, and immediately abandoned my chubbing ambitions, took a bucket of lobs from the car, and headed for the island. My favourite swim opposite the fallen willow looked perfect and when a roach accepted a bait only seconds after the cast, I knew I was in for an epic catch. So it proved, and roach came steadily all day to either lobs or big chunks of flake. By mid-afternoon, I'd taken a dozen fish to 1lb 14oz and then, after a lull in the action, I moved upstream fifty yards to fish a swim I'd been steadily baiting with mashed bread for a few hours. There might be chance of a good chub at dusk.

The first cast with a chunk of flake was followed by a firm jab on the tip, and then a steady draw. Instead of the chub I had targeted, there was a flash of bright silver, shot with crimson, as a big roach shot across stream. Immediately, I sensed this was something special and when I drew the fish over the net cord a few minutes later, I knew I had my two pounder at last. It was a special moment. There has always been something magical about two pound roach, and when my scales confirmed 2lb 2oz I was ecstatic...

My first 2lb roach - 2lb 2oz from the Leam.

Since that memorable day, I have gone on to take many more two pound river roach, but cannot really tell you a special story about any of them. They have mostly been accidental captures when fishing for chub and barbel. On these big baits I have taken fish to 2lb 7oz from the Ouse, 2lb 9oz from the Hants Avon, 2lb 5oz from the Dorset Stour, 2lb 4oz from the Warks Avon and 2lb 5oz from the Wensum. On all those rivers, the only two pounders I've taken when deliberately targeting the species are fish of 2lb 3oz and 2lb 4oz from the Warks Avon near my home in Coventry. Those were taken in a mixed bag on feeder tactics one bitterly cold day in February.

A month or so prior to that catch, I had found out that the upper Warks Avon was producing quite a few useful roach, and I decided to try it out for an afternoon. My daughter Jacqui, who was then about twelve, begged to come with me. At that time, Jacqui had never fished for herself, although she had accompanied me on trips to Queenford. I set her up with a simple feeder rig, showed her how to cast and fill the feeder, and told her where to place every cast, and then left her to it while I set my own gear up. Less than five minutes had elapsed when she shouted that she'd got a fish and I turned, expecting to see a gudgeon taking flying lessons. Instead, the rod was bending alarmingly, and I hastened to her side with the net. To her credit, she played the fish very well for her first time, and I soon slipped the net under a roach that weighed 2lb 1oz. How many anglers do you know whose first ever fish was a two pound roach!

Reservoir roach follow natural stream beds.

Stillwater Roaching

Since the early eighties, I have spent a considerable amount of my available winter fishing time in pursuit of the big roach of a Midland reservoir. The water in question was formed by damming a shallow valley and nowhere in the fishable section is there more than eight feet of water. Most of it is four feet or less. Part of the water, including the deeper dam area, is preserved as a bird sanctuary. Many valuable lessons have been learned in those years, the first of which is that coloured water is as effective for good still water roaching as it is in rivers. Being stream fed, the water can rapidly colour up after heavy rain and this always seems to encourage the roach into more sustained feeding. The higher the water temperature, the more true this is although, unlike winter barbel, the roach still feed in very low temperatures.

In a stream fed water, the first area to be affected by an ingress of coloured water will obviously be the natural stream bed, and on my water, one specific area of a few hundred yards gives access to the natural stream with a moderate cast. The deeper trench created by the stream-bed has always been a banker for a few days following the onset of the colouring. Roach act as in a river, swimming against the flow.

After prolonged rainfall in calm conditions, the colouring effect can take several days to distribute itself over the entire reservoir, during which time there will definitely be roach hot spots. However, low pressure systems in winter are almost always accompanied by moderate to gale force winds, and this leads to much more rapid mixing of the colouring effect from the incoming floodwater. This makes many more swims attractive to the roach, and for this reason heavy rain coupled with a strong blow for a few days have combined to give consistent roach sport over the years. It can be uncomfortable fishing in such conditions, but the compensation can be a roach feeding frenzy.

The other fascinating facet of the roaching is a pronounced undertow, created by a combination of factors. The two natural factors of floodwater ingress and a heavy swell caused by gales is further complicated by water withdrawal for drinking, making the undertow totally unpredictable on any one day. There is absolutely no doubt that big roach love to seek out these sub surface currents and swim against them. Such an undertow can be so strong that it will take two ounces of lead to keep the terminal rig static. When I have a heavily coloured swim, affected both by strong wind and a powerful sub current, I just know I am in with an excellent chance of roach action. Those conditions are sheer perfection.

Over the years, I have found, possibly because of the factors mentioned, that my reservoir roach are very nomadic, and for that reason I do not go in for heavy feeding, preferring instead steady introductions of loose offerings via the swimfeeder, but very accurately. I want the feeder to hit the same spot every time. This is achieved by the simple expedient of winding insulating tape around the spool at the appropriate position.

Until the early nineties, I fished for those roach with traditional legering methods, using either bobbins or swingtips as indicators, and varying the terminal rigs to suit the roach behaviour on the day. I have to say it was really fascinating fishing, making me think constantly. If I had bites I kept missing, I would try lengthening the hook link to give the fish more time on the bait. Sometimes, I would wind in crushed maggots, having not seen a bite, which would be the signal to reduce the link length, and so on. It was rarely the same on two consecutive sessions. Those years saw many frustrating days, many two pounders, but a lot of fun and comparatively few blanks.

Perhaps the most enjoyable fishing was when there was a strong undertow, perhaps needing in excess of two ounces on the feeder to stop it rolling. I would often fish in these conditions with a quivertip, sitting side on to the water, and bend the tip into the terminal rig so as to give a substantial deflection with a taut line. It was just like upstream legering a river. When the roach moved the bait, the tension would be relaxed and the quivertip straightened. Those bites were impossible to miss. It is true, though, that most days would see roach bites missed until the correct rig combination on the day had been established.

During the nineties, the bolt rig has become the method par excellence for still water roach, although it is not as much fun. But it is bloody efficient. The method involves tightening to the terminal rig until the line is as taut as a bowstring, and

A 1lb 14oz beauty.

then attaching a heavily loaded butt indicator to the line at the top of its travel. As with my quivertip technique, as soon as the bait is lifted, the tension goes out of the line and the weighted butt indicator drops like a stone. For this technique to work at its most efficient, the feeder needs to be at least 2oz.

The most important thing to remember is not to strike too hard, as it is easy to crack off when fishing a very tight line technique with a light hook link. The tension in the tackle means that the set up is virtually a self-hooking arrangement and it is normally sufficient to simply pick up the rod and start playing the fish.

My good friends Leon Tandy and Jeff Mills are both acknowledged roach experts, and perfected the bolt rig technique at Startops, where they took colossal numbers of big roach, and I am indebted to them for sharing some of their secrets with me. The essence of their rig is a heavy feeder mounted at the end of the main line, with a lighter hook link tied above the feeder so that the hook bait, usually maggots, lies adjacent to the feeder once it settles. On a clean bottom, this can be further amended into a two hook rig, with a second hook length perhaps a foot above the first.

A few winters ago, I gave a lot of thought to how the rig must look to the roach and one thing occurred to me that appeared wrong, despite the obvious success that Leon and Jeff were enjoying. With the feeder at the point of the rig and the hooklink above, as the tension is drawn into the line there would be a tendency to draw the feeder slightly towards the bank. Escaping maggots would then be left in the original position and the hookbaits pulled away from the loose feed. This I felt undesirable and so I thought up an alternative. The weight needed to be on the point of the rig to make the bolt rig work properly and so the feeder was replaced

with a 2oz bomb. An in-line feeder
was then placed on the main line
above the hooklink. When the
tension was drawn into the line
after the cast, the hookbait would
be drawn towards the loose feed,
which would be far more
preferable.

The first time I used this
variation was the last week of the
season in March 1995, when I

2lb 9oz personal best for Trefor.

fished the final six days, and was rewarded with my two biggest roach on the second
and third nights of that session. That week was possibly one of the wildest I have
ever fished, with gale force winds for almost the entire time and an incredible chill
factor that made it feel positively arctic. The first night of that week saw me land
one roach of 2lb 1oz and lose another but it was in the early hours on the second
that I was to land the fish that is the highlight of my roach career to date.

Once again I had been sitting huddled in my bivvy with the shelter creaking and
groaning from the howling elements outside. As the night wore on the wind
gradually eased and by about midnight there was pleasant respite from the buffeting
with now just a gentle chop on the water. I even sat outside for a while with a final
cup of tea before retiring to my sleeping bag at about 12.30am and had just gone
back in my bivvy when there was a sudden shrill from the alarm, the butt indicator
fell away and the reel began to backwind. Seconds later I was very carefully playing
a heavy roach and when it eventually sagged in the net I knew it was easily a
personal best. All the cold and discomfort was forgotten as the scales confirmed 2lb
11oz. The very next cast produced another roach of 2lb 3oz only about twenty
minutes later. What a tremendous confidence booster to catch two super fish like
that on the first session with a new rig.

The following night was, quite simply, bitter. The wind was back, stronger than
ever, and by dawn the temperature had plummeted to about minus six. There were
snow flurries on and off, but I was quite unworried about the carnage outside as I
lay warm and snug through the dark hours in my heavy sleeping bag.

I woke up suddenly at about 4.00am and immediately the old instincts went into
overdrive. I just knew I was going to catch a big roach at any moment and, despite
the dreadful conditions outside and trying to talk myself out of it, pulled on my big
coat and went out into the blackness to stand beside my rods. I know it sounds far
fetched, but no more than one minute later, after hours without an indication, the

butt indicator on the left hand rod dropped, the Optonic rang out and I struck into my second biggest ever roach of 2lb 9oz. Barely had I sacked that for the morning photo call when the other rod went, resulting in another cracking roach of 2lb 6oz. You will see a recurring theme through this book. Never ignore your instincts.

It was similar instinct that led to my catching six roach averaging over two pounds in thirty minutes from the water one summer night. What made that catch even more remarkable was the fact that I had long since abandoned fishing after dark in summer because of the large head of ravenous eels. A tench session was planned the next morning, and I was leaving in the early hours to arrive at dawn. I finished work the previous evening at around 10.00pm but couldn't settle. I just knew the big roach would be having a go after dark, despite evidence to the contrary in previous sessions when eels had driven me mad, and so changed out of my suit there and then, had a quick cup of tea with the wife, and set off. I arrived in the car park just after midnight, to see just one syndicate member in situ, who we knew as Big John. He used to be a minder for pop stars in his younger days, a great giant of a guy, but a man who you wouldn't want to cross. John and I had fished side by side earlier in the season and I guessed he would be in the same area I planned to fish, on the opposite side of the reservoir from the car park.

The night was pitch black, with heavy cloud cover obscuring the moon, and John was obviously oblivious to my arrival in the early hours. I had moved in perhaps fifty yards from him by about 1.00am and, before starting fishing, went down for a quick chat. It didn't occur to me that he would be half-asleep.

As I arrived in his bivvy doorway and said, "Hi, John," there was a scream from inside, and then, moments later, a very shaken John emerged.

He had, apparently, been asleep and having a nightmare when I spoke to him. I had made him jump so much he'd nearly had a coronary! As he was not in the best of moods at that precise moment, I made a tactical withdrawal until morning!

Once my swim was sorted out, my first cast was at about 1.45am, and by 2.15am there were six roach in my Queenford sack. They weighed 1lb 11oz, 1lb 14oz, 1lb 15oz, 2lb 6oz, 2lb 7oz and 2lb 8oz. Summer roach action like that was unprecedented in my experience, and I've certainly never repeated the feat. Once again, an unexplainable sixth sense had not let me down. At 2.30am, the first eel arrived and I crashed out until morning.

In the summers that have come and gone since that incredible half-hour, I've had the grand total of three big roach at night in very many hours' fishing. I count myself very fortunate to have been in the right place at the right time and that catch of pristine roach is indeed a fond memory.

Animal Magic

Fun with Bulls

I suppose every angler has a tale to tell about an encounter with bulls or bullocks, but I seem to have had more than my share. My first run in with a seriously bad tempered bull occurred on the Cherwell in 1963, and was the first time I had taken my wife fishing. We were chubbing, and had climbed a gate to fish a favourite pool about one hundred yards away. As I sorted the gear and Fran arranged the enormous picnic hamper she had brought, there was not a cow in sight. We had perhaps half an hour's peace, and then the first few cows appeared in the distance, steadily browsing their way towards us. I could see that Fran was becoming increasingly nervous, and when the nearest cow was only about twenty yards from us, she implored me to drive them away. So, doing my best Rawhide impression, I drove the herd up the field.

When I got back, Fran was on her feet, holding the rod which now had a serious bend in it. On the end was a 3lb chub, and by the time I had sorted things out the cows were back. I realised that we were never going to get any peace and decided to move Fran back over the fence and fish another swim, after I had moved the cows away to give us some breathing space. As the nearest cows retreated, I noticed, for the first time, a big, mean looking Friesian bull, who looked decidedly unimpressed by my activities. As his harem retreated, he advanced towards me, bellowing and pawing the earth. Fran started to cry in fright. This was not a healthy situation to be in. Keeping as calm as I could, I quickly detached my landing net handle and waved it at the bull as menacingly as possible. Most stud bulls are controlled by staves, and have a healthy respect for a sharp rap on the nose. So this one stopped its advance, but didn't retreat either. We had an impasse.

Keeping myself between Fran and the animal, I told her to pack the gear as quickly as possible, and then to get to the fence and get herself and the gear over it, out of harm's way. This she did, and then I started to back to the gate myself, all the while frantically waving the handle. The bull followed at a respectful distance, and then I reached decision time as I eventually felt the gate against the back of my legs. To climb the gate, I had to turn away from the bull, and I was convinced that, as soon as I turned, he would charge. For several minutes, I weighed up the options, but there weren't many and I took a deep breath, whirled round, and jumped on to the second rung of the gate with the intention of vaulting over. The bull made that unnecessary. With a thunderous bellow, he was on me in an instant. I felt a sharp pain as one horn pierced the cheek of my backside and then I was tumbled unceremoniously over the gate. I landed in an undignified heap in a muddy puddle, courtesy of the thunderstorm we had sat through earlier. More in relief than anything else, Fran broke into hysterical laughter, while I painfully climbed to my feet, rubbing a very delicate part of my anatomy.

Another incident involving a very irate Friesian bull was much more recent, only three years ago. I had spent a day on the Ouse perching and just before dusk I was heading back to the van. When I had crossed the fields before dawn, I had noticed cattle in the distance but had taken no notice of them nor had I been molested. But as I now traversed the first meadow towards the double electric fence that separated the two fields, the cattle were congregated close to the fence, accompanied by a huge Charolais bull. I dropped my pace to a crawl, so as not to alarm the animals, but about thirty yards from the fence the bull spotted me and began snorting and pawing the ground menacingly. This was looking decidedly delicate and matters came to a head when I was just a few paces from safety. I had just dropped my rod quiver over the fence when one of the cows suddenly bolted, and at that the bull charged. I did not get the other side of that flimsy barrier a moment too soon, and thank God the power was turned on. After it had a couple of jolts from the wire it backed off a few feet and stood glowering at me, bellowing.

I was now stood on a patch of No Man's land about twenty feet wide between the two electric fences, and as I watched the Charolais working himself into a frenzy I became aware of another commotion immediately behind me. I turned quickly, to see a Friesian bull in the second field, only feet from me. He appeared similarly agitated and I was now well trapped between a rock and a hard place, as they say!

I was able to move away for about fifty yards between the two fences before my way was barred by high thorn bushes, when I would have to cross into the Friesian field. It was

Calm before the storm.

The swim Jacqui's big fish came from.

A big roach comes to the net.

Three 2lb plus fish in three casts.

Great Ouse 2lb plus fish.

Daughter Jacqui's first ever roach - 2lb!

2lb 7oz fish taken on a winter's night.

My 3lb 5oz personal best rudd.

A gorgeous fish of 14lb 7oz.

very nearly dark as I tentatively crossed the fence, all the time keeping a wary eye on the bull. From here, it was perhaps four hundred yards to the fence and stile that led to the lane where the van was parked and I was perhaps fifty yards away, and breathing a little easier, when I heard the thunder of hooves behind me in the darkness. As I turned, I could see the bull bearing down from the gloom and that was one of the scariest moments of my life. It was too far to run to the stile with my gear, and all I could think of was switching on my powerful head torch to shine in the bull's eyes. Luckily for me, it worked and the bull stopped dead in its tracks, no more than ten yards from me. But it would not go away and I carefully backed to the stile, all the while keeping the torch beam in the beast's eyes. Slowly it followed, so it was still only ten yards from me when my legs collided with the stile. Having lowered my gear over the fence, all the while facing the bull, I then took a deep breath, and cleared the fence almost in a single bound. I thought I'd lost that agility years ago! I tell you, when I stood in safety, the bull was literally feet away, and for a good fifteen minutes stayed by that stile, butting the fence and making one hell of a din. It was well over an hour before I had fully regained my composure.

In the early nineties, I was fishing for big roach on the Warks Avon near my home and, as the afternoon wore on, I was becoming increasingly concerned about a small herd of young bullocks that had entered the field and were now gathered around me. As I was born in the country, cattle and other farm animals have never bothered me. Conversely, I can also tell when they are unusually agitated and this was definitely the case with these individuals. One in particular, who I learned later was being reared as a stud bull, appeared very aggressive, pawing the ground repeatedly and making short rushes. It was not playful either. Several of his fellows had felt the weight of a full-blooded head butt. While I was fishing my swim, at the bottom of quite a steep bank, I was reasonably safe, but it was not comfortable fishing. When I packed up, I had about half a mile of meadow to cross before going through a locked gate into the yard where my van was parked.

Gradually, afternoon became evening and then, at long last, I was playing a decent roach, after a dithering bite that had taken a full two minutes to develop properly. As I lifted the sparkling bar of silver in my landing net, I could see that it would not be far short of two pounds. In that I was spot on, and a weight of 1lb 14oz was registered.

In the first half-hour of darkness, I landed another three good roach, and then it was time to go. It was now bitterly cold. After packing my gear, I slowly climbed to the top of the bank with my landing net handle in my hand, which I waved as menacingly as I could at the cattle still standing vigil. For the first fifty yards or so I walked backwards, keeping the animals in sight the whole time in the bright moonlight, and they made no move towards me. Turning round, I began to walk normally and only seconds later heard the thunder of hooves as the bullocks stampeded towards me. I only just turned back in time. The most threatening of the animals was only feet away from me in full charge and luckily wheeled away at the last moment as I swung the handle. Several of the bulls were now pawing the ground and snorting, and it was getting quite worrying. There was still a long walk to safety.

The rest of the journey across the field seemed to take forever, with my walking backwards the whole way and the bulls keeping only a few yards from me. Every now and then one would make a short charge, and the only thing that came between me and a mauling was that flimsy landing net handle. At long last, I was by the gate and then found to my chagrin that I couldn't undo the lock one handed and backwards, while facing the herd. It was a stand off! I had to turn round and get my torch on the job. Seconds after I did so, I felt a terrific jolt in my back and then I was flung against the gate. It knocked all the wind out of me. I have seen mass hysteria in young bulls before and knew that at that moment I was in a dangerous situation. I had to do something positive and so I whipped round again, shouted as loud as I could and fetched the offending animal the hardest clout across the snout with the handle that I could muster. Snorting, he backed off a few feet before starting to come at me again. I hit him again, and this time he took off down the field like a jackrabbit, taking the rest of the hooligans with him.

I tell you, I was through that gate and back to the van in double quick time after that. It took me a fair while to recover my composure and after arriving home and relating my ordeal to the wife, I sank three pints of bitter in record time!

Fox Encounters

Anyone who has heard a vixen scream in the middle of the night will know what a blood curdling sound it is. You could be forgiven for thinking a young woman was being murdered. Usually, of course, the sound is in the distance, but have you ever stopped to think what it might sound like inches from your ear?

In the late sixties, my early carp exploits were at Marlborough pool, in Oxfordshire. This particular hot July night, I was sleeping under the stars, it was about 3.00am and quiet as the grave. I was using luncheon meat for the first time for carp, and the bait box was stowed under the bed chair. Unknowingly, I must have left the lid off. I remember waking up suddenly, with the distinct impression that something was pushing me in the back from underneath. As I sat up, there was a deafening scream from under the chair, and then a brown, furry thing shot out from under me and disappeared into the undergrowth. It was an hour before I stopped shaking!

Another similar incident occurred in 1984, on my first ever session at Queenford. I was bivvied up, door open as usual, and again my provisions were stored at the back of the bivvy, adjacent to my head. I was well away in the early hours, and then I woke up very uneasily. I could distinctly hear low growling. The hairs stood up on the back of my neck. I went to get off the bed chair, and again there was a sudden unearthly scream and a heavy body crashed into my ankles, stood momentarily silhouetted in the moonlight, before vanishing into the night. It's no wonder I'm prematurely grey-haired!

Horses for Courses

I have never experienced any frightening episodes with horses while fishing, but one hilarious incident at Queenford is worth relating. In the latter years of the syndicate, several horses were given freedom to roam the banks, and never caused us any problems normally. On this one occasion, though, one particular horse was attached to a heavy rope. The rope was well over 100 yards long, giving the animal plenty of freedom, but its wanderings were obviously restricted.

Several of us were fishing the well-known bream pegs on the north bank of the pit, and the closest to the horse tether point was my old mate Leon Tandy. In mid-afternoon, with nothing doing and all of us standing around talking, the horse came once more meandering down the bank towards us. It stopped by Leon's bivvy, and then went round it to the rods. Leon could obviously visualise damage occurring any moment so he set off at a run for his gear. This startled the horse, which set off back up the bank at a gallop. Unfortunately, it had gone right round the bivvy before taking off, with the result that the rope tightened round the shelter, whereupon the whole lot was wrenched after the fleeing stallion. Leon's camp was wrecked and, of course, the rest of us were duly sympathetic. Well, actually, we were wetting ourselves!

Snakes Alive

I don't like snakes, even being nervous about grass snakes. I know that makes me a wimp, but when it comes to slithery hissing things, I'm quite content to attend to my own business if they'll do likewise. Perhaps that's why I detest eels. Luckily, I had never had a close encounter with an adder, but that changed three years ago on a perching trip to the Ouse. Believe it or not, it was the day after my frightening

Beware of adders!

experience with the two bulls. I had been fishing since dawn, and by around midday, I was packed and ready to go but before leaving, decided to push my way through some dense rushes to investigate a new swim for next time. After taking a few steps, I suddenly felt the earth move beneath my foot and then a loud hissing commenced. Lifting my foot far faster than I had lowered it, I saw a very irate adder about to strike and jumped back quickly. I don't think I was in any danger with my thick waders, but I wasn't about to risk it.

After that fright, I needed a cup of tea and sat on my seat box, nerves jangling, and then became aware of a sudden loud buzzing before something heavy collided with my right shoulder. Peering out of the corner of my right eye I located the culprit, a bloody great hornet sitting three inches from my right ear. Have you ever seen a hornet up close. You can actually see the sting throbbing, looking for a victim!! For what seemed an hour but was probably ten seconds the damn thing sat there taunting me, before taking off again, leaving me weak at the knees.

Of course, the wife was no help when I arrived home.

After I had relayed the stories of the bulls, the adder and the hornet, she replied sweetly, " Well, there is one consolation. Those kind of frights can age you and turn you grey. In your case, no one will know the difference anyway."

Isn't it nice to know you're loved!

The most frightening looking snake I've encountered while fishing was at Cassien. Towards the end of our first week, Andy Barker and I were fishing the south arm in the most appalling conditions, heavy and sustained rain having seen the lake rise an incredible three feet in six days. We had decided to pack up and return to the caravan, prior to a move to the west arm. I was busy packing my tackle, perhaps twenty feet from the waters edge, when this six foot, yellow and black venomous looking serpent slithered out of the water and moved towards us. Barely ten feet away, it reared up and hissed.

"Do you reckon it's poisonous?" Andy said.

"I tell you what," I replied, "you bloody ask it. I'm off!"

The Black Rat

There can be few anglers with anything good to say about rats, horrible filthy things that thrive on squalor. I don't mean water voles, sadly disappearing as murderous mink wreak havoc, but your common or garden rodent vermin. TC pit had its share of these unwelcome visitors, and one night I had taken along an air rifle to try and get rid of one or two. I know you shouldn't take guns on a fishery, and I only did it the once, but the damn things were bugging me. I set up a low rod rest to one side of the bivvy door, to give me a steady aim. If Roland appeared in the moonlight, I had a surprise waiting. In the event, nothing transpired, possibly because I had quite an active night's fishing, taking several tench at regular intervals. The action was over by about 2.00am and, knackered, I buried myself in the sleeping bag.

I was in a deep sleep when I awoke suddenly, with a very clammy feeling that something was amiss. I had settled down with my head under the covers, to avoid bright moonlight in my eyes, but now could distinctly feel something jump on my head. I shot up, in time to see a bloody great rat scamper through the bivvy door. The rest of the dark hours I perched there, gun cocked, but the rat never returned. I got the distinct impression that devious rodent deliberately took the piss that night!

The Elstow Surprise

Sadly, I have devoted far too little of my angling life in pursuit of big rudd, for they are undoubtedly one of our most beautiful fish.

The only concerted effort I have put in was in Ireland in the late sixties with Merv Wilkinson, when I caught quite a few good fish to just over two pounds. The Irish fish were certainly true rudd, but many waters in England holding fish that look like pure rudd are now becoming increasingly suspect. A fish I long called my personal best, a 2lb 4oz specimen from a Bedfordshire brick pit in the mid seventies, was brought into serious doubt a few years later when all the big 'rudd' it had produced were pronounced hybrids.

Two of the most famous hybrid waters are Pitsford and Hollowell reservoirs in Northants, where the big golden fish they produce vary from specimens you would swear were true roach to those you would equally swear were true rudd, with plenty of obvious hybrids in between. Pitsford in particular is quite a dangerous water for the roach or rudd purist, because those fish have for years been netted and sold off for stocking coarse waters. That has led to many claims for giant roach and giant rudd for fish that were subsequently proved to be cross-bred.

The point of this preamble is that there are few waters in England where you can be sure that the rudd are pure strain fish, but some pits of Bedfordshire and Cambridgeshire still can claim that distinction. One such water is Elstow 1, a famed big carp water but also famous for producing a string of giant rudd to nearly four pounds in the mid to late nineties to anglers including Matt Hayes and Martin Bowler. I have never fished this water, my personal best rudd being taken from the neighbouring Elstow 2, which is not as popular with the carp lads as it contains far fewer fish.

I have to admit that the big rudd I was to catch on my first ever visit was down to luck, as I was actually fishing for tench at the time. Len Gurd and Matt Hayes had told me that they suspected the presence of a small head of giant tench in Elstow 2, and when I expressed an interest in going for them, Len generously gave me a ticket for the season to come.

I arrived on the water on the evening of 31st May 1997, in readiness for a two-day tench session, and after a good look round settled in a lovely bay connecting a very shallow area with the main body of the pit. An hour's judicious plumbing had

Typical pristine Elstow rudd.

revealed the presence of an interesting gravel bar at forty yards and I baited heavily along this feature with a gallon of dead maggots, six pints of casters and hemp, plus a little brown crumb. The bar was some three feet deep, surrounded by water perhaps six feet on average.

My first cast was about an hour before dark, and it is no exaggeration to say that from then until about 2.00am, the bait was not in the water more than two minutes before it was taken. All the fish were truly pristine, gorgeous rudd of between about two ounces and a pound and I have to say it was a most enjoyable few hours, albeit exhausting. When the bites stopped at 2.00am, it was like throwing a switch. Obviously, the big shoal had simply moved away, and from then until dawn at about 4.00am I was able to get a little rest. Then, just as it was getting light, I had a different class of fish altogether, in a magnificent personal best of 2lb 10oz.

During the first few hours of daylight, I was really fired up, thinking that my chances of tench were now at their highest, but there were no bites and the sun began to climb in the sky. By 7.00am I was decidedly sleepy and was just contemplating packing up for an hour and preparing a civilised breakfast in the van when the bobbin suddenly shot to the butt and the reel began backwinding furiously. The fish I hooked fought like a tiger and for a fair while I was convinced I'd hooked my tench at last, but when I saw a huge golden shape slide into the landing net, my heart nearly skipped a beat. It was a huge rudd, a magnificent unmarked specimen of 3lb 2oz. What a breathtaking-looking fish!

All thoughts of breakfast now postponed, I fished on with renewed enthusiasm, and about an hour later I was in again, this rudd being even bigger at 3lb 5oz, but not as pretty as the first 'three' as it had an ugly scar on its tail root. You will perhaps forgive me for now thinking in terms of a good catch of big rudd, but in actual fact they were the only big ones I caught at Elstow. After the 3lb 5oz fish, the little ones returned in earnest and for the remainder of the two days I must have landed over a hundred fish, with none bigger than 8 ounces. It did not matter what size of bait I used, either. In desperation, I had increased the bait size to three grains of corn on a size 6, wrapped in a big chunk of breadflake, and still caught four ounce rudd.

I returned for two more two-day sessions before turning to pastures new, and never did manage another big fish, although I caught small rudd by the dozen. I also managed to spot a large shoal of tench in the shallows one day, probably forty fish, and I have to say they were all a long way short of the double figure fish I was after. In fact, they all looked at least 8 pounds short!

I cannot leave Elstow 2 without recounting an amusing story from the winter that followed. I had convinced myself that, taking the enormous stock of rudd into account, the pit had to be a good bet for a big pike, and decided to give it a go. I arrived at the water in dawn in January on a very foggy morning, and made my way round to the swims I had fished for the rudd. Because the foliage had all died back through the winter, and the fog distorted distance anyway, I never noticed anything amiss. In actual fact, unknown to me, the water level had dropped almost three feet since the summer.

In the early morning gloom, I set up three pike deadbait outfits, and launched a mackerel tail, a herring and a sardine to fish along the bar where I had taken the rudd. Such features are often reliable for pike. Although I couldn't see the features, I measured out forty yards on dry land and clipped up the line, ensuring that the baits fished at about the right range.

As the morning wore on, the fog hardly lifting in the first two hours, I started to get strange lifts and drops back of the indicators on all three rods. I was hovering in expectation, expecting a full-blooded run at any moment. But it never happened, and for another hour these little movements continued unabated.

As the time passed, and the mist began clearing, the noise from birds suddenly became bedlam and I wondered what was going on. When the sun eventually broke through and a light breeze finally cleared the murk, everything was revealed. Hovering over my three baits, resting easily visible in about three inches of water, were about two dozen seagulls. Those strange bites I had been getting were actually gulls continually picking up the baits and dropping them!

Later that day, I was talking to one of the few regular carpers on Elstow 2, and questioned him about the pike potential, in view of the big head of fodder fish.

Rudd bay at Elstow 2.

He'd had the same thoughts, he confirmed, and the previous season had fished four days and nights every week for thirty weeks, with one rod on deadbait at all times. In that period, he landed the grand total of three pike. Worse than that, it was the same pike three times! You didn't need to be Einstein to realise that the pike stock density was probably not great, and that first pike session at Elstow 2 was also my last!

Big Barbel Bonanza

The Leviathan

My ultimate barbel destination on the Great Ouse was determined in 1990 in innocuous fashion when I was invited to give a slide show at Milton Keynes AC centennial celebrations. While I was there, I was invited to present the prizes for the biggest fish of the year. I remember giving an award for the biggest barbel to the captor of a 10lb 8oz fish from a little known stretch called Adams Mill, which had always been better known for its chub. I made a mental note at the time and promised myself a visit to this stretch in the future.

In the five years that followed, I fished other stretches, eventually attaining my goal of an Ouse double figure fish of 10lb 13oz, and at the start of the 1995 season remembered Adams Mill and decided to go and have a look. Then occurred one of those strange coincidences that often shape our lives. Only two days after deciding on my first visit to Adams, I had a phone call from my old friend Matt Hayes. He was inviting me down to fish a barbel stretch that he was just getting to know, which was indeed Adams Mill. When he confirmed that he had just caught a cracking barbel of 11lb 15oz from the stretch my appetite was truly whetted. The only

Big barbel on the shallows.

drawback was that night fishing was strictly forbidden and I would not be able to follow my normal procedure of baiting in the day and fishing through the dark hours.

The following week, Matt and I walked the banks of Adams in the early morning sun, and with the river low and clear, several barbel and chub could clearly be seen moving in and out of the holes and streamer beds. I had spotted nothing exceptionally big until we came to a swim now known as Two Trees, where a far bank raft was draped around the fallen branches of a dwarf willow. Under that raft were three barbel, and one, a very light coloured fish, was huge. Unfortunately, it was not possible to fish the swim as the only other angler on the stretch that day arrived as we did and decided to fish the swim from the opposite, and private, bank. But I had marked its card for future visits.

In the two days, Matt and I fished hard and I never had a chance at a barbel, although I managed a couple of chub. But on the second evening, Matt did have one chance, which he took with his usual aplomb. I was delighted to be on hand to photograph a gorgeous, long and streamlined barbel of 11lb 13oz. At that moment, I knew I wouldn't rest until I had become acquainted with an Adams Mill barbel of similar proportions.

That first session ended on a note of hilarity. In those days, the car parking was very close to the farm, not by the river bridge as it is now, and, as the farmer's wife had a reputation as a bit of a tyrant, Matt had told me not once but a dozen times to be as quiet as a church mouse when putting my tackle in the van and closing the doors. Once back in the farmyard, Matt shushed me yet again and we both crept around like cat burglars. I opened my van door silently, as Matt opened his car door. And then all hell let loose. His car alarm had not been turned off, and stubbornly refused to be, as the strains of what sounded like the 1812 Overture reverberated at full volume across the Bedfordshire countryside. The following season, the car parking had been moved to the river bridge, well away from the house. Nice one, Matt!

The following Thursday, I arrived early for a determined assault on the big, light coloured fish, if I could find it. I was the only angler on the bank as I made my way to Two Trees and, creeping behind the bole of the big tree on my bank, peered across river to the raft. This raft, from upstream to downstream extremities, was about twelve feet, and behind it, in a pocket of quiet water under the far bank, were four barbel and several chub. One of the barbel was the leviathan, as I had christened the light coloured fish. I couldn't believe my luck at having found it so soon.

With at least three other lesser fish in residence, it was important not to rush things. I needed to loose feed as inconspicuously as possible for a while to get the fish feeding confidently. Only then would I have a reasonable chance of the big one. With that in mind, and as the current speed was modest, I catapulted three pouches of corn and six of hemp well above the raft, so that the enticing flavours wafted right under it as the grains settled. I was using for the first time that day Pescaviva red strawberry flavoured corn, in deference to observation the previous week of fish spooking badly at plain yellow corn. The Pescaviva is a lovely dark red, smells gorgeous and has nice plump, firm grains. How could the barbel resist it! After that initial baiting, I then fed a dozen or so grains of corn every few minutes for the first hour before setting up my tackle.

Because I would be presenting my bait under the raft, I had elected to fish with 10lb Trilene XT line. I used Drennan 12lb braid as hooklink, coupled with one of my barbel rods of the time, the Barbel Supreme, the action of which was the basis for the modern Pulse barbel rods. I had already established that the barbel seemed reluctant to come to the head of the raft to feed, and I would, ideally, have liked a hooklink of at least three feet to present a bait right under the rubbish. However, the cast to the upstream edge of the raft was hampered by a trailing branch. A long link would have invariably led to snagging on the cast, and I came to the reluctant conclusion that the longest link I could use in safety would be about 18 inches. I seemed to have no alternative but to settle for that, sit quietly and low, and hope that patient feeding would draw the fish upstream under the debris.

About two hours after my arrival, I was at last comfortable on my low chair, well screened by marginal reeds, rod butt resting comfortably on my knee, as two grains of red corn rested enticingly on the clean gravel under the upstream edge of the foliage. To minimise the possibility of line bites, small pieces of heavy metal were placed on the main line for four feet above the lead to nail the line to the riverbed, out of harm's way.

After about an hour, which had been quiet apart from knocks and trembles from small fish, a sharp shower relieved the hot, sticky atmosphere, and, almost as if in response to a pre-arranged signal, the rod suddenly plunged round. One minute it lay there docile in my hand, the next the corks were straining as something angry and powerful tried to rip my arm off.

As I scrambled to my feet, the clutch was whining as a big barbel forced its way deeper under the foliage, and I quickly applied maximum left hand sidestrain in an effort to force the fish to kite into mid-river. Initially, there was a horrible grating as the fish momentarily found a sunken root, but luckily it came free quite easily and slowly began to yield to the tremendous pressure I was exerting. At last, it emerged from under the raft into open water, whereupon it saw me, panicked, and rocketed ten yards downstream, with the clutch shrieking.

With the fish now in open water, there was no way I was allowing it back under those willow branches and I could feel the throbbing pulses of pressure on the rod butt as the barbel continually attempted to regain sanctuary. But the battle was as good as over and although it lasted perhaps another four or five minutes, with plenty of hard pulling on both sides, there were no more anxious moments and pretty soon a lovely barbel folded into the net. It was not, as I had expected and hoped, the leviathan, but one of a pair I had estimated at about nine pounds. But now that the fish was in my net, I could see that it was far in excess of that. Moments later, I was confirming 10lb 8oz. What a way to start my barbel catches on a new stretch of river.

After such a fierce battle, I felt that my chances of another fish were slim, at least for an hour or two, so I went for a look around a few other swims, after introducing more hemp and corn under the raft. It was perhaps two hours later when I was again sitting quietly behind the rushes, eyes glued expectantly on the rod top. Another hour passed, and then I noticed that the river was slowly rising, the current speed now markedly sharper following heavy overnight rain. By early afternoon, there had been about a six inch rise and I was now forced to use a 2oz lead to hold across the flow under the raft, where 1oz had been sufficient in the morning. Drifting weed also began to be troublesome, and several times I was forced to clear the tackle when a weed raft caught the line, which was not to my liking as it was creating far too much disturbance.

Despite the modest rise in level, the water clarity was still good, and, by getting off my seat and creeping to the bottom of the swim, I could still see the remaining three barbel feeding, apparently unconcerned. They also seemed to be making sorties deeper under the debris, so I was still in with an excellent chance. At about 4.00pm, after having somehow pulled out of a big chub that had created further unwanted disturbance, I had just repositioned a fresh hookbait when I noticed a tremendous weed raft floating downriver. I quickly sunk my rod top to the river bed in the hope that the line would not be fouled, when there was a sudden tremendous lunge on the rod. Initially, I thought it must be a sunken lump of weed, but then an almighty boil erupted under the branches, and again I was off my chair and heaving for all I was worth. The battle that ensued was almost a carbon copy of the first, as was the fish itself when it was eventually landed. As the needle on the Avons steadied at 10lb 6oz I realised that I had achieved a first in my barbel fishing career, two doubles in a day. Naturally, I was elated.

It was then that I realised that I had perhaps badly underestimated the weight of the leviathan. My initial estimates of the four barbel were that the leviathan was possibly twelve and a half pounds, with two others about nine and the little one about seven. I had obviously landed the two estimated at nine pounds, which made me over a pound light in each case. That being the case, the leviathan was almost certainly thirteen plus. This was getting more and more exciting.

Naturally, I fished on until the appointed hour when I had to be off the water for the night, but I was not surprised that there was no more action. The remaining two barbel, though still in situ, were in a highly agitated state. I needed to get them settled before I felt I had a reasonable chance of the big one. Before I left the swim that night, I used the bait dropper to place accurately another ten droppers of hemp and corn at the head of the raft. The fish would now have a good few hours to feed in peace. Tomorrow, they would be mine!

The next morning dawned bright and sunny, and I was very pleased to note that the drifting weed problem had abated, although the current was still sharp. My first job back at the swim was to look behind the raft. For a while, all I saw were chub and then I suddenly caught a glimpse of two barbel tails slowly backing into the open water. Soon, they were in full view, the little one and the leviathan. There was no sign of the brace of doubles from the previous day, they would probably give the swim a wide berth for a while. Watching the fish closely for about ten minutes as they came and went under the raft convinced me that they were feeding avidly and I decided to have an hour's fishing with no further free offerings. The thinking was entirely sound. However when the initial cast was followed by an immediate whack on the rod top, as a roach just under two pounds engulfed the bait and dashed around with great vigour, there were two huge swirls under the rubbish as the barbel obviously spooked. I realised that I would have to patiently wean them back into confident feeding.

For an hour, I steadily fed the swim, very gently introducing hemp and red corn by dropper, and by about 8.30am I decided to risk another cast. Again, the response was immediate, this time a 4lb 14oz chub doing its best to spoil the party. Under normal circumstances, roach just under two pounds and chub just under five are more than welcome into my landing net, but this particular morning, they were a pain.

After another brief wait, another bait was in position and this time the bite, when it came after ten minutes, was from a barbel, but again not from the leviathan. I was doing things the hard way. The fish I had christened the little 'un turned out to be a lovely chunky specimen of 8lb 10oz.

The only barbel left under the raft now was the leviathan, and eventually, at 11.00am, the rod shot off the rest. As I struck, there was an explosion of spray under the raft, an almighty pull, and then the line went limp. I experienced that terrible empty feeling, and when I checked the hook, my worst fears were realised. The hook point was turned right over. The fish had been foul hooked, and my chances of catching it now looked bleak indeed.

Once again, my only option was to stop fishing and hope the big fish regained enough confidence to be a viable target. For a good two hours I steadily fed corn grains under the rubbish and after a while the leviathan was feeding steadily, but now it refused to leave the downstream extremity of the raft. Eventually, it became very obvious that the fish was not going to swim upstream to take a hookbait at the top of the raft whatever I did. I had to think of another plan.

As I pondered the problem, the germ of an idea occurred to me. From the head of the raft to the barbel's snout was about nine feet, I estimated, so what I needed was a nine foot hooklink. It was clearly impossible to cast this to the head of the raft amidst the branches, so I decided to reduce a nine foot link of braid to a few inches by coiling it around three fingers and then tying with two wraps of PVA string. The idea was that, when the PVA melted, the hooklink would extend under the raft. There were obviously problems with this. First, there was every chance the link would simply stay there in a tangled heap, and so I was as careful as possible not to overlap any coils when wrapping it round my fingers. Secondly, I would need a certain amount of extra buoyancy in the bait for the current to work on to push it down the flow and straighten the link, but not so much as to present a floating bait. My aim was a critically balanced offering that would arrive in the barbel's field of view as naturally as possible.

For an hour or so, I conducted experiments in the shallows, selecting a flow as close to that under the raft as I could, and I found that a hook made to float with foam was perfectly critically balanced when it carried two corn grains. I was gratified when two dummy runs confirmed the rig working perfectly, taking about four minutes for the PVA to dissolve and the hooklink to straighten. It was time for the real thing.

It is tremendously satisfying when a theory works as intended, and it always adds an extra sparkle to the subsequent capture. Ten minutes after the cast, the rod wrenched over, and as I struck and felt the power of the leviathan my feelings were of total euphoria. I just hoped it would stay attached this time.

The fight was fittingly memorable. The barbel knew where those roots were and continually strived for them, but I was equally determined to stop it reaching them. Not for nothing had I screwed my clutch tight. I had every confidence in my tackle and had already decided that I would rather be smashed trying to keep the fish from snags rather than having to pull for a break if it succeeded in reaching them. For several arm aching minutes, the battle under the rubbish ebbed and flowed and then, in a never to be forgotten moment, the fish sullenly emerged into the open water of midstream and swam strongly upstream, past me. For the first time, I had a really good look at it at close quarters in just three feet of clear water, and I nearly went to pieces. It was truly monstrous and I had to tell myself very sternly to do nothing stupid. The easiest mistake to have made would have been to ease off the pressure, but that could have been fatal. I had done the hard part by being unyielding, the pressure had to be kept up.

The only real problem I had was the nine foot hooklink, as the lead made it more difficult than usual to keep a totally tight line. But I needn't have worried. Au Lion D'or hooks never drop out once they are in place, and I was soon heaving the barbel of my dreams on to the bank. As it lay there on the net, I almost went to pieces, I was shaking so much. But eventually I got my act together, carefully zeroed my wet weigh sling and placed the gigantic barbel into it for the moment of truth. As I lifted and watched the needle across the dial my excitement mounted, and when it eventually settled on 13lb 8oz I knew that one of my longest held angling dreams had come true. At that moment, alone on the banks of a beautiful river, the summer sun burning my back, I had found my own private heaven.

Two Mind Blowing Days

Exactly one year later, I arrived at the fishery for one of my first barbel sessions of the new season, the intention being to start off in Two Trees, if there were any barbel in residence. In that I was disappointed, as my good friend Adrian Busby had beaten me to the swim by minutes only. He was just introducing hemp and corn under the foliage, having the advantage of membership of Potters Bar club, who control the opposite bank. We had a brief chat, during which Adrian sportingly asked if I wanted to fish the swim instead, but obviously I would have none of that. I was disappointed to have arrived too late certainly, but Adrian had arrived first and that was the end of the matter. I wished him well, and moved down to another swim which I had yet to fish for barbel, and which I had been planning to tackle for some time. I felt that being beaten to Two Trees could prove to be a blessing in disguise.

I was wrong!! I had been fishing perhaps fifteen minutes when Adrian suddenly materialised on the bank behind me, soaking wet from head to foot, but with a broad smile on his face. I knew what was coming.

"I need a photographer," he said. "I've got a 'thirteen' in the sack."

During the walk back to his swim, Adrian told me that, not long after introducing his loose feed, there were six big fish over the bait. Almost casually, he announced that they were all doubles and the biggest could go fourteen pounds. I queried the soaking, and it transpired that Adrian was only using six pound line and a size 10 hook with a single grain of corn. Obviously, having hooked a thirteen pounder, 13lb 3oz to be exact, six pound line was hardly bullying tackle in a snaggy swim, and he'd eventually been forced to go in after

it. It is no small tribute to his skill that he succeeded in landing it, but I still told him off for using what I considered inadequate tackle in the circumstances.

Moments later, we were admiring together the classic lines of a lovely, fat Ouse barbel, and I was pleased to take some photographs for Adrian. After a short rest in the landing net, the fish swan off strongly, and after congratulating Adrian once again on a magnificent capture I returned to my own fishing.

During the next hour, I had a lot of fun taking four chub over four pounds, with a top fish of 4lb 13oz, which really seemed to like the new boilies I was trying. And then Adrian was behind me again, but this time the story had a different ending, with his hook having pulled out of an estimated twelve pounder. What an amazing hour he had experienced. Little did we know what was to follow.

At midday, hot, hungry and thirsty under the now baking sun, I decided to knock off for an hour and retire to the van for a meal and a fresh mug of tea. Just as I was winding in, I heard a shout and knew immediately that Adrian had scored again. Once more, I found him dripping wet with another beaming grin on his face. It transpired that this second capture had given him all kinds of problems, and he had spent over half an hour in the river with the fish before he was able to extricate it from the snag it had ploughed through. Finally, his patience had been rewarded with another magnificent fish of 12lb 8oz, to complete a quite stunning brace. In fact, it was the biggest brace of barbel I'd ever seen at the time. As I was taking the photographs, I remember wishing, although I was pleased for Adrian, that I'd arrived at the water ten minutes earlier!

It was then that Adrian told me that he had to leave at about 2.00pm for a prior appointment, and he suggested that I should move into the swim on his departure. I had grave reservations about whether the remaining three barbel would be catchable after the disturbance created by the two captures and the lost fish, but Adrian assured me that they still seemed to be feeding on the corn with abandon, and it was an opportunity not to be missed. This was certainly true, as one of the as yet unhooked barbel was definitely fourteen plus, and in truth was difficult to ignore. Consequently, at a little after 2.00pm, I moved my gear and Adrian bade his farewells. His departing words were prophetic.

"Ring me after four if you do any good," he said. "I'll be back home then."

Although I was aware of Adrian's success with light tackle, I was not happy with that approach. From my previous captures, I knew that hair rigged corn on a size 6 to 10lb line would give just as subtle a presentation as corn mounted directly on a size 10, and I would have the power necessary should I be lucky enough to hook the monster.

I set up a hair rig using 2lb mono, supergluing two grains of corn face to face, leaving only a quarter inch hinge from the hook bend. Longer than that, and I had found that barbel bites were often missed as the fish turned with the bait in its lips, but not the hook. The characteristic lunging bite of barbel is caused by them turning downstream with a bait held in those thick lips, and then I think swallowed shortly afterwards. For this reason, I had never had success with long hairs for barbel fishing.

Having prepared the hook bait, I disguised the hook by winding a twelve corn grain stringer around it, so that when the PVA melted, the hook would be buried under a little mound of bait.

At about 3.30pm, without any prior warning, the rod almost flew off the rest. As I struck, an impressive vortex momentarily opened a hole in the midst of the *Gorgeous Adams Mill.*

rubbish raft, and then the barbel made a determined try for the roots right under the far bank. I was prepared for that, and already had maximum sidestrain on, with the rod parallel and low to the water surface. In situations like this, I fish with my clutch really tight, so that only when there is imminent danger of breakage will it yield line. Fishing like this demands knowing the limitations of your tackle, and having total faith in it. I knew the tackle would not let me down, and therefore hung on grimly as the barbel battled for those roots. The corks bent under my hand, the rod bent into an exciting, pulsing arc, but still neither of us would give way.

For possibly a minute, although it seemed longer at the time, there was stalemate, and then the rod top eased back a fraction as the fish began to wilt under the relentless pressure. Suddenly, it gave up, shot out from under the foliage and rolled in mid-river, showing a great expanse of deep flank. The barbel was massive, close to if not over my personal best, and my heart began to beat a little faster.

Once in the open water, it was a matter of keeping control of the situation, and a few minutes later my prize rolled into the waiting net. I knew it was well over thirteen pounds, and when my scales confirmed 13lb 5oz, I reflected on the incredible fact that the swim had now produced two different thirteen pound fish as well as a twelve pounder and another fish of at least twelve pounds lost.

By the time I had ensured that the fish was safely recovering in a capacious carp sack, and had regained my composure, it was 4.00pm, and I phoned Adrian. He was genuinely delighted for me, and promised to be back down in about thirty minutes to do the honours with the camera. Now in contented mood, I recast a fresh bait under the raft, and settled back in the warm afternoon sun. There were still two fish to go at, was any more action possible?

Adrian duly arrived on cue, and after the customary bout of mutual back-slapping, we got down to the serious business of organising photographs, at which Adrian is a natural. The first time he photographed a big fish for me, he told me that he was very inexperienced with cameras, but the shots that he has taken for me are among the best I have ever had. He has the instinctive knack of framing a good angling shot. Anyway, photographs duly taken, I had just returned the barbel to a sack for a few minutes recovery before putting it back, when my rod, which I had neglected to wind in, suddenly took off, literally. It was in mid-air when Adrian grabbed the butt, as he was nearer to it than I was. I remember him panicking and telling me that he thought the clutch was stuck, because it wasn't yielding line. As he handed me the rod, I told him that the clutch would slip if the fish pulled hard enough, and then gave him a demonstration of the advantages of playing a big barbel in snags with adequate tackle. Afterwards, he said that he had never seen a rod bent like that in his life, and vowed to step up his gear in future!! This he has now done, and as a result has taken many tremendous fish since.

After another pulsating scrap, yet another double figure barbel lay in my net, a fish that looked almost small in comparison to the others. But, at 10lb 11oz, I certainly wasn't complaining.

After both fish had been returned, Adrian and I sat talking for a while before he eventually had to leave, this time confirming that he would not be able to come back down if I caught another. One of the things we discussed was the possible weight of the final fish under the snag. As he had fished the swim all morning, when they had made the occasional foray away from the branches, he knew that one of the barbel was substantially longer than the others, although they were all huge. He repeated that he thought it could be fourteen plus and wished me luck with it as he made his way to his car.

That evening, there was to be one final drama, but the end result was not so happy. At a little after 8.00pm, the rod flew round for one last time, but when the fish rolled I realised immediately that I was in trouble, as it surfaced right alongside the far bank snag. I had made almost too good a cast, propelling the bait further under the foliage than previously, and as the fish took the bait it was probably already behind that immovable root. My initial fears were soon confirmed, because I could not win an inch of line from that fish, despite getting in the river and pulling from all angles. Eventually, the inevitable happened, and I recovered a hook that had straightened under the incredible pressure I had been exerting. In that I was grateful. Better that than leaving a hook in a fish.

My mind was in turmoil on the journey home that night. I had enjoyed a tremendous day's fishing, but it had been soured slightly by losing that monster at dusk. I knew at that moment that I would never rest until it lay in my net.

The next few days at work seemed more like a month, so impatient was I to get back down the river for round two, but eventually I stood in the early morning sunlight watching about a dozen average barbel cavorting in the swim. It is difficult to describe my initial disappointment adequately in words. During the week, I had hyped myself up with the thought of that fourteen pounder, but there were no fish in the swim anywhere near that calibre. For ten minutes, I stood watching, trying to decide upon my next course of action, when a movement under some streamer to my left caught my eye. As I peered through the clear water at the spot, an enormous barbel emerged, and leisurely drifted downstream, to disappear under the foliage of the branches. Immediately, I knew that was the fish I was after.

I had a new problem to overcome. I had not been expecting to fish for the barbel where it would have competition from so many other lesser fish, and knew from experience that fishing prematurely could ruin my chances. I had to get all the fish into a feeding frenzy, and then leave them unmolested long enough for the big one to establish feeding dominance. With that in mind, I determined at the outset that I would steadily feed the swim for an absolute minimum of two hours without putting a line in the water, being quite prepared to wait far longer if I felt the situation demanded it.

That morning, the river was low and clear, and rather than risk disturbance by using a bait dropper, I decided to press my chest waders into service. I could just about manage to wade to the head of the raft, by standing on tiptoe, from where I was able to bait by hand, simply lowering handfuls of hemp and corn to drift directly under the branches. About two and a half hours after commencing this procedure, I was again in position, topping up the loose feed. A huge barbel head emerged from under the raft, no more than a few feet from me, and watched with interest as the corn grains left my hand and slowly started to drift downstream. Without a doubt, it was the fish I was after, and appeared to be on the case!

Not long after, therefore, hair rigged corn was in position, again accompanied by a giant corn stringer, and I cannot remember ever being so wound up as I awaited the hoped for bite. I was on the edge of my seat, like a coiled spring, and had to tell myself out loud to sit back and relax.

As the minutes and then the hours slowly ticked by with no indication whatever, I started to question my technique and began to curse myself for not baiting for longer before putting a hook bait in position. By late morning, the sun was scorching, well into the eighties, with the river apparently dead, and I was getting uncomfortably sticky. I quietly erected my umbrella to give some relief from the sun, and had only just settled again when the rod suddenly took on a life of its own and plunged round. I struck and heaved all in one movement and, following an impressive swirl under the branches, the barbel lost the battle with a fatal error of judgement. Instead of going full tilt for the snag, it shot downstream into a thick bed of streamer, but away from those all-important roots. Once away from the danger, a combination of heavy pressure and left-hand sidestrain kept the fish kiting into mid-river, and then he emerged from the streamer, heading upstream quite fast.

That was when I saw the full length of the barbel for the first time and at that moment my heart nearly stopped. It was indeed a giant amongst barbel.

I have to say that that barbel never had a chance, I played it like a man possessed. The fish had won round one last week, with round two there was only going to be one winner, me! I'll never forget the moment that fish crossed the net cord and folded into the mesh, and I realised just how big the fish was. It was indeed a heady occasion. There, glistening in the summer sun, was one awe-inspiring barbel.

Minutes later, weigh sling dampened and scales zeroed, I faced the moment of truth and watched with elation as the needle raced round the dial, to settle at 14lb 7oz.

That moment provided one of the most intense rushes of adrenaline I've ever experienced in my big fish career, and the memory of it, and similar moments over the years, ensures that I will remain a big fish angler until the day I die.

A day to forget

As well as my 14lb 7oz fish in 1996, there had been other big barbel landed at Adams Mill that year, including the recapture of my fish at a mind numbing 15lb 10oz to my good friend Adrian Busby. With other different fish to 14lb 14oz being recorded, there were still obviously targets to chase, and the start of the following season, in June 1997, again found me at Adams. My first session of the season is well worth recounting, as it redresses the balance a little against the charge that angling writers always seem to have good days.

As this was to be my first trip of the new season, my first job after arrival was to walk the banks, looking for barbel. In 1997, the river was becoming progressively more popular and the fish a lot more nomadic than they had been previously. It was one of those muggy, overcast mornings, with the threat of rain in the air, but oppressively sticky. Locking the van, I donned a lightweight jacket, calf length boots, and set off on my voyage of discovery, involving more than two miles walking. I was just at the downstream extremity of my searches, perhaps a mile from the van, when the heavens opened almost without warning. Within a couple of minutes, the wind had picked up to gale force and the rain become so heavy I could barely see through it. I was completely soaked in seconds.

After sheltering for a miserable fifteen minutes under the scant protection of a tree, as the rain lashed down, the wind began to die and the rain abated to just a steady downpour. I could actually have got no wetter, so I decided to continue my searches for barbel before returning to the van to change.

In that I was successful, locating a massive barbel under a far bank willow, a swim I had never before fished. I had often seen chub under there, but never barbel. For several minutes, I watched that huge fish, possibly 14lb plus, as it came and went in the clear water, and then an even bigger fish joined it. This new arrival was gigantic and had to be over 15lb. I had certainly found what I was looking for.

Making my way back to the van entailed negotiating a horrendous, high fence, topped with barbed wire, which I am sure has been erected deliberately as a devilish angler trap. I had reason later to curse that fence. Back at the van just as the heavens opened again, I stripped naked (not a sight for the squeamish, let me tell you), towelled myself dry and then made myself a hot mug of tea. Those barbel could wait another ten minutes, they weren't going anywhere. Tea over, and the rain still steady, I realised that it could be set in for the day, so when I emerged into the elements for the second time I was swathed in my waterproof suit and waders.

Soon I was back at the high fence, now soaked from the inside with sweat, and lowered my tackle over the obstacle before negotiating it myself. I was so intent on not tripping over the barbed wire on top of the fence that I never saw the rusty nail on the first rung down. What happened next seemed to occur in slow motion. With my right foot trapped behind the nail, I lost my balance completely and fell off the fence, face down into a deep pool of water, which was conveniently full of stinging nettles, just to add extra spice to the proceedings. Plastered in mud, my hands on fire from a thousand stings, I was decidedly short on temper as I eventually reached the swim.

The swim itself was quite difficult to fish, with a high sloping bank waist high in nettles and rushes, and by the time I had made it habitable, I was once again soaked in perspiration. During this time, the rain had again reached monsoon proportions, and for half an hour all I could sensibly do was crouch under my umbrella and hope it eased.

Things could only improve, and improve they did quite suddenly, with the rain stopping, clouds parting and early morning sunshine at last lifting my spirits. It also appeared that the passing of the storm re-awoke the fish because, as the sun at last broke through, one of those huge barbel rolled noisily under the willow. It was time to put a baiting programme into operation, and to do this I needed a far clearer view than was possible from my bank. Luckily, close to my swim was an area of gravel shallows, which allowed easy access to the far bank. Although the fishing on that bank is private, access to the public is not restricted and it would allow me a much closer look at the behaviour pattern of the resident barbel. It would also ensure baiting accuracy for the loose feed, which would be traditional early season fare of hemp and corn.

At the deepest point, the shallows are just over knee depth, but quite deep enough to fill my right boot with water from a hole I suddenly discovered I had in my new waders. Obviously, the trip on the fence had damaged mote than just my ego. Soaked again! I faced another trek back to the van for yet another change of clothes. Sometimes I wonder why I put myself through this torture!

Before doing so, however, I continued with the plan of action. I introduced ten droppers of hemp and corn in a slight depression a few yards downstream of the willow for the two big barbel, and another ten droppers of corn only at the upstream extremity of the willow to occupy the dozen or so chub that also cruised around. I have found on the Ouse that barbel appear to tolerate small regular amounts of corn loose feed, but definitely shy away from big beds of the stuff. Chub, on the other hand, cannot get enough of it so a simple ploy to segregate chub and barbel is to lay a substantial corn feast out for the chub, leaving the barbel to feed in peace somewhere else. It is not foolproof of course, nothing in angling ever is, but works well enough to swing the odds in my favour.

All preparations taken care of, I once more squelched my way back to the van, and, half an hour later, now on my third pair of trousers and socks, second water proof suit and chest waders, I was ready to start fishing. Now, those barbel would pay for the previous few hours.

However, I suppose I should have known that the day was destined to be a disaster, for it was not long before I discovered the next problem, and one that proved insurmountable. Although I had noted the current speed picking up in the last hour, I hadn't given it much thought until my first cast to the far bank stayed in place precisely thirty seconds before being washed away by a submerged drifting weed raft. This was to happen a further four times in a matter of minutes. When a 2oz back-lead, directly under the rod top in the near margin, failed to solve the problem, I realised that fishing a far bank run now that the rain was lifting the level and bringing down tons of rubbish - would prove impossible for the rest of that day at least.

All the walking, the soakings, the baiting, the wasted hours, were in vain. I had no choice but to cut my losses. I can confirm that I did not go back to the van with a spring in my step, singing.

Over another steaming mug of tea, I weighed up my options. With the rain having returned, the river would obviously be still out of sorts the following day, so I had to move venues. I decided to head for another section I knew well, where I could fish after dark, and which featured two or three near bank swims which would be fishable even if the drifting weed problem worsened. As I pulled away from Adams that morning, I reflected on the far from auspicious start to my season's big barbel campaign.

The second venue looked much more promising, several minutes watching the current from the road bridge showing no evidence of a drifting weed problem. I was soon settled in a favourite swim, the only problem being that a cold north wind full in my face was making things distinctly unpleasant in the continuing heavy rain. It is never easy using an umbrella to counter a head wind on a river, but eventually I managed it after a fashion and at long last managed a few hours relatively relaxed fishing.

It was several hours before my first bite, and then I experienced a mad hour that at least saved the day from being a depressing blank. First on the scene was a brace of 4lb chub, followed, a short while later, by barbel of 9lb 3oz and 9lb 9oz in successive casts. Things were on the up, and I looked forward to some more good barbel during the dark hours. I should have known better!

At about 8.00pm, all thoughts of fishing had been abandoned as a tremendous thunderstorm raged, and all my efforts were directed towards keeping dry by hanging on to my umbrella for dear life in the strong headwind. Suddenly, it uprooted itself and took off over my head. At first I thought the wind was responsible, but then I found that a frisky herd of Friesian bullocks had taken a liking to it, and thought it would be fun to tear it to pieces. By the time I had retrieved it, every rib was broken away from the canvas.

I was a beaten man. Soaked yet again, and now with no means of protection and no further weatherproof clothes to change into, I was forced to admit defeat. Within half an hour, I was on my way home, a full 24 hours early. I started laughing on the return journey. I actually write fishing articles advising others how to fish. What a bloody joke that was!

The record in waiting
After that early season disaster, I was very pleased to find the river in normal summer trim when I arrived for a one day session the following Friday. The water was low and clear, although fish were a little difficult to spot early on as it was very grey and overcast, although dry and humid. For possibly two hours, with the river to myself, I was in a frenzy of indecision as to where to fish, as I hadn't located barbel in any swims. But then, I caught a fleeting glimpse of an orange pectoral in a mid-river depression, and stared intently at the spot. This is where I struggle a little compared with anglers such as Adrian. I have never had very good eyesight, being very short sighted, but since a haemorrhage behind my right eye in 1991, leading to permanent blurring in it, my vision has deteriorated further. Often, Adrian, or Trefor, have pointed out barbel that they can obviously see clearly, only for me to have to really stare and concentrate before the outline of the fish can be

made out. Anyway, on the morning in question, having pinpointed where I should be looking, the shapes of several barbel began to materialise, and when I had the assistance of the sun breaking through the murk, I could see that there were perhaps a dozen barbel in that hole. There didn't appear to be any really big fish in residence, although one of them could have been over twelve. But they were barbel, and after the totally aborted session I had undergone the previous week, any barbel would be welcome.

I had decided on a maggot blitz approach, the method so expertly perfected by Stef Horak, and which I had used with such great success on the Cherwell in the eighties. Consequently, the first four hours were spent in patient baiting, introducing a pint of maggots and a pint of hemp every half hour or so, until a gallon of each had been put in.

It was early afternoon before I carefully placed a hookbait in the middle of the depression. That day, I had kept faith with the method that had stood me in such good stead on the Cherwell, a bunch of fifteen maggots on a size six hook.

Slowly, the hours ticked by and, although barbel continually flashed and cavorted in the swim. I seemed as far away from a bite as ever. From my position behind a high reed bed, I could clearly see the bottom of the swim, and, although barbel briefly inspected the feed, they never seemed remotely interested in serious feeding. As they had been undisturbed for hours, it was quite unusual behaviour, especially over maggots which normally turn them on strongly. Although rare, I had experienced this before, as I know Stef has.

In mid afternoon, I began to suspect that perhaps my large hook bait might be a factor, so I switched to hair rigged double maggot, superglued to a short length of 2lb mono, but still retaining the 6 hook. For an hour, that made no difference whatever, and then I saw a big fish flash almost under the rod top. Cautiously peering over the rushes, I saw three smaller fish feeding with abandon only a couple of yards down from me, and the tail of a much bigger barbel protruding from the foliage almost at my feet. The bed of bait in the depression was being totally ignored. It was baffling. By now it should be seething with fish.

As I pondered the situation, I remembered that the dropper had twice opened prematurely as I had baited the main swim, depositing the contents in the margins. The evidence suggested that the fish were happy to feed over a sparsely baited area but were avoiding a heavy concentration.

It was time to rethink my strategy, and as I did so, a very big fish rolled right in front of me. It was now about 6.00pm, still with almost four hours of daylight, and I wanted to be able to introduce a bait quietly and then not touch it until it was taken. With the fish being so close, I could not afford regular disturbance.

Accordingly, I made up a PVA bag with maggots and dried hemp, still keeping faith with hair rigged double maggot, and then quietly lowered the lot off my rod top, to rest no more than two yards from the near bank. As the near bank area was alive with minnows and fry, I did not want to strike at anything I was not sure was a barbel bite, and so I was using only a six inch hooklink with a two ounce lead. I would not miss a barbel bite on that rig!

My 14lb 2oz fish that became the record for Ray Walton at over 17lb.

Just before 8.00pm it was party time. The rod was resting on my right knee, as normal, with my hand loosely cupped around the reel seat, and for a moment my attention had wandered to a pair of kingfishers cavorting in the trees opposite. Next second, the rod butt flew up, literally wrenched from my grasp, as the rod went round at least a yard. If I hadn't been using 10lb line, I could easily have been broken on the bite!

As soon as I struck, I knew that here was something really special. If you've ever caught really big barbel, you'll know that they do not dash around like their smaller cousins, but fight deep, slow and with great power. This one was no exception, a real brute of a thing that just did not want to yield. But it showed no inclination to actually go anywhere either, relying on its strength to resist the pressure I was exerting. Throughout the encounter, it gained not one inch of line off me. Nor, however, did it relish being bullied, pulling hard enough to prevent my gaining control. For several minutes, we had stalemate.

Up to that point, the battle had been fought out under a streamer frond, but then the fish suddenly came through to just under the surface and tried to go upstream across the shallows, where there was a tangle of fallen branches. I had no intention of allowing that and applied maximum sidestrain. For a few moments, the barbel strained for those roots, with me equally determined to stop him, with the rod at an alarming curvature, and then it suddenly gave up the effort, rolled and came back under the rod top. The battle was now as good as over. When the fish had rolled, displaying its incredible depth of flank, I knew that I was once again playing a truly awesome barbel.

Moments later, it was all over, and the magnificent creature sagged into the net. As soon as I felt the dead weight, I knew that I had again been lucky enough to connect with the fish of a lifetime. My first thoughts were 15lb plus and it was with increasing excitement that I zeroed the weigh sling, before placing the fish inside. It transpired that I overestimated the fish, but even so a weight of 14lb 2oz left me in a state of complete euphoria.

What was very special about that barbel was the fact that it was so short and so exceptionally deep. It was only just over 30 inches from nose to fork, and built like a little pig. It was also an unknown fish at that time, one that even Adrian Busby had never seen, and he has fished the stretch probably longer than anyone.

Since that day, that barbel has gone on to become one of the most famous in barbel fishing history. It has been caught several times in the three years since my capture, at ever increasing weights, culminating in the record to Ray Walton at well over seventeen pounds. Despite its regular appearances on the bank, it is still in absolutely magnificent condition, a tribute to the caring anglers who have caught it, and I would certainly have no objection to making its acquaintance. It might be eighteen pounds next time. Now that would be a story worth telling!

Biggest Brace

During the 1998/99 season, I was only to have one session of two days at Adams Mill, the rest of my barbel fishing time being devoted to the intensive bait trials that my good friend Matthew Bodily and I conducted on a different stretch of the Ouse. Those trials revolved around boilie, long term food baits, and when I decided on my Adams session in early October, I wanted a complete change in approach. Initially, I had opted for another maggot blitz but, after talking to a few people who had fished Adams since the summer, it seemed as though there was evidence of barbel spooking at the big beds of maggots being introduced, largely because the technique had become common knowledge. Also many of the newcomers to it did not know how to apply it properly. After much thought, therefore, I opted for a very similar technique, but using mass baiting with casters.

My approach was entirely parallel, baiting patiently for several hours with casters and hemp with no attempt being made to introduce a hook bait until I was sure that the barbel would be feeding confidently. On the Thursday morning, I had spotted three good fish in the same swim I had taken the 14lb 2oz fish. This time, instead of baiting the depression itself, which had produced disappointing results the year before, I placed the loose feed right at the edge of overhanging foliage at the upstream extremity of the drop off, almost under the far bank.

My first cast was made a little after midday. Because I was using two casters hair rigged on 2lb mono, to a size 12 Drennan Super Spade hook to 12lb brown Dacron, I once again elected a bolt rig, using only a six inch hooklink coupled with a 2oz lead. A small bait like casters is very prone to attack by small fish and I wanted to wait for a really positive pull from a barbel, without being tempted into an unwarranted strike at a lesser fish.

The only worry I had was that the small fish attacking the bait could actually shell the casters and leave me with no bait on the hair. In the first couple of hours this paranoia led me to wind in four times following particularly savage plucks from roach or dace. But each time, the bait was unmarked, and it seemed my worries were groundless.

At about 3.00pm, after a series of bumps and bangs on the tip that had lasted a good fifteen minutes, the activity ceased abruptly and for ten minutes nothing happened. This might mean one of two things. Either this time the bait really had been destroyed or the barbel were in the swim and on the prowl. Moments later, I had my answer when there was a sudden vicious pull, a shriek from my tightly set clutch, and then an impressive bow wave under the far bank as a big barbel set off downriver like a torpedo.

When I'm fishing near to snags, as I've said before, I play fish hard and they have to fight hard for every foot of line. It is very rare for me to lose ten yards of line to a barbel in those circumstances, but this fish did exactly that, despite the tight

Matt Hayes landing a good fish.

clutch setting. Had it elected to hurtle upstream instead of down, where it could have found sanctuary under tree roots, I would have been done for. But, as it was, all it headed for was a thick clump of streamer, into which it dived and then went into an immovable sulk.

The trick with a barbel embedded in streamer is to get below the fish, when they will come out easily under constant pressure, and that is the approach I adopted. Slowly, I drew the fish out of the weed, and then eased it slowly towards the waiting net just under the surface. Once again, the fish was having none of it, and this time did elect to rocket back upstream, past where it had been hooked and under those trees. I just about stopped it in time, and then the battle developed into a to and fro affair, with the barbel and me alternately gaining and losing a couple of yards of line. After ten minutes or so, it was visibly tiring, and I increased the pressure even more. After a token gesture of a final half hearted kick at the net cord, it surrendered and soon a long, slender and very pretty barbel was gracing my landing net. Had it been as deep as the 14lb 2oz fish it would have weighed over 16lb, as it was close to 33 inches long. But as it was, the scales recorded a very satisfying 12lb 10oz. I was elated.

I was particularly interested in the state of my hook bait, fully expecting it to be totally mangled after all the attention it had received before the barbel bite. But the casters were still as good as new. I could now fish on with renewed confidence.

Before recommencing fishing, I crossed to the far bank briefly for a look into the swim, where observation was far easier. There had been three good fish in residence in the morning, including the one I had just caught, which still rested in my Queenford tube, whereas there were now four. The two newcomers were considerably bigger, both estimated over 14lb, and the fishing suddenly took on a new dimension.

Before starting fishing again, I devoted half an hour to introducing more bait to allow the swim to settle, and by about 3.45pm two more casters were waiting in ambush. An hour passed, a fine drizzle started and then, just before 5.00pm, there was a repeat performance. This second barbel was just as athletic as the first, but did go upstream straight away, right under those worrying roots. I was, however, lucky in that the fish negotiated the obstacles without snagging me and within a few minutes the fish was circling in the open water under the rod top. Few fish can do much against sustained pressure from directly above and I had no further anxious moments before a second gorgeous barbel reposed in my weigh sling. This fish was about two inches shorter than the first, although more portly, and spun the Avon dial to 12lb 7oz, to complete my biggest ever barbel brace.

Before leaving that evening, I introduced another two pints of hemp. If I could get the same swim tomorrow I had to be in with a chance of one of the really big fish.

On the Friday morning, I was indeed first out of the blocks and managed to secure the swim I wanted and, after introducing two more pints each of hemp and casters, crossed to the far bank again for a look. In the dull light, I could only make out one fish over the bait, but it looked mighty big. The excitement was building.

I followed the now familiar pattern of patient baiting until I knew the barbel were confident, and only five minutes after my first cast, around noon, the rod shot off the rest. This fish gave me no problems at all, and I was soon recording a nice double of 10lb 4oz. Once more I stopped fishing temporarily and crossed the river and this time what I saw, now in good light, were two monstrous fish feeding greedily. My name had to be on one of those, if not both.

By 2.00pm, another bait was in place and after only about ten minutes a succession of hard knocks had been followed by a whack that I simply had to hit. But I felt nothing, saw the casters were still sound, and put it down to a determined dace. Within an hour, I was getting bumps and grinds from small fish every few minutes, but I was now full of confidence in leaving the rod alone. It appeared that the casters, free to move in the current on the quarter inch hair, were quite difficult to mouthe by the small fish and that's why they were not getting shelled. So I fished on.

By 4.00pm, all this activity had ceased and I hovered over my rod expectantly until it was time to leave the fishery, every second expecting it to crash round at last. But it wasn't to be, and eventually I was forced to call it a day and wind in. There was a distinct feeling of anti climax, soon to be replaced by stunned disbelief as I examined the hair. All that remained was the tiniest fragment imaginable of one caster shell. To all intents and purposes, I had been fishing for two enormous barbel with a bare hook, possibly for several hours. Yesterday, I had retrieved the bait several times unnecessarily after the attentions of small fish, but today I had been confident enough to leave it in place. In reality, therefore, I had got it wrong both days, a classic example of Sod's Law in action!

Winter on the Thurne

In the early eighties, Trefor and I were regular visitors to Norfolk, to sample the wonderful chub and barbel fishing on the Wensum as a guest of Dave Plummer, and it was inevitable that we progressed to the piking on the Norfolk rivers and broads.

The Thurne in particular was attracting attention for the huge fish it was producing, and at the beginning of the 1984 season, Andy Barker and I jointly invested in a sturdy 14ft boat. This was to be kept permanently moored in the boat dyke just off the river at Martham, so that we could go piking at a moment's notice without the hassle of towing a boat all the way from Coventry, some 180 miles away. The previous season, Trefor and I had acquired a smaller boat, intending to tow it backwards and forwards each week, but we only ever did it the once. The long journey and preparation required really was a pain. Also, the one time we used it we realised that it was inadequate for two men. Although we fished out of it successfully for a while, it was dangerously overloaded, an accident waiting to happen. Sure enough, on the second day, we were moored by a Bure boat dyke and, after landing a small pike, my foot became trapped under the seat as I bent forward to unhook the fish. This led to my sliding along the seat to one side of the boat, which tipped under water. Momentarily, I couldn't move, and only Trefor's quick thinking in diving to the other side of the craft, stabilising it, prevented our sinking completely. As it was, everything in the boat was awash and had to be decamped onto dry land. It was a hairy moment, and we were really lucky not to have lost everything.

The only problem, of course, in keeping a boat so far from home was the ever-present possibility of vandalism or theft, despite the fact that it was well padlocked. During the 1984/85 winter, when my Thurne campaign was at its height, I never had a problem, although Dave Plummer had twice found the boat deliberately sunk in the dyke and had baled it out for me before my arrival. One or two sad local anglers didn't like competition from Coventry. Eventually the padlock was wrenched off and the boat stolen in 1986. Although I have no proof who was responsible, I have my suspicions.

Before I embarked on my big pike campaign in November 1984, I had no illusions. I knew that the fishing would be slow. Dave had told me how temperamental the fish were, and susceptible to changing weather conditions.

Living where I did, I could not hope to be fishing when conditions dictated. I had to fish on Thursdays and Fridays and hope that conditions were favourable. In this regard, I was unlucky on my initial trips, mainly because of drifting weed. Thursday morning always seemed to coincide with a spate, bringing tons of debris downstream, making fishing impossible.

Bait was another problem. The Thurne was primarily a livebait water. Although the pike would pick up deadbaits, it was very slow going. The main reason was the lush bottom weed, which was at least two feet thick. Traditional legered deadbaits were obviously masked, and buoyant baits proved inferior to livebaits fished free roving or paternostered just above the weed. The pike obviously cruised through the bottom foliage, in ambush, waiting for a meal to present itself overhead. This stalking behaviour made the free roving livebait the most effective method by a mile, and Dave Plummer had exactly the same experience.

By February 1985, I had only managed a handful of fish, best 17lb, and although I was certainly losing no enthusiasm, I needed a boost. And that is exactly what I received shortly after arriving at Dave's house on Thursday 7th February. Over coffee, Dave swore me to secrecy before confiding that Neville Fickling had just broken the pike record with a massive fish of 41lb 6oz from the Thurne. It was not common knowledge at the time as Neville was still in negotiation with the media, but I was absolutely delighted for him. Fish of that stature often go to anglers who do not deserve them, but that certainly could not be said of Neville's record. He had fished very hard for that reward, enduring many long, cold nights in his boat, and

The Thurne at Martham.

Trefor with Broadland specimens.

thoroughly deserved the accolades that followed.

The next day proved to be memorable for two very different reasons. Dave fished with me for the morning, anchoring just inside Martham north broad, for which he had a ticket, while I anchored up in the free water of the Thurne just off the mouth of the broad. The wind was quite strong that morning, and I managed the grand total of one infant pike to a paternostered roach while Dave took a magnificent brace of twenties to free roving livebaits off the broad. After Dave had said his good byes on the way to work, I decided on a change of approach. Between Martham north broad and the boat dyke was perhaps one and a half miles, and for the bulk of it, from a winding section known as Dungeon Corner to the dyke, you could fish from the bank. I decided to head downstream to Dungeon Corner, moor the boat, and then work a free-swimming livebait from the bank, covering as much water as possible.

By early afternoon, there was now a distinctly chilly edge to the wind, and I was glad to be off the boat and engaged in more active fishing. One rod was fished statically, presenting a paternostered roach livebait, while I worked a six-ounce crucian free swimmer for thirty yards above and below. The line on this rod was well greased to allow the bait unfettered movement. After half an hour or so, the paternostered bait was moved fifty yards downstream, and the procedure repeated. In this way, every pike for several hundred yards of river was bound to see one of my baits.

I was on my third move, and the crucian was working the far bank reeds. Briefly, I sat on my seat box and put the rod on a rest while I enjoyed a coffee and sandwich. After a few minutes, the crucian suddenly became very agitated, then shot across river until it was only a couple of feet from the reeds on my bank. Then, in an incredible swirl, the float vanished and a few feet of line zipped across the surface. No sooner had I picked up the rod than the line fell slack. The float never re-appeared, though, and seconds later I caught sight of it, about two feet under the surface, unmoving. It was obvious what had happened, a pike had ambushed the crucian from the bottom weed and dropped back down with it. I was uncertain of what action to take next. I felt it most likely that the bait had not been taken properly and that the pike was simply holding it in its jaws. It was, after all, quite a big livebait. On the other hand, it was just possible that a massive pike had wolfed the crucian down in one gulp, in which case further delay could lead to unwanted deep hooking. It was a dilemma, but in the end I realised I could not risk the possibility of a very big pike being badly hooked, and started to tighten gingerly to the fish. If I could get it to move off, it would be far simpler to put in an effective strike.

The pike, however, did not oblige me by moving off, but simply allowed itself to be lifted off bottom. From the impressive curve in my rod, I knew I had a big fish on the end, and sure enough a monstrous pike emerged from the bottom weed, gripping my bait firmly cross ways. Immediately, I could see that a strike would have simply pulled the bait straight from its mouth, and just as I slackened off again to enable it hopefully to be turned for swallowing, the pike gave an angry shake of its head, throwing the crucian clear. A huge tail broke surface as the pike vacated the area in haste, leaving me cursing on the bank and thinking about what might have been. I will never know how big that pike was, but my best guess would be at least 35lb. After that sad episode, I was obviously a little down, but did have the small crumb of consolation of my biggest fish of the campaign later in the afternoon, a chunky 17lb 10oz specimen that tail-walked several times before eventually coming to net.

On my winter trips to Norfolk in the eighties, I would usually fish the Thurne from first light to mid-afternoon, moving to the Wensum for dusk, when I would give it a go for a few dark hours in search of barbel and chub. There was nothing different that afternoon, and after returning the seventeen pounder, with about an hour of daylight remaining, I motored back downriver for the thirty mile drive back to Norwich. During the drive, the wind had picked up again and was now bitter, carrying the first few flakes of snow. By the time I pulled into the Wensum syndicate car park, the ground was covered in a fine white carpet and I debated for a while whether to fish at all that night or drive straight home. In the end, I felt that the snow would probably soon fizzle out, and, as I was well wrapped against the elements, decided on a couple of hours chubbing before setting off for Coventry. A barbel was probably expecting too much. In deference to the weather, I decided to concentrate on one swim, so that I could enjoy the comfort of my umbrella, and about fifteen minutes later I was snugly ensconced in a swim known as the Top Tree, a very reliable area for big chub.

Under my shelter, I was very comfortable, taking a 4lb chub after an hour, and would possibly have stayed late had I not needed to attend to a call of nature after perhaps a further hour. In the dark, I had been unaware quite how hard it was snowing, but now, as I scanned my umbrella with my torch, I could see that at least five inches had fallen in around two hours. This was obviously getting serious if I intended getting home that night, and I packed up immediately, struggled back to the car, and only just managed to drive through the car park on to the road. At the nearest call box, I pulled over to phone my wife, explaining that I could be late as we had snow in Norfolk, and she advised me not to even attempt coming home that night. Apparently, the snow had started around midday in the Midlands, and driving conditions were already very hazardous. Accordingly, I returned to Dave's house and begged his couch for another night. Next morning, there was an incredible sight. The snow appeared to be two feet deep everywhere, and was still falling. When I rang the wife again, she confirmed that the situation across the country was diabolical. I hadn't heard any news, but we'd had one of the worst blizzards in living memory, many roads were impassable and even snow ploughs were having problems clearing all but single lanes of motorways. Worse, the snow was set to continue and the temperatures stay below freezing for at least a week. I had to get home in those circumstances, so told Fran not to worry and that I would be home as soon as possible.

The 150 mile drive from Norwich to Coventry was a nightmare I shall never forget. Without exaggeration, I never got above third gear and twenty miles an hour for the entire journey. I obviously kept to major roads, and even they were down to one very narrow path down the middle, with huge drifts either side where the snow ploughs had forced through. Roads were continually being covered in fresh snow in the strong wind, and that, together with a road surface of sheer ice, made driving treacherous in the extreme. Everywhere I looked there were abandoned and crashed cars and lorries, and the eerily deserted scene on my way home looked for all the world, like the aftermath of a war in Siberia. When I eventually arrived home in mid-afternoon, after nearly eight hours, my wife was nearly frantic with worry. I was so stressed out following hours of intense concentration that I was suffering from a blinding headache and flashing lights in my eyes that were later attributed to snow blindness. Never again do I want to experience a drive like that one.

Having been so close to a mega pike, I was champing at the bit to get back down to Dungeon Corner for another crack at it, but the weather had well and truly closed in. The big freeze was set in with a vengeance, and it was a further three weeks before a trip to Norfolk looked remotely feasible. At the start of the last week in February I rang Dave and he told me that the ice was steadily thawing.

Conditions for piking, he said, should be about perfect at the back end of the week, when all the ice should have gone. That was all I needed to hear, and, armed with a good supply of crucian livebaits, I set off for the Thurne in the early hours of Thursday, February 28th. The intention was a dawn start, many of the really big Thurne fish having come in the first hour or so of daylight.

However, the good old British weather proved as fickle and irritating as ever because, barely twenty miles from home, fog began to close in. The further east I travelled, the denser it became until I was reduced to an absolute crawl as visibility shrunk to just a few yards. It was ridiculous carrying on in those conditions, with still a hundred miles to travel, but I am nothing if not stubborn when it comes to my fishing. Common sense told me to turn round and return home, and the thought of a big pike told me to carry on. There was, therefore, no contest. I carried on.

Having passed Cambridge, the fog did mercifully thin enough to allow reasonable speed, but notwithstanding that it was still a good two hours after daybreak when I finally arrived at the boat dyke, not in the sweetest of moods. Half an hour later, boat packed, I was motoring steadily down the dyke, turning right onto the Thurne, and then chugging towards Dungeon Corner, a mile or so upriver. The next problem was not long in manifesting itself. No more than four hundred yards from the dyke, the margins of the Thurne were still iced and the further upstream I motored, the wider these margins became until finally the river was fully iced over. Several hundred yards short of my destination, I was forced to stop. The ice was thick enough to halt any further progress, and I pulled over into the reeds and jumped onto the bank to re-think my strategy.

At first, I was well and truly brassed off, as I had been totally obsessed, during the enforced lay off, in fishing Dungeon Corner again. But that was now clearly impossible, and so I mulled over the alternatives as I enjoyed a hot coffee in the bitingly cold wind. As I stood there in the bleak Norfolk landscape on that murky morning, I could hear regular creaking and cracking noises as the ice continually moved, and then it suddenly hit me that I was in exactly the right spot. Where better to fish for pike, after three weeks rest from anglers, than a spot that has only just become ice-free. As if to reinforce that belief, a floe some three feet across broke away and drifted slowly downstream as I watched.

Soon, I had formulated my plan of action. I would fish a paternostered livebait right at the edge of the ice, and work a free rover up to forty yards downstream, covering every inch of the river. As ice broke away during the day, I would steadily move the paternostered bait upstream to coincide with the new ice margin, similarly covering the rest of the newly ice free water with my free rover. It was a simple and logical tactic.

After the first hour and one 4lb jack to the static bait, there was a very noticeable shift in the wind, which became warmer and fresher, so that, by midday, it was blowing quite strongly. It felt ten degrees warmer than it had on my arrival and, consequently, the break up of the ice accelerated rapidly. Every few moments, there would be another loud crack as more broke away, and by around 12.30pm another hundred yards upstream of my commencing point had become ice free. Following my plan, I repositioned the paternostered bait and then commenced a thorough search with the free rover. I knew conditions could hardly be better, I had to make the most of this opportunity.

In the next hour, I think I covered every inch of that river for 80 yards downstream of the ice without response, and I was nearly back at the point where I had moored the boat. The crucian was just working across the mouth of a small bay in the opposite bank reeds when the float simply vanished. There was an audible plop as it went away, and then the most impressive whirlpool and vortex appeared. Immediately, I knew that was caused by no jack. Just like the Dungeon Corner fish, this pike never moved after intercepting the crucian, and again I faced the same dilemma. Should I stick or twist. Thankfully, this pike took the decision for me, as, in one of the most impressive moments in my angling career, a huge shape rose to just under the surface, a shape I could see was at least four feet long. Then, in an awesome demonstration of acceleration from a standing start, it rocketed downstream as though jet propelled, keeping just under the surface such that it created the most incredible bow wave. As I struck, the speed merely intensified, the rod slamming over irresistibly as forty yards of line whistled off the spool. The scream of the clutch rose to a high pitched whine and never before had I felt such power from a pike, which I have never rated as one of our stronger fighters.

Even in that moment of high drama, I could laugh at a comical incident. A pair of mallards had been fussing around in the reeds downstream as I struck into the fish, and they both looked up as this awe inspiring bow wave approached them at a rate of knots. It must have seemed like Jaws approaching. The pair looked at each other as if to say, "let's get the hell out of here," and then they both took off at the same instant, colliding head on in mid-air. There was a big cloud of feathers, and next second they were both on their backs in the river, whereupon they started fighting. Obviously, they blamed each other for the impact. Seconds later, they were airborne again and were last seen heading for the coast!

When that initial surge had finished, I commenced pumping the pike back towards me, and slowly won back the line I had lost. Soon, it was circling in front of me, giving a good opportunity to estimate its size. I knew my first length estimate of four feet was about right and I also knew that Neville's record had been about

four feet long as well. The possibilities were all turning over in my head, and I had
to tell myself very sternly to keep calm and not rush things. Eventually, the fish was
beaten and I drew it towards the waiting net. It came over the arms and I began to
lift to engulf my prize. But the net wouldn't budge, the mesh was stuck fast on an
unseen underwater snag. It was a panicky moment. I had an awesome pike at my
mercy, and I couldn't get the net around it. As I struggled to free the mesh, I could
see the pike gathering it strength, and then, with an angry flip, it was off the net
arms and surging downstream again. I was powerless to stop it.

Keeping as calm as the circumstances would allow, I waited until the pike had
stopped running, about ten yards. Then, keeping the tension in the rod with my left
hand, lay flat on the bank, groping around in the freezing water with my right to
locate the snag on which my mesh was tethered. This turned out to be a clump of
sunken brambles, which I tore free, and scrambling back to my feet, I recommenced battle with the biggest pike of my career. This time there were no last
minute dramas and, a few minutes later, a massive pike folded into the net.

The first thing I noticed, apart from the awesome size of the fish, was the fact
that it was deeply-hooked. Exactly the scenario that had worried me three weeks
previously had obviously occurred. The crucian had been gulped straight down.
After a short while trying to extricate the trebles, which were in a delicate position,
I realised that it was a job more safely carried out by four hands rather than two. As
I knew Dave and Neville were due on the river any moment, I bit the line well up
from the trace and carefully sacked the fish to await their arrival. Before placing it
in the water, I did a rough weighing, which, with my shaking and the strong wind,
gave me a reading of somewhere around 32lb. It was an overwhelming moment.

My 32lb 1oz fish.

No more than forty minutes later, Dave's boat chugged into view, and Dave and Neville were as delighted as I was, they both knew how much that pike meant to me. Extracting the trebles proved no problem with two of us on the job, and then Dave and Neville carried out an accurate weighing for me. 32lb 1oz was their verdict and, at that moment, the hundreds of miles driving, the hours of facing cold east winds, the hassle of arranging livebaits all became insignificant. A long held ambition of a thirty-pound pike had been realised and that night, around Dave's fire, the story was told and re-told until the early hours.

At the time of writing, fifteen years later, I still await my second thirty.

The Upper Great Ouse
My Private Paradise

I first fished the Upper Ouse system in the summer of 1961, when I was introduced to the Claydon Brook, about two miles upstream of Buckingham, where it joined the main Ouse itself. It was to be the best part of ten years before I fished the main river, as I had little reason to look further afield than the Claydon Brook. The fishing for those ten years on that beautiful little stream was quite exceptional, with many five pound chub and three sixes coming to net, as well as dozens of big perch and roach.

My love affair with the Claydon Brook ceased abruptly in the early seventies. A ruthless dredging which totally denuded the previously lushly vegetated banks, the sinking of a new bore hole to supply Milton Keynes also lowered the water table dramatically. In addition, the destruction of the magnificent big perch population as a result of the infamous perch disease, combined to tear the heart and soul out of my beloved stream.

In the early summer of 1971, therefore, I was seeking pastures new, and a letter in Angling Times caught my attention. Ian Howcroft, who acted as fishery manager for Dick Walker on Dick's famous stretch of the Upper Ouse, had invited applications from readers to fish from the palatial fishing hut that Dick had constructed in the early sixties. I had devoured every word written by Dick in his

books and weekly column and the thought of possibly fishing his water filled me with excitement. I wasted no time in penning my application and, by return, I was offered a choice of weekend dates. When I studied the map that Ian had enclosed, I realised how close to Dick's stretch I had been fishing for my ten years on the Claydon Brook. It was no more

Dick Walker's famous fishing hut.

than five miles away.

On a pleasant Friday evening in August 1972, my excitement mounted as I stood on the threshold of that famous hut and when I finally entered the luxurious interior the aura of the place was simply overwhelming. I stood drinking in the atmosphere for several minutes, contemplating how many renowned anglers had trodden those same boards. Only once since have I experienced that same sense of awe. The day I took my first steps on the dam at Redmire!

Early next morning, I was quietly fishing a swim known as the Small Cabbage patch, laying on stewed wheat in the hope of a big roach, when there was a faint rustle behind me.

I glanced round and then a voice said, "Good morning, my name's Walker."

All thoughts of fishing were temporarily forgotten and I jumped up to shake the hand of the man I had admired so much over more than ten years, and whose writing had put me on the road to successful specimen hunting.

The fishing that weekend was good without being spectacular but to me the fishing was really irrelevant. Later on Saturday, we were joined by angling legends Pete Thomas and Fred J. Taylor, and I avidly devoured every word these angling heroes had to say. There were the wonderful tales of the Redmire monsters, monstrous Avon barbel and the huge Ouse chub they had all seen. There were the hilarious accounts of Dick's early poaching exploits and the story of the wooden chub.

This was a very lifelike carving of a large chub which Dick and Fred attached to the riverbed in a shallow swim called White Bottom, where a lively current created sufficient ripple to give the fish some "life." They had Peter Stone casting baits at that chub for hours before they let him in on the secret!

I also discovered much of Dick's generosity and quite what a remarkable man he was. Pete Thomas told me the story of how Dick had always claimed his best Redmire mirror carp at 31lb 4oz although it actually weighed 34lb. This was solely because he did not want to overshadow Bob Richard's previous record mirror of

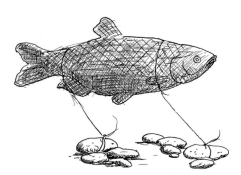

31lb 4oz, having already taken the record with the common of 44lb. It was many years later, after Bob Richard's death, that the story ever came out in the press.

Sunday of that weekend was very interesting. Dick and I fished together for the whole day. A fond memory is watching him catching crayfish in the manner he had written about so often, wading alongside the high bank of a swim known as Two Willows and reaching into all the bankside holes for those freshwater crustacea. That method is one I refused to use then, and would refuse to now. I asked him how often he got it wrong and received a rat bite for his troubles. His answer was never, but I still wasn't convinced!

The evening was spent roaching, Dick trotting a little swim known as Rook Run while I laid on again in the Small Cabbage Patch with Wheat. About a dozen roach to 1lb 14oz rewarded our efforts and before leaving for home at dusk the fish in my net were transferred to Dick's. He was making a film for the BBC the following day and the roach in the net were insurance against any lack of piscine response on Monday!

That weekend was the only time I ever met Richard Walker and the only regret I have is having no photographs of such a treasured memory.

After that first weekend on Dick's stretch, I was told I could fish whenever I wanted and so I visited the river often over the next few years, catching many good chub and roach. Sadly, the perch, as on the Claydon Brook, were just a memory.

Hard Fighting Bream

In the summer of 1976, the year of the great drought, I stayed in Dick's hut twice more. During the first trip, I decided to have a crack at the big bream Dick had told me about in a swim known as the Large Cabbage Patch, and spent part of the first evening baiting it in readiness for a dawn assault the next morning. I was accompanied that weekend by a very good match angling friend, Fred, and at the crack of dawn we cast simple porcupine float gear to fish laying on with large lobworms, in small clearings in the cabbages. When it was fully light, I could see that the water was noticeably colouring from the activities of feeding fish. Just as I was contemplating introducing more feed, a large bronze back broke surface, all but submerging my float. Immediately afterwards, the float shot away, and I was in contact with a fish that fought like no other bream I had ever hooked. It was as strong as any big chub, and I was very relieved when the net mesh finally closed around it.

Bream of 5lb 2oz, 5lb 10oz and 6lb 4oz.

Fred Starkey with his five pounder

During the next hour the activity was hectic, with three more good bream coming to net. As suddenly as the action had started, it finished, the water cleared again and the bream were gone. The fish had gone completely off the feed as soon as the sun began to come up. The three bream I took in that spell weighed 5lb 2oz, 5lb 10oz and 6lb 4oz, and I also landed four perch to about a pound and a lovely roach of 1lb 10oz. Fred's solitary bream of just over five pounds was far and away the biggest he'd ever seen, so he was well pleased. No more than three hours after starting fishing, we were back at the hut tucking into bacon and eggs.

First Five Pounder

Although I'd taken many five pound plus chub from the Claydon Brook, a fish of that size from the main river continually eluded me, but that was to change on a foul winter's day when the conditions could hardly have been worse for chubbing. On my arrival at dawn, I was disappointed to find a horrible brown surging torrent, still rising and carrying tons of debris. I knew I was up against it, but I had driven over fifty miles and was determined to give it a go.

After a fruitless morning roving from swim to swim, getting colder and wetter by the minute, courtesy of the torrential rain, I realised that perhaps my best hope of a bite lay in concentrating on a known swim containing a slack that resident chub could migrate to. Just such a swim was Two Willows, where there was a very inviting crease swim between the two sets of trailing branches.

As it was by now virtually impossible to detect bites by quivertip, because of the gale force wind, I had to rely on touch legering, with the line over my right index finger. I sat unmoving in those atrocious conditions for what seemed an eternity, and then, quite suddenly, there was a sharp pluck on my finger. Moments later, a steady draw was followed by a firm strike, and a big chub kited into midstream. A short, exciting battle in the heavy flow followed, before I managed to guide it back to the steady inside glide, where there was only going to be one winner. I was soon extracting my hook from a very precarious hook hold in a chub I knew to be my Ouse five pounder at last, and when my scales confirmed 5lb 2oz, the appalling conditions were forgotten. I often think of that fish when conditions are against me. In big fish angling, there is rarely such a word as impossible. Providing you can get a bait in the water, there is always a chance, however remote.

Early Upstreaming Experiences

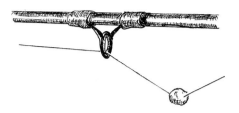

Above Dick Walker's stretch of the Upper Ouse, upstream of a little weir, the river was totally different in character. The water was of uniform, steady flow with no current variations, and the only interest was provided by the opposite bank, which was lined with trees and waterside bushes, many of which hung in the water. A riot of fallen timber littered the riverbed under that foliage, an obvious chub haven.

The Coventry Specimen Group was going strong when the stretch was first discovered, and as we all agreed that it screamed big fish we decided to give it some serious attention. Our early forays saw several big chub lost in the jungle opposite. We were fishing traditional across and downstream techniques, placing hookbaits just above small rubbish rafts, and hooked chub, which invariably turned downstream after taking a bait, were in snags almost as soon as they were hooked. What we needed, therefore, was to get the fish to take baits at the downstream extremities of rafts, when there would be a good chance they would move downstream initially, into clearer water, allowing vital extra time to strike the hook home and pull the chub out of danger.

Hence there developed the upstream legering techniques that have stood us in such good stead since. The principle was the exact opposite of traditional downstreaming in that we would be fishing for slack line bites rather than pulls, requiring a bite indication method that would allow a big chub to pick up the hookbait without feeling resistance but register bites immediately. Those few seconds where we could catch a chub off guard were crucial.

We therefore decided to use the old dough bobbin principle, but with the bobbin set to drop rather than rise. After casting across and upstream, the line was drawn as tight as possible without shifting the hookbait, a dough bobbin then being placed on the line between butt ring and reel. The bobbin had to be heavy enough to keep maximum tension in the line but not so heavy as to move the bait. As soon as the hookbait was picked up, the tension would reduce dramatically and the bobbin would drop sharply, ensuring that the chub felt no resistance initially as the bait would appear unfettered.

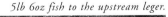

5lb 6oz fish to the upstream leger.

Far bank raft.

This new approach to our chubbing brought immediate success and, in fairly quick succession, Merv Wilkinson took a fish of 6lb, Keith Walton one of 6lb 3oz and Trefor West his personal best of 6lb 4oz.

A couple of weeks after Trefor had taken his big fish, I was fishing a nearby swim which featured a veritable jungle of fallen branches under the opposite bank. It was early evening and, after a bright, sunny winter's day, the light was fading, bringing with the gathering dusk a very sharp frost. These conditions had been with us for a while and, as a consequence, the river was low, clear and cold, the flow being negligible. So sluggish was it that my sliding leger link was comprised of a single swan shot, perfect for delicate presentation of a small piece of bread crust.

Because of the unusually light link, it was quite difficult balancing line tension with a bread paste bobbin, but when that was achieved the set up was ultra sensitive. Because of this sensitivity, the bobbin dropped to the floor twice from false bites in the first hour, but the third indication, an hour after dark, was the real thing.

This time, my sweeping strike was met with a living resistance, and a muscular adversary shot into the tangle of branches before I could haul it into the open water of mid-river. Luckily, the chub came free quite quickly, although the fight thereafter was heart in the mouth stuff as the fish was towing a large branch around. That branch almost cost me my prize as I went to net it, several twigs fouling the net mesh by the chub's head, but fortunately it broke away and I heaved a sigh of relief as a superbly conditioned short and stocky chub sagged into the net. That fish weighed 5lb 6oz and was to remain my biggest from the main Ouse until the late eighties.

Revival of a River
In the late seventies, it was becoming obvious that something was seriously wrong with the river. When I had enjoyed the company of Dick Walker in 1972, he bemoaned the deterioration in the fishing since the sixties. Once I started fishing his stretch seriously, it was obvious that the average weight of the chub was down on the heady peaks of a few years earlier. Having said that, they were still deep and well conditioned, but there were insidious forces at work. My diaries reveal that, in

the summer of 1979, there were suddenly no crayfish to be found, from a stretch that once crawled with them, and the riverbed was becoming coated with horrible, black, slimy weed.

Near bank raft.

The decline in condition and numbers of fish was quite extraordinary, and in my long angling career I have never witnessed such a rapid decline in a fishery, other than from an obvious pollution.

I have never heard a satisfactory explanation of what caused the problem, but the fact remains that for almost ten years the Upper Ouse was a sad caricature of its former self.

And then, in 1988, friends in Buckinghamshire started reporting good catches of roach, plump pristine fish regularly exceeding two pounds in weight. In the 1988/89 winter, one friend had six two pound roach at a sitting, in a catch of over forty fish, and also a bonus chub of 5lb 13oz. Apparently this chub was as fat as butter. Seemingly, the recovery was as dramatic as the decline, and I couldn't wait to renew my acquaintance with my beloved Upper Ouse.

My very first chub session, in the winter of 1989, was memorable.

As most of the catches of big roach had come from a stretch some miles upstream of Dick Walker's fishery, I decided to start operations there. It was an area I hadn't given that much attention to before, although I had taken several average chub in the mid-seventies. Before even taking the gear from the car, I walked the entire stretch, from the road bridge to the bottom boundary some two miles downstream, identifying a bewildering number of cracking-looking chub swims. As I had decided to devote much of the winter to this chubbing, the game plan was to pre-bait ten swims with mashed bread, and continually commute between them. Initially, I would concentrate on the top meadow, and on each subsequent trip gradually work downstream until I had a thorough working knowledge of the entire length.

That morning, I covered the upstream four hundred yards, depositing six handfuls of well-mashed bread into ten areas I fancied. Each area featured an area of slightly steadier water than the main flow, where the mash would settle.

One area in particular was an absolute screamer. The river made a sharp right hand bend around a protruding high bank, and right on the bend stood an elder bush with branches trailing in the water. Better still, downstream of the bend the

A good Ouse chub taken in sub zero conditions.

river deepened suddenly, before shallows some thirty yards downstream. Last but not least, a substantial crease had formed as the main flow hit the high bank. Fishing the hot spot appeared a simple matter of lowering a bait almost at my feet. It was an absolutely classic chub swim.

That swim was the third I fished that morning, having taken only a modest roach from the previous two. After studying the set of the currents again for a few moments, I lowered a large chunk of crust right on the crease immediately behind the little raft created by the elder branches. It settled no more than two feet from the near bank, in around six feet of water. The response was literally instant, with the quivertip jabbing towards the water surface with great purpose. As I was right over the fish on a short line, I had the upper hand from the word go, but did that chub scrap. I only lost about two yards of line on the first plunge, but the fish simply would not come off bottom. It continually tried to find snags under the near bank and I had my heart in my mouth right until the moment the net closed around it. As I swung my prize ashore, I could see that it was easily my biggest ever from the main river. When the Avons confirmed 5lb 10oz and I closely examined the chub I knew that the reports I had been receiving were spot on. The fish was in truly immaculate condition, short, exceptionally deep, and with no missing scales or split fins in evidence.

Gorgeous Adams Mill.

My 14lb 2oz fish that became the record for Ray Walton at over 17lb.

Brace of 10lb 11oz and 13lb 5oz.

My 32lb 1oz personal best.

A gorgeous Thurne '30'.

My 5lb 10oz chub of 1989.

In all honesty, I did not need another bite that day, but on my second visit to the same swim, perhaps two hours later, the sequence of events was almost identical, resulting in another superb chub of 5lb 5oz. What was most intriguing was that, in the other nine swims, I totally blanked, apart from the early roach. It was early days, but possibly the chub population had shrunk to a modest number of exceptional specimens. Time would tell.

A Red Letter Day

After that magnificent brace of five pounders on my first visit, the rest of the winter, and the winter that followed, followed a very similar pattern, with few fish but of good quality. Several more five pounders were landed, but none to beat 5lb 10oz.

And so we come to February 1991, which was an exceptionally cold month with severe frosts and lying snow. I remember the day in question being bitterly cold and bleak, with an icy wind to make the ears tingle. The Ouse was frozen over in the slacker areas, the only fishable areas being where sufficient current prevented ice formation.

That morning, I had a definite plan in mind. The stretch I had selected was one of the hardest on the river, but the chub were exceptional, even for the Ouse. It had produced a cracking specimen of 6lb 7oz recently to my old mate Merv Wilkinson. Over the previous weeks, I had identified five swims that had produced chub. Four of these were ideal for prebaiting, and my plan of action was to prepare these four with mashed bread, and leave them well alone for at least six hours. I also decided to use strawberry flavoured mash, with similarly flavoured crust baits, for no better reason than I wanted to experiment.

The fifth swim, at the upstream boundary of the fishery, where I had caught chub most consistently, was a long glide along a crease. I would sit in that swim for those first six hours, progressively fishing down the crease, and periodically doing a tour of the other four swims to keep the feed topped up.

Lying snow crunched crisply underfoot as I slowly made my way upstream, and, all preparations over, I settled into the crease swim for a few relaxing hours. That morning, my crust baits searched the long crease for several hours without response, but by mid day there had been a detectable change in the weather. A milder air stream was becoming very noticeable, and ice floes were breaking away all along the river. Although conditions were certainly promising, I was still on a blank as I moved into the first of my prepared swims in mid-afternoon.

This swim featured a steady near bank glide disappearing under the trailing branches of a gnarled old willow. A substantial build up of flotsam around the trailing fronds was welded together by a raft of ice, giving any chub present immunity to attack from above.

The first cast into a prepared pitch is often the most vital, and my pulse raced as the first strawberry laced crust offering drifted into position, under the trailing willow branches in mid-river. Soon, the quivertip eased back into a normal slight tension as the bait settled. I sat expectantly, eyes glued to the quivertip.

I doubt that the tip was stationary more than thirty seconds, before plunging round savagely. As I struck, an impressive vortex formed near the ice floe and a powerful chub surged downstream in an impressive run. That chub gave a tremendous account of itself, making several short rushes in an attempt to make the sanctuary of the overgrown opposite bank, but it was overcome eventually by a power greater than its own. Eleven feet of carbon fibre had done its work well. That February chub was majestic, perfect in every fin and scale, weighing in at 5lb 3oz.

After consigning the fish temporarily to a keep sack, I decided to call it a day early. I would get a few shots of the chub first, and then head for home. The previous evening, I'd had a very heavy fall on the ice and bruised my back badly. The longer I fished, the more excruciating the pain was becoming.

Having made that decision, I wandered slowly back to the van to pick up my tripod for some self portraits, but as I was painfully making my way back to my tackle in the gathering dusk, the rain started, a fine deluge of cold drizzle and sleet. Within minutes, the rain was a steady downpour, and I was in a dilemma. I never use an umbrella for winter chubbing and if I attempted self-portraits in the rain and dark, I risked needless damage to my camera. After considering the options for a couple of minutes, I decided to fish on for a short while, despite the intense pain from my back. I was convinced that the rain was just a passing shower, would be over in short order and then I could get my photographs.

Barely had the bait settled when the quivertip again plunged round to the attentions of a second big chub, and I was again locked in battle with a worthy adversary. By the time this second specimen was safely ensconced in the net, it was fully dark, and the torch beam confirmed a satisfying 4lb 7oz. I had been delighted with the five-pounder, but such a brace was a real bonus, and I would get a shot of the pair when the rain stopped. A second carp sack was put to use.

With the rain easing, I cast a third bait under those inviting branches, not for a moment expecting further action, and I swear the crust never even settled. As if by magic, the rod took on a life of its own and I once again found myself in plunging confrontation with a big chub, which eventually pulled the scales to 4lb 8oz. Something very special was occurring.

By the time I had consigned this latest capture to my third and last sack, the rain had stopped, but I now had no intention of packing in just yet, despite my back now being agonisingly painful. Three chub in short order from that stretch of river was unheard of and I realised that I must be in with a real chance of an extra big fish. Something, either the weather conditions or my baiting technique, had turned the chub on and I had to take advantage, at least for a while longer.

Red letter day. Chub of 5lb 10oz, 5lb 3oz, 4lb 8oz and 4lb 7oz.

Ten minutes passed painfully slowly, and I do mean painfully. With the passing of the rain, the sky was clearing, the temperature dropping fast and a frost making my fingers tingle. All was still and silent in the moonlight, and then, suddenly, the line crooked loosely around the index finger of my right hand tightened urgently, before the glowing betalight arced towards the water surface.

I knew that chub was exceptional as soon as it was hooked, it just had that dogged, heavy resistance. There were none of the histrionics of lesser chub, this one relied on brute force. For several minutes it hugged the riverbed, only rising in the water grudgingly, and the longer the fight went on the more excited I became, and the more the agony increased from my back. The chub sullenly refused to be bullied, but, thankfully, the battle was eventually over, and my net sagged to the weight of a big fish. As I examined my prize, I knew that I had caught my biggest chub ever from the Upper Ouse. The confirmed weight of 5lb 10oz equalled the fish I had taken the previous winter, and also meant that for the seventh time in my angling career, I had taken two five pound chub in a session.

With no more sacks left, and by now in so much pain that I had to question my sanity, I really did decide to pack up, and after a few minutes organising photographs of a memorable catch, I returned those lovely chub to their home under the old willow.

I remember thinking that the weather must have held its breath for my photographs, because just as I commenced the long hobble back to the van the heavens opened, and I was soaked by freezing rain that stung my face and chilled me to the bone. All I could think of was a hot meal, warm fire and straightening my back out on a soft bed.

But then the old instincts played up. As I passed the last of the swims I had baited earlier, but had not fished, I knew I had to have a cast alongside that little clump of rushes, which was drawing me like a magnet. This kind of sixth sense is hard to explain, but I have learned never to ignore it, and I knew with absolute certainty that I was only moments away from another big chub. I will not even try to explain it. I just knew.

Moments after the cast, another leviathan chub snarled away with the bait. For about five minutes the battle ebbed and flowed through the foliage. Eventually, a broad silvery flank glided over the rim of the net, and even without the torch I knew I had cracked another five pounder, achieving a feat unique in my long angling career, three five pounders in a day. 5lb 5oz that final fish weighed, the last act of a quite remarkable session.

After returning this latest capture, which I did not attempt to photograph because of the freezing rain, I continued on my way back to the van. It is perhaps stretching the truth to say that I had a spring in my step, but the intense euphoria I felt at that moment provided effective pain relief. Today truly had been a red-letter day.

A Day of Mixed Emotions

At first light on 9th December 1999, I arrived at the Upper Ouse for a two-day session to find a river well below normal winter level, but still carrying a tinge of colour. I had commenced my chub campaign in late October, and so far things were going quite well, although I hadn't yet managed to find a very big fish. As I studied the flows on that crisp morning, I felt that, although not perfect by any means, the conditions were certainly reasonable for a chub or two.

The plan was to walk a good mile from the van, and then slowly fish my way back during the day, settling in to a couple of swims near the road for the after dark fishing. On my way downstream in the morning, I would prebait any swims I fancied with a dozen samples of my special cheesepaste. With a bit of luck, I could reap the benefits on my way back later.

I was settled in the first swim not long after dawn, which features a lovely crease behind dead rushes, presenting a cherry-sized piece of cheesepaste on a size 6 Au Lion D'or to a 12" 6lb Invisiline hooklink. Three swan-shot were sufficient to hold the bait on the crease, while shifting easily to present a rolling bait by a gentle tug on the line. The swim is around thirty yards long, and for several contented hours

I searched it thoroughly. However, by 2.00pm I was still biteless, and moved into a lovely long glide terminating in a fallen tangle of branches. On my arrival at first light, I had deposited paste freebies around those branches. That was my ace in the hole.

For half an hour I fished the run progressively, until I eventually placed a bait hard against the foliage, which produced the goods at last. I was soon admiring a chub of 3lb 14oz, no monster by any means, but very welcome after several blank hours. The next cast produced another strong pull, but this time the battle was dour and I knew a much bigger fish was responsible. Once again, there were no mishaps, and I was soon weighing an immaculate, fat Ouse chub of 5lb 7oz. The prebaiting had achieved the desired result.

That double success flattered to deceive because the rest of the daylight hours saw a repeat of the morning's performance, with nothing to show for fishing several more perfect looking swims. Although I was to take one more fish of 3lb 14oz just after dark, the gale force wind was becoming really trying and by 9.00pm, I was brewing up in the van and preparing a hot curry.

When I went over the events of the day, it was difficult to understand why I had failed to get indications in so many swims. Perhaps the water temperature was the critical factor. Although I had registered 43°F, it had fallen four degrees in a few days, certainly not ideal.

When the next morning dawned clear and frosty, but mercifully calm, and

Trefor plays a good Ouse chub.

especially after I registered a further degree fall in water temperature, I decided on a changed approach from the previous day. I would abandon the mobile approach, with frequent recasting, but instead settle into one swim, which I felt chub would colonise and fish it much more statically. With that in mind, I moved to a swim featuring a far bank raft. I had fished it for about half an hour the previous day without result but today I intended giving it far longer. It was an awkward little swim to fish, with my having to cast over a dead rush bed in mid-river, which would certainly make landing any hooked chub an exciting affair.

Again, on my arrival, I had introduced a few cheese paste freebies under that enticing looking raft, and then gone for an exploratory walk while the swim settled. It was around 10.00am before my first cast, but things remained quiet for about an hour until the tiniest nudge on the quivertip brought me to attention. In the next ten minutes or so, two further delicate indications kept me on my toes, before a full-blooded thump had me on my feet at last, playing a real powerhouse of a chub. I know that it is notoriously difficult to estimate a fish weight from its feel, but I am as convinced as I can be that that chub was a monster. Sadly, I was not destined to see it. Several times, it made powerful rushes under the raft, each one being countered with the rod at maximum fighting curve, and I felt things were going my way. It was obviously huge, and I couldn't wait to see it in the net.

Eventually the fish was in open water, whereupon it promptly snagged me on a dead rush stem. Unworried, I moved downstream of the fish, maintaining tension, and then gently increased pressure until I felt it yield. At least, that's what I thought. In the event, I retrieved a nice clump of rush stem, but no chub. It is an understatement to say I was gutted. I was convinced I had just lost a six pounder.

When I examined my hook, the sense of bad luck was further compounded when I discovered that the hook point had broken away at the barb. I had been using Au Lion D'or hooks for thirty years, and that was the first one that had ever broken on me. It was just 'one of those things', or so I thought. I tied up a new hook link, again with a size 6 Au Lion D'or.

To give the swim time to recover, I put in six cheesepaste freebies and had a wander along the bank, annoyed that I had just lost an obviously big fish, and possibly ruined the swim. For a while, I contemplated whether I should move out of the swim, but eventually decided against it. I was fishing a fairly substantial raft, possibly containing numbers of fish. So long as I gave them sufficient time to recover, the chub would continue feeding.

Two hours passed uneventfully after I had eventually recast, and then the rod flew round, more like a barbel bite. I struck, missed completely, and the terminal tackle landed in a tangled heap in the undergrowth at my feet. The air was blue as

I sorted the mess out, eventually swinging another bait into position. At least that was the intention. Actually, it landed in the tree and I had to pull for a break!

After again tackling up afresh, I no longer felt competent to fish for chub, and once more put a few freebies out before going for a walk to let the swim settle all over again.

The day's disasters were by no means over, because I was to lose another monster in mid-afternoon. After successfully landing a chub of 4lb 4oz, I only had ten minutes to wait before I was in again. I did the hard part, pulling it out from under the branches, not allowing the chub to get its head down. With the fish in mid-river, over clear water, it rolled on the surface, showing a vast depth of flank. My heart skipped a beat as I felt this chub could be nearer seven pounds than six, and I reached for the net. And then the hook pulled out! Or at least, I thought it had pulled out. In actual fact, a second Au Lion D'or had snapped at the barb. After an angling lifetime without a breakage, to have two failures in quick succession was sinister. Why did it have to happen on two monstrous fish? Sod's Law I suppose.

After the trauma of this second lost fish, I really did wonder about the wisdom of carrying on in the same swim, but decided to stick it out, and how glad I am I did. After having again retackled, this time with a size 6 Drennan Continental Boilie hook at the business end, I again swung out a bait to the far bank raft.

The action I was to enjoy in the next thirty minutes or so went some way to compensating me for the disappointments of the day. In that short time I had four very positive pulls, one of which was inexplicably missed, and the others yielding good fish of 5lb 2oz, 4lb 14oz and 5lb 4oz.

That day raised several fascinating questions. What had caused the chub apparently to group up, leaving usually good swims barren? What had caused my usually reliable Au Lion D'or hooks to suddenly become mischievous? With the chub so obviously reluctant to feed over most of the river, why were they feeding with such apparent abandon in my swim? And why were normally spooky fish still feeding when I had created such a disturbance in the swim by a combination of bad luck, bad casting and landing fish?

I have gone on record as saying that a group of big chub would not tolerate the disturbance of one or two of their fellows being taken from a swim, as barbel will. In the main, I still believe that, but that Friday gave clear evidence to the contrary. By the time the final three big chub came to net, I'd missed two good bites, cast into the tree and lost two big fish after quite a commotion.

I'll never fully understand the mentality of big fish. Just as you think you know the answers something happens to disprove all the theories. When you think about it, that's why this big fish angling is so enthralling. Long may it continue.

The Sixth Sense

All those of us with many years' experience can relate stories of the occasions when big fish were caught as the result of following instinct, as opposed to the application of logical thought processes. Certainly, in my case, I learned many years ago never to ignore my instincts. Many would have us believe that there is no such thing as instinct, or 'a sixth sense,' suggesting that what we are following is simply a process of applying latent memories, or subconsciously making decisions based on a similar set of conditions faced years before, but long forgotten. I remain neutral on this point, but it is a fact that I have taken several big fish, when I have followed unconscious urges that have not made sense under cold analysis. I don't pretend to understand what causes such urges, other than perhaps the vestiges of a long atrophied primeval hunting instinct.

In March 2000, I was to follow a sudden overwhelming compulsion to fish an area where I had never before enjoyed any success with chub whatever, and my reward could not have been more dramatic. I had been joined on the bank by my old mate, Bob Roberts, who fancied a crack at some winter chub. I had enjoyed some wonderful chub fishing over previous weeks, and my main objective was to get Bob stuck into a good fish! With that in mind, I suggested that he fish a swim where I took a fish of 6lb 3oz in March 1999. Of all the swims on the fishery, that one probably responds the best to a steady build up of liquidised or mashed bread, which I knew was the method that Bob favoured.

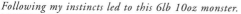

Following my instincts led to this 6lb 10oz monster.

I had decided to fish the glide upstream of Bob, and after the first hour I'd had a 3lb 14oz chub and Bob his first of 4lb 4oz, with which he was absolutely delighted. Not long after photographing Bob's fish for him, I became increasingly unsettled and knew I had to move to the bottom meadow of the fishery. What made this instinct more surprising is that the bottom meadow had not

Bob Roberts' chunky five pounder.

produced me a single bite in the previous three winters, or to any of my friends. Two friends who are heavily into summer chubbing have reported many times that they never see a fish down there and it is, in their words, a chub desert.

Nevertheless, I could not rest, and was soon humping my gear the long trek to the bottom of the fishery. Once there, I selected an area facing far bank trees, and introduced ten lumps of my cheese paste under the foliage. You will have to believe me when I tell you that I knew I was going to catch a big fish, there was absolutely no doubt about it. And this was despite consistent blanking over the years.

Sure enough, my hookbait had not been in position more than five minutes before the tip kicked back as the lead moved and a chub made off with the paste. I knew I was connected to a monster immediately, as it held in the flow, and then pulled away like a barbel. After a lively battle in the good current, I was able to get the fish over my net, and lift it ashore. I knew straight away that here was a fish that would come close to my personal best of 6lb 12oz, and when the scales registered 6lb 10oz it was a moment of pure euphoria.

Although I used my watercraft in selecting the exact area I eventually placed my bait, if I had followed normal reasoning I would not have been anywhere near that bottom meadow. Over previous seasons, I had wasted countless hours there.

When I eventually reached Bob to tell him my news, I found that he had a fish in the sack that I weighed for him at 5lb 9oz, so he was also over the moon. All in all, quite a memorable session.

Obviously, 99% of all specimen fish are going to be caught by the application of sound angling principles, and by elimination of basic errors. The most consistently successful anglers hone their skills and watercraft continually. Occasionally, however, as I have proved to my satisfaction, something will insist you fish a particular swim or venue that you would not normally consider. If it happens to you, don't ignore it. I don't. It has caught me too many good fish for that.

The Agony and the Ecstasy

During the winter of 1998/99, I went through one of those spells that afflicts all big fish anglers from time to time, in that, no matter what I tried, I kept blanking. During the previous summer and autumn, Matthew Bodily and I had enjoyed some wonderful fishing on the middle Ouse, on a special bait we had put together, and in Matthew's case that continued right until the end of the season. In my case, for whatever reason, bites just dried up. Even on those days when Matthew and I fished together, using the same rig and bait, Matthew was catching and I wasn't. It got to the stage where I was suffering a total lack of confidence and although I had targeted the Middle Ouse for my winter campaign, I felt that a change of venue might change my fortunes. I had fished through a similar period on the Wensum, when I couldn't catch a double figure barbel whatever I tried, when others were taking them regularly.

So, in February 1999, I decided to switch my attentions to the upper river and revert to chubbing with the traditional methods, using either bread crust or cheese paste hookbaits, depending on water conditions. To my chagrin, the barren spell continued, and by late February I had caught very little for three months. It reached a low on the first Friday in March.

I had arrived at the river the previous morning to find a tinge of colour, the water about a foot above normal level, and the weather mild and drizzly, conditions that screamed chubbing with cheese paste. Following my normal procedure, having the river to myself, I prebaited several swims with paste and then fished in rotation, not packing up until about three hours after dark. The day summed up the previous few weeks. The only chub I hooked that felt any size stuck solid on a tree root and I eventually had to pull for a break, and I went on to take two chub of around three pounds and a four pound bream after dark.

A reliable big chub swim.

I was up and about at the crack of dawn next morning, the plan being to cover exactly the same ground again, the thinking being that the previous day's freebies may well have drawn in chub overnight. The first swim I fished, quite close to the car parking area, has long been a favourite of mine, where I had taken many big fish in the

past. The previous winter, it had
produced several five pounders,
including one of 5lb 12oz, to
edge my main Ouse record closer
to that 6lb target I had set myself.
The swim is a lovely glide
between two willows, the
downstream branches hanging
right in the water just as the
current slows, an ideal set-up.

I decided to give this swim a
couple of hours, and I baited with
about twenty freebies before
going walkabout to bait the other

Two Willows, a very famous swim.

swims. It was perhaps 45 minutes later that I made my first cast. Half an hour later,
I had taken a chub and a bream, the chub weighing about a pound and the bream
about three pounds. Then I had a better chub of just over three pounds, and then
nothing. After a blank hour, I decided on a move, but before doing so put in
another dozen freebies

My second visit to the swim was around midday, when a good pull after a few
seconds to my first cast heralded the arrival of another three pound chub. I was
pleased to be getting bites at last, but when was I going to catch a big fish. Again,
that solitary chub was all the response I had, so once again, an hour or so later, I put
in more freebies and rested the swim. That is when it all went pear-shaped.

I had settled into a glide perhaps a hundred yards away when I suddenly became
aware of other anglers arriving at regular intervals. Quite a few were familiar faces
and it transpired that they were all members of the Chub Study Group, who were
on the Upper Ouse for their AGM. The most obvious implication of this was that
the sudden activity would severely hamper my mobility, and I had just decided to
go back to my favourite swim and sit it out when Paul Fickling arrived and stopped
for a chat. This was about mid-afternoon. Paul and I had met for the first time
earlier that season and had already become firm friends. He was also surprised to see
so many bodies about, and announced that he would go back towards the car park
where there were still a couple of vacant swims. The one he fancied, he said, where
he had left his tackle, was situated between two small willow trees. I was too late.
Paul has since told me that, had I told him I was returning to the swim, he would
not have fished it, but that was simply not an option. When I prebait swims, it is
in the full knowledge that other anglers may arrive and fish them. After all, they pay

their membership fees and have as much right to be there as I have. So, I wished Paul well, and decided to sit it out where I was.

Some three hours later, by now pitch black and raining hard, I was concentrating hard on my glowing quivertip, when a tap on my shoulder made me jump. It was Paul, who had crept up behind me unnoticed. I will never forget the brief conversation that followed as long as I have breath in my body. It went like this.

Paul "Tony, I need you to come and take some photographs for me."

Me   "Got a big fish, mate?"

Paul "You could say that!"

Me   "Well, how big is it?"

Paul "Exactly seven pounds!"

Me   "How bloody big!"

A few minutes later, Paul produced from a sack the most impressive chub I've ever set eyes on. Incredibly, it was in perfect symmetry, suggesting that it was by no means at its maximum weight. Paul was understandably totally overawed by the event. That was the first chub he had ever caught from the stretch, and after the photographs were over he confided in me that he didn't think he could fish any longer. There didn't seem much point somehow.

As I made my way back to my swim, rain lashing in my face, I pondered the injustice of it all. I am ashamed to say that, for the first time in my angling career, I was annoyed at someone else catching a big fish. Thankfully, the feeling soon passed, but I still felt, much as I was pleased for Paul, that I deserved that chub for all the preparatory work I had undertaken over two days. Needless to say, Paul took it on cheese paste, under the trailing branches I had baited earlier. As I drove home, about two hours later, still biteless, my mind was in a turmoil.

Seven days later I was back for the final six days of the season, determined to end the season on a high. I had caught next to nothing since December and badly needed a result.

For the first three days of the week, the river was quite heavily coloured, although it improved day by day, with the level steadily falling from semi-flood conditions to normal winter level. As this was accompanied by a corresponding steady increase in water temperature, conditions were approaching perfection. Considering the less than perfect conditions over those first three days, I was quite pleased to have taken two chub of just over five pounds as well as two lesser fish and several nice bream. There were no blank days and my nightmare was gradually coming to an end.

On the Thursday, the colour suggested that I would be better using bread crust than cheese and I spent a very enjoyable day wandering from glide to glide bouncing my crust baits along the flow accompanied by regular infusions of bread mash. Three chub to just under five pounds rewarded these efforts, plus bream of five and six pounds after dark, so the day was most enjoyable.

On Friday morning, the conditions were as good as they can be for winter chubbing with bread crust. The river had a perfect colour, the water temperature was well up, it was exceptionally mild and windless. That day, if I couldn't tempt a few chub, I never would. On my very first cast, fate was once again to play a cruel trick on me. Before leaving home for this final session, I had religiously renewed the lines on my spools, using a brand new bulk spool of 6lb for my chub reels and 10lb for my barbel reels, just in case heavy rain forced a change of species. I had of course tested both lines and both broke at or slightly above their nominal rating.

So, the first cast I made was down a long glide towards a fallen tree, and was perfect in that the crust alighted only inches from the raft that had formed. Moments later, the tip twitched and then pulled round decisively. The chub I hooked was big, as proved by the tremendous swirl it made at the surface of the relatively shallow water on feeling the hook. Several times, that chub tried for the sanctuary of the fallen branches, with my heaving it out each time. After a few minutes, it was well clear of trouble and I pumped it closer to me to retrieve a little line, and then the main line just parted. There was no snagging, no sudden lunge, the line simply gave way. I was using Drennan Specimen Plus main line of 6lb, coupled with a 6lb Invisiline hook link, and it was the main line that had snapped. Suffice it to say that I was gutted, and when I subsequently found that the line was breaking at little over 3lbs I cursed my luck long and hard. Despite my precautions, I had refilled my spools obviously from a suspect batch. Crestfallen, I started the long walk back to the van to pick up some new line.

Back at the van, I did some more testing, and found that not only had the line on the spool lost half its strength in a matter of days, the two bulk spools I had in reserve had also suffered the same fate. The only line I had that was reliable was the 10lb barbel spools, hardly the most delicate approach for chubbing, but I had little choice.

Maybe I was totally paranoid when I arrived back at my tackle, but I decided to carry out some tests on the 6lb Invisiline as well, and to my horror found that was breaking at around 4lb. Although it had given me no problems so far, my confidence had been shaken and so I went the whole hog and selected a 10lb Invisiline hooklink as well. Yes, I know, totally over the top for chubbing, but I couldn't have stood another big fish coming adrift.

I felt that I had made these tackle adjustments after the horse had bolted, so to speak, I cast out to the same spot, not expecting any further action for a while. I was therefore amazed when the tip was flying round barely two minutes later, and even more amazed when I hooked what was obviously another exceptional chub. With the security of the strong gear, I was grimly determined that nothing would go wrong this time, and I piled on the pressure from the off, dragging the fish from danger in short order. Despite the gear, the chub fought well, rocketing up and down in mid-river, but never really giving me any anxious moments. At last, it was ready for netting, and as I lifted it clear of the rushes I knew that my long wait for an Upper Ouse six pounder was over. As the scales settled on 6lb 3oz, I stood quite still for a moment, drinking it all in.

An hour later, a good friend of mine, Shaun Simpson, who had responded to my excited telephone call for a reliable photographer, stood beside me and together we admired the classic lines of a superb, unblemished Upper Ouse leviathan. In that moment, all the frustrations of the previous months were forgotten. I was even able to forgive Paul Fickling for pinching that seven pounder off me!

My Greatest Catch

I would like to end this chapter by describing what is undoubtedly the greatest catch of big chub I have ever taken, or am ever likely to take. On this most memorable morning, a bitingly crisp February morning in 2000, I arrived to find the trees cloaked with frost and the grass crackling underfoot. A quick look over the road bridge confirmed that the water clarity was perfect for crust fishing, which was very pleasing as, until then, the river that winter had been consistently too coloured for bread. The only negative was that the water temperature had fallen sharply since the previous week, now standing at only 38°F. Nevertheless, conditions still looked reasonable for chub and I was full of expectation. When the water becomes very cold, I always find it has the least detrimental effect when bread fishing.

Given the lower than hoped for temperature, I decided to concentrate my efforts on one large swim, a thirty yard crease of steady water culminating in a very enticing far bank raft around draping alder branches. It was a swim I had caught chub from before and one in which I felt fish could be grouped under the prevailing conditions.

I followed what has become a common approach to my chubbing with crust, in that I commenced operations by introducing six large handfuls of mashed bread immediately on arrival, and then two smaller introductions every hour until midday, while I actually fished progressively down the crease. I would not contemplate fishing under the raft itself until early afternoon when, hopefully, any resident chub would be feeding hard.

In deference to the cold conditions, I did not want my hook bait too mobile, so elected a much shorter link than normal, of two inches of 6lb Invisiline.

This 6lb 5oz fish had a partly digested lamprey in its throat.

Bait was a good chunk of crust on a size 6. I would not be moving the hook bait as much as normal, the plan being to allow each bait to stay still where cast for ten minutes before placing the next cast a further five yards downstream and so on. Similarly, I varied my link weight, to allow presentation on an inside line, mid-river and far bank. Normally, the swim fishes best towards the far bank at the edge of the faster flow, but possibly the chub may have moved to my bank to find steadier water in view of the temperature drop.

At just after 8.30am, my first chub of the day was safely ensconced in the net. It weighed exactly three pounds. A modest start, which gave no clue to the dramatic events that were to unfold later. Over the following three hours, I covered every inch of that glide. I raised the interest of plenty of infant roach, and then, right at the base of the swim, static water tight under the near bank, a vicious pull preceded a tremendous scrap from a chunky chub which pulled the Avons to 5lb 2oz. A cracking fish to have in the bag any day. The significance was not lost on me that the bite had come from still water.

I was comfortably installed in the raft swim itself by early afternoon, casting above the debris and allowing the steady flow to take the crust under the leading edge. For two hours, I fished intently, periodically decreasing link weight and/or increasing bait size to try and drift it as far under the raft as possible, but all to no avail. By 3.00pm, I'd had not the slightest sign of a chub bite. But I knew they had to be there. My problem was that the raft was about ten yards long, upstream to downstream, and some four yards deep from the opposite bank. Perhaps the chub were tucked right under the downstream end, where it was impossible to drift a bait and still achieve a good presentation. If I fished light enough to get the bait where I wanted it, the mid-river flow pulled it out of position.

5lb 13oz fish taken on a cold winter night.

So I stopped fishing for ten minutes and considered the problem. Getting off my seat, I walked downstream so that I was opposite the bottom edge of the raft. Actually upstreaming the bottom edge was impossible because of the geography of the swim and a whole mass of fallen branches that would have made snagging inevitable. However, about two yards up from the downstream extremity there was a small gap in the outer branches and a patch of clear water beyond which was not covered by dead rushes and other debris. The water at that point was barely moving and I knew immediately that was where I had to position the bait.

That was easier said than done as a very difficult cast was involved to propel the bait through a gap in branches no more than eighteen inches wide to land at least a yard beyond them into the slack area. I also had to consider that the intervening current must not then pull the bait out of position by current action on the line, so I changed my light lead for a three quarter ounce flattened bomb. Once in position, the bait would stay where it was cast until I, or a chub moved it.

At the third attempt, my bait sailed perfectly into the required area, and I paid a little line out as I moved back to my upstream sitting position, so that a shallow line angle would assist in keeping the bait in position. Within ten minutes, my change of tactics was vindicated. A savage plunge on the tip was followed by a spectacular battle with a chub that went wild on feeling the hook. Several times it took line as it continually dived under the branches, but I was able to keep it out of snags and eventually gain the ascendancy. As it folded into the net I was convinced I had a six pounder, but the scales stubbornly settled on 5lb 14oz. What a magnificent creature it was, perfect in every fin and scale, short, deep and as fat as a little pig.

Feeling very pleased with a difficult day that had produced two fives, I did not imagine what was still to come. At 4.00pm, back in my little slack, another good pull heralded the arrival of my fourth chub and third five pounder of the day. This one weighed 5lb 6oz, and when that was followed half an hour later by another giant fish of 5lb 11oz I had taken four five pound chub in a day, in fact in only about five hours, the first time I had ever achieved that feat.

However, there was still one act of the drama to unfold.

In the gathering dusk, the frost was starting to bite once again and I was contemplating calling it a day much earlier than usual, when there was a small jab

Trefor baiting the Bristol Avon.

12lb 2oz from the Ouse, on red strawberry corn.

Truly magnificent 13lb 3oz specimen.

Pristine 13 pounder.

12lb 6oz from the Ouse, on boilie.

A unique shot - 9lb 12oz, 10lb 3oz, 11lb 11oz.

Exactly 10lb of green beauty.

One awesome tench - 11lb 11oz.

on the quivertip followed by a very determined plunge. I was in business again and completely in fitting with the size of the chub, the fight was special. Rather than trying to tie me in the branches, as the others had done. This one shot out of the cover into the main flow and then rocketed downstream, taking ten yards of line against the clutch. It is not often a chub does that to me against a fairly tight clutch setting. Using the current to full advantage, the chub continued to battle, more in keeping with an average barbel than a chub. Eventually, a long shape surfaced and although I could see it was not as deep as the 5lb 14oz fish earlier, I knew immediately it was a six pounder. And so it proved. Of all the fish taken that day, that one was probably in the poorest condition, having quite a pronounced scar on its right flank, and it was certainly a lot leaner looking than the five pounders. At 6lb 2oz, I certainly was not complaining, but I would love to have made that fish's acquaintance when it was in its prime. In the same condition as the 5lb 14oz fish, that chub could have gone close to seven.

So there you have it, six chub on large chunks of bread crust on a bitterly cold day, a catch which included four five pounders and a six pounder. Chub fishing does not come much better than that!

Orchid Delight

In the summer of 1996 it had been four years since I had enjoyed any serious carp fishing, and one of my targets was a carp to beat my relatively modest British best of 27lb 4oz. At the time, my good friend Marsh Pratley had not long purchased the fabulous Orchid Lakes, and I had a long standing invitation to sample the wonderful carp fishing they had to offer.

On a June morning of my first visit, over a gallon of tea, Marsh showed me mouth watering photographs of some of the giant fish that had been taken in the previous few weeks, and two in particular impressed me. One was the famous common called Arnie, just over 35lb at the time and now sadly no longer with us, and the other was a chunky Italian mirror of 32lb 4oz. My remark at the time that "either of those will do," was quite profound in the light of subsequent events.

After giving me a comprehensive guided tour of the water, Marsh advised that there had been consistent carp activity in recent days around the beds of lilies along the left hand bank, in front of a swim known as the Island Dug Out. This was where I was soon erecting my temporary home.

A matter of only feet out from the bank to the left of the swim was the right hand extremity of the substantial lily bed, while open water straight out and to the right would allow an unhindered cast to the edge of the large island, about sixty yards out.

There are good stalking swims at Orchid.

My initial plan of action was to fish a boilie on the right, but to fish corn under a lift float just over the edge of the pads on the left, about two rod lengths out. Having prebaited the boilie swim with about a hundred Frankfurter Sausage boilies, and the lily pads with four pints of hemp and a tin of Pescaviva

Owner, Marsh Pratley with an 18 pounder.

banana flavoured corn, I leisurely set up camp.

It was around lunchtime before I was finally relaxing behind my rods in the warm sun. I had a fresh cup of tea in my hand, watching the Drennan crystal waggler riding serenely alongside the lilies, with an ear cocked for the Optonic on the second rod. Two hours passed uneventfully, and then an impressive carpet of frothy bubbles rose around the float. Tench, obviously, and soon the float sailed away as a three and a half pounder found two grains of flavoured corn irresistible.

During the next three hours there were myriad lifts and knocks on the float but no more positive bites, and, obviously, the coarse carp gear, consisting as it did of 14lb line and a size 4 hook, was not exactly conducive to delicate presentation. By 5.00pm, with just the one tench landed, I knocked off for an hour and it was back to the van for a steaming curry.

Back at the swim an hour later, I introduced more hemp and corn, and this fresh baiting seemed to turn the swim on. No more than ten minutes later there were bubble patches all over the swim, and I had a mental image of a great gang of tench in a feeding frenzy. However, despite the obvious activity in front of me, the float did not move for half an hour.

At around 6.30, I made a promised mobile phone call to my wife, and not long after we started talking the float gave a little dip, and then slid away with great purpose. As I struck with my free hand, there was an explosion of spray under the pads, the rod hammered over and an obviously big carp shot through the lilies. Yelling down the phone to Fran that I'd call her back, I tossed it onto the bedchair, and gave battle with the unseen monster snarling through the aquatic undergrowth to my left.

The Pads.

My first action was to cram on every ounce of pressure possible to prevent the carp getting deeper into the foliage. A short stalemate followed, and then, grudgingly, the carp yielded, before surging from under the pads and heading out for open water at top speed. As the fish had turned, I had caught a tantalising glimpse of a deep flank and knew that I was certainly playing a twenty plus mirror.

Being conscious of my second rod, I applied maximum left hand sidestrain to prevent the two lines tangling, in which I was successful. In a last effort to outmanoeuvre me, the big mirror turned abruptly, and shot back towards the bank and ploughed at speed under the marginal vegetation almost at my feet. Once again I was forced to clamp down on the fish to prevent it snagging me in the tangle of branches and brambles. With the rod bent alarmingly, the fish was forced back into open water and out of danger.

Disaster almost struck during the netting. I could see my hook in the corner of the carp's mouth and then the fish rolled right over the float and hooklink, pulling the hook out. The carp was momentarily lassoed, but luckily was now over the mesh and I was able to quickly lift the net and engulf my prize.

Only when I peeled the folds of net back did I realise quite how big the fish was, and then, suddenly, Andy Little stood beside me. I hadn't even known he was there, but he had tactfully remained silent during the battle so as not to distract me.

"I reckon that'll go thirty," he said, and after extracting the hook from where it had lodged in the gill plate, I confirmed his diagnosis. The fish was the big Italian mirror, at an impressive 33lb 2oz. At that point, Andy was a tremendously calming influence, and I am eternally grateful to him for the superb photographs he took of one of the highlights of my angling career to date.

A little later, with the carp safely returned, I couldn't resist going down to Marsh and saying, "Right, I've had the Italian, what else do you want me to catch?"

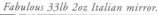
Fabulous 33lb 2oz Italian mirror.

There is quite an amusing, or sad, postscript to this story, which demonstrates quite how one-dimensional some carp anglers are in regard to bait, not using anything else but boilies. I was relating the story of the capture to another angler nearby, and he asked me what it had been taken on. I replied quite honestly that I had used float fished flavoured corn in the margins. "Bugger me," he said. "Who'd have thought that big carp would take sweetcorn!"

More Barbel Bits

A Wensum Double

Of all the venues I've fished in my big fish career, the only one where I can honestly say that I do not believe I caught the big fish my efforts warranted was the River Wensum, as far as barbel were concerned. My record there in some ways is quite amazing. Whereas most other anglers who fished for the barbel saw one fish  in three being in double figures, I only ever caught one double, and I took over sixty Wensum barbel in my years on the river. However you slice it, I can justifiably claim to have been unlucky.

You will not be surprised to learn, therefore, that that fish meant an awful lot to me, and that the details of its capture are permanently etched in my memory. Let me take you back to early September 1987.

I had arrived at the syndicate stretch on Thursday morning, and for once had got my timing about right. We'd had the first flood of the autumn and the river was two feet up but fining down nicely. I had fished the stretch the previous week, and although I had taken a couple of seven pounders, I had been driven mad by the eels, a seemingly inexhaustible supply of which had been devouring my meat baits as soon as they hit bottom. I had therefore been working on a new bait at home, and had devised a paste with no meat content whatever, consisting of shortcrust pastry and crushed hemp, set in gelatine so that it could be cubed.

It was early evening before I was ready to make my first cast with this new bait, and I settled into one of my favourite swims, known as The Copse, and swung out an inch cube to rest in the small mid-river depression. I couldn't have scripted it better. Obviously, I needed a bite on the bait quickly to give me confidence in it, and that is exactly what happened. Within five minutes of that first cast, I was returning a 4lb 10oz chub to the river. It wasn't a barbel, but if chub found the bait to their liking, the barbel would also.

A second chub quickly followed, after which there was a quiet period before I moved downstream a few yards into a swim I called the Long Glide. As dusk slowly settled over the Wensum valley, the rod suddenly flew off the rest and I found myself attached to a muscular barbel which proved to weigh just over six pounds. Two more of similar weight followed quickly and then the swim went dead. Half an hour later, I was on the move again, this time settling into the bottom swim, but to no avail. After a biteless twenty minutes, I decided to try meat, and was immediately pestered by eels. Back on the hemp bait the eel bites stopped and I was really pleased to have found a solution to that particular problem.

Well after midnight, with no more fish landed, I was seriously knackered, and decided to call it a night. Before doing so, I introduced a few baits into several swims for the next day, and then set off for the car park.

That night featured one of the most amusing incidents I can recall in Norfolk. The farmer on whose land the syndicate water was located had given us permission to use a car park access down a very quiet country lane. You entered through a rickety old farm gate and drove into a small area bordered by a tiny side stream. Next to the hard standing was a small, raised foot bridge, across which was the pathway to the river, about fifty yards away. That pathway led through reeds and shrubs well over head height, it was literally a mini jungle.

I knew my way along the banks of the river and through that dense vegetation like the back of my hand and never used a torch to light the way. A torch impairs your general night vision.

I came along that path in the early hours with everywhere as quiet as the grave, only lighting my way with the bright beta light on my rod top. As I neared the edge of the undergrowth, and the little foot bridge, I noticed a faint glow in front of me and as I drew closer I could see that it was a car, gently rocking backwards and forwards. I obviously don't need to draw you a picture. This car was parked adjacent to the bridge, whereas my van was at the other end of the car park, behind the hedge, out of sight of the road. Quite conceivably, the young couple in the car would have been unaware it was there.

As I stepped onto the bridge, there was a blood curdling scream, and then the car engine started, before the vehicle screeched through the gate on two wheels. I heard it howling down the road like a bat out of hell. Then, I drew up the mental image of what the young lady must have seen. In the blackness, there had suddenly appeared a mysterious, disembodied, eerie green glow, getting closer and closer. And then, a terrifying dark figure had materialised from nowhere, like the creature from the black lagoon!.

The more I thought about it, the funnier it became. I have no idea to what stage their lovemaking had progressed, but I tell you one thing. I bet the withdrawal method has never been used as rapidly as it was that night!

Next morning, I could see that the river had dropped an inch or two and quite honestly, if I couldn't catch barbel today, I never would. I spent a good part of the morning wandering from swim to swim, topping up the bait and doing work here and there, removing little branches that could impede me after dark, that kind of thing. Although I fished a few hours in the afternoon, it was not particularly serious stuff, and it was not until after my evening meal at 5.00pm that I moved in to my first prepared barbel swim, the copse once more. Again, I was greeted with an instant confidence booster, in the shape of an eight pound barbel, but that was to be the one and only bite for several hours.

Sunset on the Wensum.

Well after dark, I made a decision on impulse to cross the river and go right downstream almost to the disused railway bridge. There was a swim there that looked a classic in high water, but which I couldn't get to from the syndicate bank. Accessing this swim was a major hassle. I had to walk back to the car park, actually away from where I was heading, out on to the lane, down the lane half a mile, over the railway bridge and up the other side, with my gear, in the dark and drizzle. I felt I must be mad, but the old instincts were giving me grief, as they have so often in my angling career.

It was probably forty minutes before I was settled into the swim I wanted, but it looked perfect and I knew something special was going to happen. It was very easy to fish. The striking feature was a pronounced crease that emanated on the near bank, right under my feet, and then progressed across the stream, along the path of the natural bay and cattle drink that is evident at normal height. Fishing the swim was a breeze, all I had to do was lower a bait under the rod top.

After half an hour, progressively fishing down the crease, thoroughly absorbed in what I was doing, I was suddenly distracted by movement on the bridge, about forty yards away. There was now a bright moon, and the activity on that structure was captured in stark relief. I saw a man climb up onto the top of the safety rails, and balance there precariously for a while, before getting back down, undress, and then climb right over to stand on the narrow ledge between the rails and the edge of the bridge. Remember, this was 30 feet above a flooded, cold river, at night. I watched, fascinated, not believing what I was seeing. Slowly, he lowered himself off the side of the parapet until he was dangling by his hands, when he started to swing backwards and forwards.

Just as I started to realise that the man might seriously be contemplating suicide, the line, which was loosely crooked over the index finger of my right hand, gave a sudden vicious tug, the rod plunged round, and the clutch screamed. A big barbel powered away upstream with great purpose, straight into marginal rushes, where it stuck fast. As I tried to heave it clear, it came to the surface, rolled, and luckily came free before racing across river. In that brief glimpse in the moonlight, I knew I had my double at last. I had waited a long time for this moment, nothing must go wrong.

Although the fish fought hard for a good ten minutes after that, I felt in control during the entire proceedings, and it was a gratifying moment when the net closed, at long last, around a Wensum double. Trefor had taken many doubles from the river, including twelve pounders, but none of them could have felt any sweeter than this. The important weighing ceremony having confirmed 10lb 5oz, I then broke out my tripod and camera, finding to my extreme annoyance that the flash gun had been left in the van. After debating the issue with myself for a while, knowing that I faced a mammoth walk to fetch and return with the flash gun, I decided to go for it. If I didn't get photographs of my only Wensum double, I would always regret it. After carefully sacking the fish, therefore, I set off on the long hike back to the van, first making my way downstream to the bridge.

And then I remembered the man doing the Tarzan impressions. There was no sign of him, and when I crossed the bridge myself, there were no signs of any clothes either. Presumably, he changed his mind about jumping in, if that was his intention. Whatever the truth of the matter, it was very odd. There are, without doubt, some strange people about.

It was a good hour before I arrived back at my gear, and half an hour later, photographs taken, the fish was returned and I was on my way back to the van, to make the long drive home. I was obviously delighted with the night's work.

I know we've all heard the one about the angler claiming to have caught a big fish and then saying that the photographs didn't come out. Yes, I'm always as sceptical as you. In the case of my one and only Wensum double, however, that is exactly what happened. When I received the film back, all the shots taken of that fish were blank, although the rest of the film was fine. I was gutted, even having bought a new flash gun for the occasion. Puzzled, I retrieved the gun and camera from my gear, and suddenly my mistake dawned on me. For years, I had used a disposable bulb flash gun, and now I had an electronic, automatic version. I checked the camera and, sure enough, it was not set for synchronisation for electronic flash. What a stupid error. I know I have caught dozens of barbel bigger than 10lb 5oz, but that particular ten pounder means a lot to me. I would dearly love to have a picture of it.

Floodwater Barbel

The reputation that barbel have for fighting hard is well justified, and I have caught very few indeed that did not give me a good scrap. But, there are two fish that stand out in my memory as being truly exceptional although, as you will see, in both cases they had the assistance of very high floodwater. Let me go back first of all to March 1989, and the banks of the Bristol Avon at Lacock Abbey.

My final week of the season had actually begun on the Wensum, but the weather was clear and anticyclonic in Norfolk, in total contrast to the wet and windy conditions in the south west. After two days of relative struggle, I had been contacted by Trefor, via my wife, to tell me that the Avon was fishing its head off and that I should get down there. It made sense, and with four days of the season to go, I set off on the 200 mile trip across country.

When I finally joined Trefor in the car park at Lacock, he told me that the river was carrying at least six feet of floodwater, but it was warm for March and the barbel were having it. He'd had an 11lb 10oz fish that morning, which I was pleased to be able to photograph for him, together with a ten pounder he'd caught while he was awaiting my arrival.

After a cup of tea and bite to eat, we set off on a reconnaissance down a stretch of river I'd never before seen. It was already late afternoon, and the look round was sketchy in the extreme, not that I was able to glean too much information about the normal river configurations. Trefor obviously acquainted me with the normal swims, but fishing tonight would have to largely disregard that. I would fish to

Trefor with a Wensum 12 pounder.

appropriate flow, and smoothness of flow, features, which might be, and probably were, in totally different areas from the normal hot spots.

Thinking back on it, fishing my first session on the Bristol Avon, in a high flood, at night, was stupid. I'd ignored one of the most basic safety rules of the lot, which is, know your river before night fishing. As it was, I got away with it, but I was lucky.

I had arrived at this high, sloping bank, and could see in the moonlight a smooth surface under the near bank, turbulence on the far bank and a patently obvious crease between the two in mid river. The inside line screamed barbel, and I wasted no time in propelling a good chunk of meat into midstream, and then working it round under the near bank. It was taken on the roll, a good thump heralding the arrival of a barbel which turned out to weigh 7lb 14oz. As I stood up to play the fish after setting the hook, my feet went from under me on the slippery bank, and I found myself sliding down the wet grass into the river. Luckily, there were a few tough clumps of gorse below me, and one of these halted my descent. How it held firm against my weight I'll never know, but thank God it did. Inch by inch, I was able to dig my heels into the bank, until I had formed a little, secure step from where I was able to land the fish.

Next morning, I was to discover that swim was the best part of twelve feet deep, counting the floodwater, and moving like a train. Had I gone in, dressed in heavy winter thermals, I would have been in serious trouble.

That day, I spent many hours assessing the river conditions, and establishing swims I fancied, simply by studying the flows. Interestingly, Trefor informed me that all but one of the areas I picked were recognised swims, the one exception normally being only inches deep. It was this latter swim that was to produce the highlight of the night.

When I arrived at it, in the early hours of the morning, I was in very contented mood, already having landed seven barbel, although nothing big had hit my net. Carefully moving into position to the left of the stick marker I had put in position in daylight, I gently swung out my meat bait just beyond mid-river, where I knew was a gentle glide below a submerged weed bed of indeterminate pedigree. For ten minutes, fifteen, I waited, at peace with the world. Nothing stirred, no sounds disturbed my concentration, and then, without warning, the rod doubled over.

Seconds after the strike, the buzz from the clutch rose to a high pitched whine. That fish was really moving, and I do mean motoring. I have never known, before or since, a barbel move so fast. I must have lost fifteen yards to the initial dash, and then there followed an arm aching wrestling match for what seemed an eternity. It took me perhaps ten minutes to win back the line I lost until the fish was circling deep under the rod top. But it simply refused to come off the bottom. The more I bent into it, the more stubborn it became, and after another ten minutes my right wrist was really painful. The fish would insist on making sorties downstream in the fastest flow, so that I had to pump it back against the heavy current.

As the minutes passed I started to have visions of twelve pounders, so it therefore came as a surprise when I eventually landed a comparatively ordinary sized fish. Even on the bank, it wanted to fight me, but eventually it calmed long enough for me to confirm 9lb 2oz, not an exceptional weight by any means, but certainly an exceptional fish in every other way.

Elsewhere in this book, I have described the events leading up to my long awaited first double figure barbel from the Great Ouse, and this eventually materialised in the summer of 1994, in the shape of a 10lb 13oz fish. My second Ouse double was to come calling in November of that year, on a night when there was one fishable swim on a stretch of river swollen by almost eight feet of raging floodwater.

My heart had sunk as I surveyed the Ouse after my long drive from Coventry, but the more I looked at it, the more convinced I became that one swim could be

Trefor with lovely 12lb 12oz fish from the Bristol Avon.

I had a spectacular battle with this 23lb Ouse carp on special barbel bait.

a real hot spot in the prevailing conditions. It was an area of normally zero interest, a stagnant bay with no flow, off the main push of the stream. All that could be caught normally were small roach and perch, and the swim was popular with club anglers who did not like coping with the current, but were content to fish for bits with very light float gear.

The flood had transformed this swim. The demarcation between the raging main flow and the gentler inside line was now quite close in to the near bank, where it was normally almost on the far bank. Obviously, the very tall upstream rush beds had been flattened by the heavy current and high water, so that the flow had been more centralised, but the vegetation was still holding back and diverting the main push, leading to the steady, smooth flow I was now examining. It looked perfect. In the conditions facing me, I could well believe many barbel and chub taking up residence here, out of the fiercest flow.

That night, I fished through appalling weather conditions. Sometimes the rain was heavy, sometimes torrential, but it was uncannily warm for November and with a water temperature over fifty Fahrenheit I knew the conditions were good. Dusk came and went, as did a couple of washed out looking chub, but at midnight I'd still had no sign of a barbel. But I had not the slightest intention of packing up. I knew there had to be barbel there, it was just a matter of time.

By 1.00am, my eyes were drooping, but I was determined to fish through till dawn, so I decided to stop fishing for half an hour, go back to the van for a hot meal and fresh tea, and then come back refreshed. This involved climbing a muddy two hundred yard steep hill in the rain, so let no one tell me I didn't deserve the fish I was later to catch.

By 2.00 I was back on the case, fresh as a daisy, and ten minutes later it was Show Time. The rain had stopped at last, a fitful moon was peeping through gaps in the clouds, and then the rod took on a life of its own. Following a ferocious jerk of the line on my finger, which almost sliced it open, the rod bent round to the butt. I struck and, to quote Dick Walker, it was like hitting a sandbag. The fish just never budged. More and more I bent the rod, and not one inch of line was gained. It was as if the fish was saying, "right, now what are you going to do?"

This weird stalemate perhaps lasted four minutes, before the fish suddenly woke up to the fact that someone had actually dared hook it. It started off for midstream, not fast, just irresistibly powerfully, the classic sign of an extra big barbel. I don't know how long I played that barbel, but it must have been twenty minutes or more, and in all that time it never took more than a few feet of line. But I couldn't win any either, and every time one of those heavy thumps came on the rod top I feared for my hook hold. This barbel was testing the gear for weaknesses.

Even when I landed the fish, I don't think it was beaten. I think it was bored, because it was brimming with energy when I secured it in my Queenford sack in readiness for the dawn.

That superbly conditioned barbel weighed 11lb 6oz and is, without doubt, one of the most beautifully proportioned fish I've ever taken.

Boilies and Crashing Takes

Following on from our bait experiments in the 1997/98 season, Matthew Bodily and I conducted an intensive campaign on a stretch of the Ouse from June 1998, with a new bait designed along the lines suggested by a very successful carp angling friend. It featured a high quality base mix, with low flavour level, and Matthew would introduce it sparingly for the two weeks prior to the season, and from then on the baiting would consist of the unused hookbaits being introduced as we were leaving after a fishing session. As Matthew was fishing up to four times a week, the baiting was very regular.

We had elected boilies from the off, largely to combat the large bream population on the middle Ouse, and from the first cast on June 16th the results were, quite simply, awesome. I won't bore you with a long list of statistics, but that bait just took the river apart. In one season, Matthew had over twenty double figure barbel, as well as a stack of lesser fish, from a not particularly prolific stretch, and no less than 35 chub over five pounds, with six over 6lb. Compared to Matthew's spectacular achievements, my results were comparatively modest, as I fished the bait very little in comparison. I was doing other things much of the time but keeping a close eye on developments. But one of my sessions that is

Special high protein bait took this nine pounder.

unforgettable is a night in a swim called The Point, which is where I took my first ever Ouse barbel.

The point is not known for producing bags of fish, but is generally reliable for a chub and perhaps a barbel in an average night. The first night I used our new boilies there, I had thirteen chub, including no less than twelve four pounders and one five, a quite astonishing average. On my second session with the bait, I had from one swim barbel of eight and nine pounds, two four pound chub and a 24lb mirror carp in two hours. Obviously, the bait was working.

The knowledge of bait and bait application gained in 1998, for a long term food bait, has, I believe, given me knowledge that will revolutionise my fishing for ever. As I write this chapter, August 2000, Matthew has taken the principles to another stretch of the Ouse. It is not overly dramatic to say that he is taking it apart; the catches so far are mind blowing. I am sworn to secrecy at the moment, so will say no more, but when he gives me permission to release details of the current campaign, the statistics will be found to be, quite simply, staggering.

But, back to my own fishing, and continuation of the learning curve in the summer of 1999.

I had decided to take the baiting principles to Adams Mill, knowing that the one technique I could not employ there was pre-baiting. It was too far from home, and too popular to make it viable. I wanted to see whether those ultra spooky, ultra educated barbel would succumb to the baits.

The 1998 bait had been very low flavour dosage, a deliberate ploy for a long term bait with regular topping up. But, at Adams, I could not arrange regular topping up. I gave it a lot of thought, and in the end decided on the same bait in principle, but doubling the flavour level. The fishing at Adams Mill demanded a more instant attract bait. The first session was encouraging, the fishing progressing in a way that gave me exactly the information I required.

In July 1999, I arrived at the river at the appointed hour and, luckily, was first there and had my choice of swims. I knew where I wanted to be, and settled into a secluded little copse, opposite a tangle of trees on the opposite bank, under which was a favourite hiding place for barbel. I would not be fishing for three hours. The first act was to introduce a dozen of my boilies, as tasters. I didn't want to overdo it, I wanted the fish to be on the look out for more.

There is little more to say about the day, because precisely nothing happened. Not a twitch. However, I was half expecting that, and, before leaving the swim at dusk, I introduced a further twenty baits, hoping against hope I could get the swim again the following morning.

In that, I was successful and I know it sounds terribly arrogant after the event, but the day went exactly as I thought it would. After about two hours fishing, I had my first pull, a savage affair that produced a modest fish of 8lb 4oz, and then, an hour later, I was on my feet heaving a cracking barbel from under the far bank trees. This was a beautiful barbel which had been nicknamed Teardrops by Adrian Busby, on account of two marks under its left eye that look for all the world like tears. Teardrops took the scales to 13lb 3oz and, fittingly, Adrian had arrived for a chat just in time to do the honours with the camera.

There was to be a third fish that day, in late afternoon, yielding another spectacularly conditioned Ouse fish of 12lb 6oz, to complete a superb brace.

At home later, I wrote down my thoughts. The bait had worked like a long term food bait, in that it had not produced on the first day, but had the second. With only two days a week to fish, prebaiting not being an option, and uncertainty over which swims might be available, I still needed to tweak the bait a bit more to arrive at the more instant attract version I was seeking. Consequently, on Sunday morning, I made another batch, re-doubling the flavour level once more.

The following Thursday, I was again lucky enough to secure the swim I wanted, and this time the first bite came only two hours after introducing twelve boilies on my arrival. Unfortunately, the fish responsible was lost when a Dacron hooklink chafed on branches and parted, but that was only a temporary upset as I went on that day to take fish of 13lb 1oz, 11lb 12oz, 7lb 8oz and 8lb 4oz. The next day, fishing the same swim, I had three others of 9lb 8oz, 9lb 14oz and 12lb 12oz. It

Returning a twelve pounder.

Trefor trundling meat down the Bristol Avon.

was all starting to come together, and I drove home on Friday night deep in thought. Those two sessions had took my learning on to another plane.

I must finish this chapter by telling you about the smallest fish I caught that session, the 7lb 8oz fish. All anglers know about the legendary smash and grab bites that barbel can give at times. They would pull the rod in if you let them. But that seven pounder was a bit special. As always, I was fishing with the rod butt on my knee, the top supported by a rest, and my hand loosely round the reel seat, the line over my index finger. Nothing had happened for a while, and I decided to have a cup of tea from my flask, which was standing by my right calf. Leisurely, I enjoyed my tea and, cup drained, I momentarily released the reel seat while I picked up the flask and screwed the cup back on. At that precise moment, the rod butt flew up with such force it catapulted the flask in the river, and then the rod took off, literally, heading for the downstream trees. I leapt out of my chair, making a grab for the butt, and just managed to grab the butt cap. The force of the bite, however, sheared the cap straight off and I had to jump in the river to catch the rod, which was rapidly disappearing downstream. It took me several minutes to gain any kind of control, with a demented barbel whistling all over the swim, and I was dumbfounded when I eventually confirmed the actual size of the fish.

How the hell do barbel generate that kind of speed on the bite from a standing start. It's a mystery to me but I tell you what, it's one of the main reasons they're one of my favourite fish.

Tench - The Later Years

Since my early tenching exploits in the sixties, you could say that my tench fishing has come full circle. My early forays were all geared to the Midland reservoirs, and tench were taken from Napton Reservoir, near Coventry, plus other waters such as Clattercote, Boddington, Welford and Sulby. Those reservoirs were then superb mixed fisheries and I caught tench from all of them without taking a big one or any particularly interesting catches. As an aside, today's young anglers will not be allowed to follow the same path. Apart from the Coventry & District AA water of Napton, which is still a good mixed fishery, the other mentioned waters have been ruined by British Waterways' policy of raping good mixed fisheries to turn them into grossly overstocked carp holes. But, I digress.

In the mid seventies, Trefor and I had progressed to Sywell Reservoir, near Northampton, searching for that first elusive six pounder but, as you will read in the chapter on TC Tench, quickly moved on when the incredible tench fishing at that Oxfordshire gravel pit came to our attention. In the next seven years, TC occupied my time, taking my personal best tench to 7lb 13oz, but then, in 1984, my blossoming friendship with Alastair Nicholson led me to the banks of not only Queenford Lagoon for giant bream but also Deans Farm, near Reading. I was only ever to fish two sessions at Deans, but they were to take my tench fishing up another gear.

From 1984 until the early nineties, I was to do very little serious tench fishing, my summers being taken up increasingly with carp and barbel, but in 1991 a water I had long been associated with for its superb winter roach fishing, Stanford Reservoir, started producing a few tench of very interesting sizes. I was to have my first serious sortie there for the tench in July 1991 and by 1993 it was obvious that we had an exceptional tench water on our hands. That is the tench water I am still involved with today, so now, nearly forty years on, I am back where I started, fishing a Midland reservoir. But, before I tell you about the incredible events of the last few years, let me first look back at the summer of 1984, and take you to the banks of Deans Farm.

Deans Farm

I first met Alastair Nicholson in March 1983, when I called in on him at home on the way back from a Cherwell barbel session. During an earlier telephone conversation, he had mentioned a water he was fishing which had produced several tench over nine pounds in weight and had, obviously, whetted my appetite more than somewhat.

I spent several hours with Alastair, and during that time he showed me many slides of the incredible tench he and his friends had caught over the previous two seasons. One of the slides was of a face I recognised instantly, Eric Edwards from Merseyside, who had broken the tench record the previous summer from an undisclosed water with a fish of just over ten pounds, the first double figure fish ever recorded. Immediately, I put two and two together and then Alastair showed me another slide of Eric holding a massive tench, on the back of which was the caption, "Eric's ten pound tench - Deans Farm"

At the time, I thought it might be just carelessness on Alastair's part that had blown the secret of the new record tench venue to me, but in fact it was quite deliberate. He had information that the following summer could be the last when the brilliant tench fishing they had known would be enjoyed. The water was being developed as a Marina, involving cutting through to the adjacent River Thames, after which the area where the best of the tench action had occurred would be out of bounds. Alastair said, and I believed him, that he wanted to give access to the water to me and Trefor to see what we could extract from it.

With that background, Trefor and I planned an early season assault at Deans, but events transpired to delay my own first session. I found out during the close season that I had to be in Greece on business on the 16th June for a few days, and Trefor started at Deans on his own. It would be ten days before I could join him. Those ten days were very hard work for Trefor, and he never managed one tench. There were precious few tench caught on the entire lake, although Eric did manage a solitary fish of nine pounds, and Trefor had formed the definite opinion that the head of fish was very low.

I remember well how pent up I was as I joined him at dawn after my return home. I was expecting to hear exciting news and couldn't comprehend that Trefor was still on a blank.

After we'd had a good look round together, I told him that I'd have chosen exactly the same area to start operations. It was fairly shallow, with three parallel bars out in the lake, and a perfect set up for when the fish began spawning, which they hadn't at that time. The only thing I felt I would do differently was fish on the crest of the bars, rather than in a trough as Trefor told me he was doing. Two hours later, I had made up my mind and set up about forty yards to Trefor's right for a three day session.

The next job was to identify where I would be placing my baits, and half an hour's probing about on my inflatable boat soon identified two prime areas. The three bars I mentioned ran parallel with the bank, one at about twenty yards, one at fifty and the last at about eighty. I decided to ignore the farthest and concentrate my efforts on the other two. When I examined the features closely, I became more convinced that I did not want to be fishing the gullies between the bars. Unlike other pits I have fished, these gullies were completely devoid of weed, other than a thickly weeded marginal area no more than ten yards out from the bank. The

A six and two eights from Deans Farm.

bar crests, however, had a fine coating of silkweed, and I was as convinced as I could be that any visiting tench would probably browse these areas in preference.

This thinking was strongly reinforced when I found a large oval of sparkling clean gravel on the shallowest part of the nearer bar, barely three feet deep. This was so uniform I felt it likely to have been caused by browsing fish, and on this spot my first marker float was placed. To hedge my bets, I then looked for similar clues on the second bar, and although I never found anything so glaringly obvious, I did fancy a sparsely weeded section of this bar, where a definite hump made this also about three feet deep, whereas the bar was generally about five feet down. My second marker float was brought into play.

In early evening, it was time to bait up and each area was baited with half a large bucket of yellow breadcrumbs laced with maple crème flavour, plus two handfuls of chopped lobworms, the intended hookbait. You may be interested in my choice of free feed. I knew from Alastair and indeed from Trefor's first ten days that the head of tench was meagre, and as the pit was large, I believe in excess of eighty acres, I felt I needed good attraction in my bait to lure the fish on to it. Visually, I had found yellow to be a great tench attractant from my TC fishing, while I felt the pungent aroma of maple crème could be helpful. I wanted the loose feed to be difficult to ignore, if you like.

The next morning dawned bright and sunny, as most of that early summer did, but my alarms remained stubbornly silent. In fact, there was no sign in front of me that there was any fish within a hundred yards. I was, therefore, delighted when Trefor had some action at last, it was certainly no more than he deserved. In quick succession in, he landed tench of 5lb and 6lb 15oz, but that was a little oasis of activity because a further 24 hours were to pass before anything else happened.

On the Friday morning, I was up and about well before dawn. It was so warm and humid I couldn't sleep, and just as the first hint of light was appearing in the eastern sky, I sat quietly, enjoying the first cup of tea of the day, contemplating the glassy stillness of the lake in front of me. I could just about make out my marker floats in the half light, and then I saw, quite distinctly, the unmistakable profile of a tench dorsal slicing through the surface film right alongside the nearer marker. Instantly, I was alert.

Ten minutes passed, by which time it was fully light, and then the Optonic gave a single bleep, and the bobbin trembled. That was the first sign I'd had since arriving at the water 48 hours previously. There was a second bleep, a little jump of the bobbin, and my hand hovered over the rod butt. I didn't have much longer to wait. Moments later, the bobbin rose steadily to the butt and I struck, hard and far back,

Creating a new tench swim.

and connected with a heavy resistance kiting to my right. For a good five minutes, that fish pulled and bored, battling every inch of the way, but there were no anxious moments and soon I was folding the net mesh back to examine my first tench from Deans Farm. At first glance, I knew it would be close to a personal best, but when Trefor and I confirmed 8lb 4oz I was in a dream. I had been lucky. My summer target was 8lb, and to achieve this with my first fish on my first session was obviously fortunate. Trefor was full of congratulations, but he must have pondered on the injustice of it all.

Had that been the only action that morning, I would have had no complaints, but in fact it was only just beginning. About an hour later, the same rod was away again and this time the fish I hooked was exceptional. It came in to the marginal weed fringe easily enough, but then really started to battle. Twice it dived into the vegetation and stuck fast, but twice I was able to heave it clear, on the second occasion having a clear look at it as it rolled. Just as I thought I had the battle won, the hook simply dropped out. Obviously, the heaving and hauling had loosened the hook hold. To say I was gutted would be an understatement. The fish I had just lost made the one still reposing in my sack seem small. I knew I had just pulled out of a fish that could have exceeded ten pounds, even the record.

I did not have the luxury of being gutted for long. No more than ten minutes after the loss, the same rod was away yet again. That clean oval of gravel I had observed on my first day obviously had been significant. This third fish could not have provided a greater contrast to the one I had lost. It fought with little spirit, more or less allowing itself to be wound in. For that reason, I was fooled into thinking it was of average size only. Only when I lifted the net did I realise my mistake, and then I knew instantly that here was another eight pounder at least, it might even be nine. I shouted Trefor, and moments later we confirmed 8lb 14oz. This was becoming unreal. We were still admiring the fish when my other alarm sounded, and I was soon landing another good tench of 6lb 1oz to complete a quite remarkable sequence of action.

I have to say that I felt guilty that day, as Trefor deserved better fortune than he had. To rub salt into the wound, he had a good bite just after I had my six pounder, and proceeded to land one of the smallest tench caught at Deans in years, barely 3lb. But when the luck's against you, it's against you.

Those frantic few hours on Friday morning saw all the tench landed I was destined to catch, although I lost a further two fish by pulling out, neither for any reason I could find. Obviously, when I left Deans Farm on Saturday morning, I was well pleased with my first session and couldn't wait to return the following week.

My 8lb 14oz Deans Farm tench.

During the days that followed I analysed all the evidence from my first trip. Firstly, I knew I had made the right choice by fishing the shallow tops of the bars, but wondered why it had taken the best part of two days for the tench to home in on my feed. I thought about the colour and flavour, and decided to build on those principles by adding more maple crème flavour for the next session. I also thought about ways of achieving greater flavour dispersion, and hit upon the idea of incorporating a good quantity of dry sausage rusk in the loose feed mix. This would explode once it became water logged, hopefully blowing a cloud of flavoured particles far and wide, increasing the pulling power, I hoped!

On Thursday afternoon, I put these theories into operation, and within an hour had all the evidence I needed that I may be on the right track. Tench were rolling regularly over the markers, whereas I had not seen one tench actually roll on my first session. Despite the obvious activity in the swim, there were to be no bites that evening or in the dark hours, and nor did this change at dawn. It was almost mid-morning before the bobbin suddenly rocketed to the butt and the alarm shrilled. That was a lovely, clean, spawned out female of 7lb 2oz, closely followed by a 5lb male, and I had thoughts of a big catch of fish. But the swim died as quickly as it had burst into life and it was the early hours of the following morning before any other action occurred. In the space of four hours, my last three Deans Farm tench

were landed, two 5lb males and another good female of 7lb.

When I drove away from Deans Farm that morning, I didn't plan that to be my last session; far from it. In fact, I thought I was really starting to get somewhere, and an exceptionally big fish could be close. I don't know why I never went back, and certainly regret not doing so. It was not planned, it just happened, but I have always had the unshakeable conviction that, had I kept faith with Deans Farm that summer, I could have caught a fish to shake the tench world.

My First Nine Pounder

My first tench season at Stanford was in 1991, and I was to make several interesting observations about tench behaviour that differed completely from the gravel pit fish I had been accustomed to. First, I found that the traditional dawn start was once again very important, being a very reliable time, where this was not necessarily the case on pits. Second, night fishing was very unproductive. On gravel pits, especially in the TC days, I had taken many good tench in the dark, but at Stanford, although I did take two tench one night, I had much more chance of a good roach and a very high chance of rigs being wrecked by eels.

Third, and most fascinating, I found the tench tackle shy, even in early season. I will never forget on the 16th June 1991 sitting alongside a good friend, fishing the same feature, both of us blanking on 6lb hooklinks. Then John switched to 4lb and started catching regularly. Initially, I put it down to coincidence, but eventually I scaled down as well and the tench switched on immediately. Lastly, there was the question of bites. I had never had a problem with twitchy tench bites but the early experiences at Stanford were frustrating, with more bites being missed than was

good for me. Eventually, we were all on bolt rigs and short hooklinks, in conjunction with heavy butt indicators, with the main line taut. That set up converted all the bites to real screamers, for that season at least.

It took me a few sessions to get my head round all these factors, but then I started to catch good tench with satisfying regularity, taking in successive weeks 8lb 12oz and 8lb 14oz fish to first shake and then equal my best from Deans. I felt it just a matter of time before I caught a fish to exceed the new target of nine pounds, but the summer drew to a close with that dream unrealised.

Plans were drawn up for the start of the 1992 season, but Stanford is a very frustrating fishery as you are forever at the mercy of drinking water and irrigation demands. As we can only fish the shallow car park end of the reservoir, the bulk of the water being a SSSI and out of bounds to anglers, it is very common for there to be no water at the fishery end. Added to that, Severn Trent needed to de-silt the dam in the 1992 summer, which led to them drastically lowering the water level until the winter. All the fish were concentrated in a deep trench in the bird sanctuary area and our end was literally dry. I was forced to be patient until June 1993.

I was only a few hours into my first session on June 16th when a fresh subtle difference in the tench behaviour manifested itself. I had commenced with the bolt rig and heavy butt indicator arrangement that had served me so well two years previously, and from dawn until about 8.00am I had four real churning bites, yielding a 5lb male tench plus two belting females of 7lb 2oz and 8lb 11oz, as well as an unexpected opening day bonus in the shape of a 2lb 5oz roach. And then the bites just stopped, or at least I thought they did.

In the next two or three hours, I had several single bleeps, accompanied by trembling on the butt indicators, but certainly nothing positive to strike at. At least twice I had wound in to rebait and found crushed maggots and I was convinced tench were responsible. The first thing I changed was the hooklink, dropping it from six inches to three, and reducing from 4lb to 3lb mono, as well as substituting a size 16 hook for the 12 I had been using. That, however, made no difference and the annoying single bleeps continued. So then I tried a much lighter swimfeeder, coupling that with my lightweight bobbins rather than heavy drop arms, and that made all the difference. The next single bleep that occurred was followed by a steady crawl to the butt of the bobbin, and the answering strike met with the solid resistance of a scrappy 6lb male. The next three hours were followed by three more fish, including another big one of 8lb 8oz, and I felt that I had learned an extremely valuable lesson, which I have carried through to my present day tenching. At the really hot times of dawn and dusk, the bolt rig does produce screaming runs, but they soon fizzle out. The tench become more circumspect as the day wears on, and I then switch to light bobbins, which register good, hittable bites when the fish appear unwilling to move against undue resistance.

If that opening session of 1993 was a valuable learning exercise, the second saw the reward for that learning. I had arrived at dawn on Thursday morning and, working to a pre-arranged plan, attacked the swim initially with a gallon of scalded maggots and two pints of casters via my baiting cone, the cone being sealed with a small quantity of brown crumb flavoured with Tutti Frutti. To my knowledge, no one had yet gone for the big, particle bait carpet, and I was interested to see whether it would work quickly. With only two days to fish, I was conscious that I might well be preparing the ground for an angler to move in after me on day three, but I was willing to take that risk.

Baiting complete, I gave a lot of thought to my terminal rig. As I felt that the likelihood was that the tench would not feed for a while, I set up immediately with light, open ended feeders, and a 12" hooklink of 3lb mono to a size 14 Drennan Carbon Specimen, baited with two Tutti Frutti flavoured maggots. I would be using my light bobbins from the off, and after putting two baits in position, lit the kettle and settled back to wait.

The hours passed. As elsewhere around the lake the odd tench was being caught, I started to have doubts about my baiting programme. I knew it would work eventually, I just worried how long that would be. The sun rose high in the sky, and by about 9.30am it was warm and sunny, following the dissipation of the chilly early morning mist. I stared at the bobbins, willing them to move. Suddenly, one did. One second all was still and unmoving, the next my left hand reel was backwinding furiously as the tench galloped off with the bait.

The frenetic battle that followed told me immediately that I had hooked a big male, and I had to play it with kid gloves on my light hooklink. But there were no mistakes, and I was soon weighing a gorgeous fish of 6lb 2oz, with pelvic muscles like rocks.

That first fish opened the floodgates, and in the next few hours I was to take no fewer than nineteen tench, mostly males, but including females to a satisfying 8lb 2oz. That action continued right through until dusk, when the first eel put in an appearance, and I wound in for the night. Before crashing out, I set the alarm for dawn.

The next day, June 25th 1993, was indeed memorable. As daybreak approached, I could see tench breaking the surface near my markers regularly, and decided not to introduce any more loose feed initially. By 4.00am, two baits were in position, and no more than fifteen minutes later I had recorded two more lovely fish of 6lb 14oz and 7lb 13oz. What a start to the day!

After that heady spell, there then followed a quiet hour, and I decided to fire a few more cones of bait into the swim. It was as if I'd rung a dinner gong, because the next three hours saw a succession of good tench hit the bottom of my landing net, the best being yet another eight pounder at 8lb 7oz. I had about fifteen fish in that frenzied period, with several seven pounders.

At midday, having had no action for quite a while and being absolutely knackered into the bargain, I decided to have a break and a gentle walk back to the van to cook myself a hot chicken curry. I say a gentle walk. Actually, the area I was fishing involved a walk from the car park of just under a mile, which reminds me of a story that is funny to relate now, but was far from funny at the time. In the summer of 1991, I had arrived at daybreak for a three day session, and it took me a fair while to hump the gear round to the swim. As I had no trolley or wheelbarrow, and have not yet reached the wimp stage, it took me two trips to get the gear into position. The mathematicians among you will already have calculated that I had now walked the thick end of four miles. It was a humid morning, and I could not contemplate doing anything else until I had a brew. So, I broke out the kettle, tea bags, milk and then searched desperately for the water bottle. I'm sure you must have experienced that horrible, sinking feeling as well. Sure enough, my drinking water was still in the van, a mile away. As there is no way I will ever drink lake water, having seen a friend nearly die of Weil's disease, I had no alternative but to set off on another two mile hike.

On my return, every inch of my body was soaked in sweat, and I slumped on the ground, feet ablaze. After a moment to get my breath back, I filled the kettle, and opened my box of provisions to find the matches to light the gas stove. Then I remembered. I had used the last match the week before and had intended to get a fresh supply. The only light I had was an old cigarette lighter, and that was, you've guessed it, back in the van!

I did eventually get my cup of tea that morning, at about 7.00am, after arriving in the car park at 4.00am and then walking eight miles. And my wife reckons fishing's a lazy man's occupation!

After a much appreciated hot meal, and a pleasant chat to some of the syndicate members fishing the opposite bank, I was back at my tackle in mid-afternoon, and the first job was to fire in another couple of pints of dead maggots and casters. By 4.00pm, I was sitting peacefully behind two rods, not a care in the world, but just after 6.00pm I had undergone the extreme lows and highs that this sport of ours can

9lb 10oz fish from 1993.

provide, in the space of just ten minutes. Let me explain. At about 5.40pm, the bobbin suddenly shot off the line and I set the hook into a slow and ponderous tench, but one that was obviously very big. It did not want to yield and yet I knew it was not a male. Several times it showed itself twenty or more yards out and it was a very big female indeed, a definite personal best. My excitement was mounting and then, suddenly, the line was slack. My light hooklink had parted. I could have cried. The one fish I wanted above all others had eluded me; I would cheerfully have traded all the fish I'd had that day just to have landed the one I lost.

Ruefully, I gazed at the hooklink, and at that moment decided I would not fish as light as 3lb for the rest of the session. Accordingly, I put on a 5lb hooklink, a size 12 hook baited with three maggots, and recast. It was one very disgruntled angler who settled back to wait, but the wait was no more than five minutes. Again, the bobbin flew up, again I connected with a big fish, but this time the outcome was far different. With a greater margin of safety, I was able to keep the fish out of the offending weed bed to my right that had contributed to my earlier downfall. Soon, the tench was circling in front of me and then my good friend Clive Goode, who had come round from the next swim to join in the fun, slipped the net under a colossal tench. As it cleared the rushes and I saw its full bulk for the first time, I let out a whoop of triumph. This fish was monstrous.

I allowed Clive to undertake the all important weighing ceremony, and moments later he announced 9lb 10oz, one of the biggest tench ever to come from the water. Moments before, I had been in despair. Now, I was on cloud nine. Doesn't that just sum up specimen hunting!

Day of the Doubles

Following the incredible events of that 1993 summer, which saw three more eight pounders caught after that fabulous 9lb 10oz capture, all the syndicate members were obviously impatient to renew acquaintance with those fabulous tench in the summer of 1994. But frustration was around the corner. As I said earlier, we are very much at the mercy of water requirements, specially in a dry summer, and whereas the 1993 summer was wet and windy, 1994 was hot and dry. Consequently, by mid-June, the fishable area of bank was only a foot deep and fishing was a non-starter. The same problem was to transpire in 1995 and in 1996 Severn Trent were again forced to lower the water level for further work on the dam. 1997 was the year of the weed, and although we had water in our end of the reservoir at last, there was only a handful of tench caught by the members. For some reason, the fish stayed in the bird sanctuary end.

And so we come to June 1998, after five years of total frustration. At last, conditions seemed in our favour. It was a more normal summer, that is, wet and windy, and the reservoir was full. One or two of the members who did pre-baiting trips reported seeing rolling fish, so things looked extremely promising. Our season at Stanford now starts on June 1st, but unfortunately I could not be on the bank for the start as I was abroad. On my return, however, the rest of the lads had stunning news for me. In the first weekend, several members had recorded personal bests, with a handful of tench over ten pounds. This was exciting stuff, and the time dragged oh so slowly until the following Thursday, when I was at last on my way.

I arrived a good hour before daylight, with the express purpose of finding which swims were vacant and making a decision where to settle in time for a start at first light. As might be expected, there was a good turn out of members, and most of the known swims on the productive bank were taken. After mulling it over for ten minutes, I decided to cut a new swim, which only entailed making access through high reeds and moving some fallen timber. A couple of false casts with a feeder confirmed the weed present to be very sparse, so I could now concentrate with getting some feed out without further ado. This turned out to be the most critical facet of that summer's tenching for me, as you will see later.

That first morning, I baited with a gallon of dead maggots, two pints of casters, a gallon of hemp, about four pounds of cereal in my baiting cone, and a tin of red corn. After the baiting, which took about half an hour, I leisurely set about arranging my camp. It was around 6.30am when my first hook baits were in position. I had started as I finished in 1993, with a short, six inch hooklink of 5lb mono, and a medium weight block end feeder, coupled to my light bobbins. Bait was two Tutti Frutti flavoured maggots to a size 12 Drennan Super Spade. I was full of confidence, brewed a cup of tea, and sat back to await my first bite.

A brace of nines.

It never came. As the hours passed, I began to wonder about my presentation, my swim, in fact everything. When nothing is happening, we all do it. By midday, I was still biteless, and then a good friend Ken arrived, and set up perhaps thirty yards to my right. He would only be fishing a few hours, so did not bother with any loose feed whatever, contenting himself with simply chucking out two blockends. It worked, though. While I still sat biteless, two hours later Ken was on his feet, playing an obviously serious tench. I was privileged to net it for him, the biggest tench I had ever clapped eyes on. It weighed 10lb 7oz, a fish in truly magnificent condition.

I returned to my swim in thoughtful mood. I did not think at that time I was doing anything wrong, it was just one of those things. Having said that, I had known occasions before when initial heavy baiting had taken a few hours to kick in. I was still, therefore, quite happy with my approach. Happy or not, however, I was still biteless as I wound in at dusk after the first eel.

Next morning, I awoke at the crack of dawn to steady drizzle and a really humid atmosphere, and the first two hours were bedlam. At last, the tench had found the dining table and in that period I had a succession of five males, the smallest 5lb exactly and the biggest a personal best of 6lb 14oz. This was brilliant fishing, but a little frustrating. Where were those net busting females.

The bites stopped as abruptly as they commenced, and it was then around 1.00pm, after at least seven biteless hours, before the left hand rod was suddenly away. By a weird coincidence, this was also to herald five fish in a two hour spell, and just as strangely, they were all females this time, weighing in at 6lb 10oz, 6lb 12oz, 7lb 6oz, 8lb 2oz and 8lb 11oz. When you look at those weights, and think

Casting my cone feeder.

back to the days when a six pound tench was as rare as an intelligent swan, I should have been over the moon. But I was puzzled. Two other friends had arrived that morning for short sessions, neither had introduced any feed apart from their feeders, and they had landed just one tench apiece. Those fish weighed 9lb 14oz and 10lb 2oz, and yet I had had ten fish, superb sport admittedly, with nothing close to those weights. When I eventually drove home on Saturday morning, with no further fish landed, my head was buzzing. Had I just been unlucky, had my friends been very fortunate, or was there more to it? The only difference had been the loose feed, and I would have to re-assess the situation the following week.

Over the week that followed, I mulled over the events of my first session, and came to the conclusion that I must just have been unlucky in the size of my biggest tench. After all, ten fish in a day was super sport, so I had to be doing something right. I would take the same approach on my second session. This week, I would crack that double figure fish!

When I arrived, a member was ensconced in the swim I had created, which would have been my first choice, so I wandered down to a swim we know as the Poll Tax, so called because a friend of mine, Clive Goode, spent so long there a few years ago that the joke was he had told his postman to deliver the Poll Tax demand there!

This swim is a lovely secluded spot, surrounded by trees, and for the two days I spent there I was entertained by a green woodpecker, perched no more than ten yards behind me. It was a wonder he didn't wear his beak out, the hammering he gave that bloody tree!

My approach was identical to the first session, although I had cut down the amount of maggots a little, and this time I only had to wait until midday for the action to start. Significantly, I now feel, the first two tench were again males, good fish of 6lb and 6lb 8oz, followed by two blank hours, and then two good females of 8lb 3oz and 8lb 13oz. This is obviously terrific tench action, and I was quite content when another of the members, Andy, stopped for a chat. He was on his way to the next swim round for just a few hours. All he had with him was two pints of maggots, no loose feed of any description. Andy left my bivvy at around 6.00pm and by 7.30pm he was back, asking me to take some photographs for him. His first cast into an unprepared swim had yielded a colossal fish of 10lb 10oz.

For the rest of that evening, which produced two more males of 5lb 12oz and another personal best of 7lb 7oz, I sat in my bivvy deep in thought, almost oblivious to the torrential rain that had started. It kept going round and round in my head. I had now mustered sixteen tench to 8lb 13oz over well prepared beds of bait, whereas three friends had had one singleton apiece, without preparation, and all three fish had been monstrous. I can put down one fish as chance, two possibly coincidence, but not three. No, something strange was definitely occurring. It was an enigma I was determined to solve.

On the Friday and Saturday, there was no let up in the monsoon conditions, and over

Landing a big tench.

about thirty hours fishing before I had to go home, I managed but two other tench. One was yet another male, a third personal best of 7lb 9oz, and then I was absolutely delighted to record only my second nine pound tench, a lovely sleek female of 9lb 3oz. I was getting closer. But the Friday also saw two disasters.

The one drawback with the Poll Tax swim is that it is a swim requiring waders, as you have to go out a good ten yards to cast past reed headlands. When I'd started fishing, I'd wondered about my 5lb hooklinks in this swim, as the fish were significantly bigger than in 1993, but had stuck with them in the end. I was to pay the price with a big fish in mid-afternoon, which kited round the left hand corner of the reeds and stuck fast. Two other fish had done the same thing, but had come free. But it was third time unlucky, and the hooklink broke on me. I am as sure as I can be that was the biggest tench I'd hooked, and I was not a happy man.

Filling my cone feeder.

After that sad episode, I decided to switch the hooklink to one of 7lb Blue Chip braid, which a match angling friend had recommended, but only an hour later had decided to throw the spool in the dustbin! I was well in control of a tench that looked around 7lb when the braid just parted. Just like that, not even any serious pressure. Testing the material later, I had breaks at pressures as low as 3lb and as high as 9lb. The damn stuff was so inconsistent it was worse than useless for a big fish. Another lesson learned the hard way.

When I analysed the events of my first two sessions, and especially the order in which the fish had come, and when, it definitely seemed to indicate two possibilities. One, fairly obviously, the heavy baiting was eventually attracting a good head of fish, and the less circumspect males were first to feed. Second, the very big females were either being spooked by the bait in the first place, or by other smaller fish getting to the bait first and being caught. So the decision had virtually made itself. On my next trip, I would use minimal bait, but of a type making the tench search for it. I decided on a couple of pints of mixed casters and mini trout pellets spread in the fishing area. I would deliberately not keep the bait in too tight an area.

The following Thursday morning found me in the swim where I had witnessed the 10lb 10oz fish the previous week, the swims nearer the car park again being occupied. Following my pre-planning, the first job was to introduce the bait via my baiting cones, and, that job complete, I took my time setting up home.

I had also given some thought to the terminal rig, and had decided to move onto hooklinks of 10lb Herculine braid, which I had used for chub and barbel and never had a problem with, and Sod's Law was to dictate that the first fish I hooked was a big pike as I was winding in, and promptly bit through the braid!.

I have to say that my confidence level was not unduly high, as I do like to be fishing over a good bed of bait for tench. Even that lowered confidence gradually drained away as the blank hours piled up, and in early evening I was still biteless, as Andy's dad John arrived for a few hours fishing. I bet you can guess what's coming next!

No more than an hour after setting up some thirty yards to my right, John had lost a good fish and then landed a second, another absolute monster of 10lb 7oz. Once more I was behind the camera when I was itching to be in front of it!

As I indicated earlier, the time when you are most likely to play around with your rigs is when you are not getting action when you feel you should be. Most of the time, you know what you are doing is right, but you still mess with it anyway. So it was with me that Thursday evening. Having just witnessed another monster, when I had sat there all day for nothing, I felt I had to be doing something wrong. I became paranoid about my Herculine, although I knew it was the same diameter as 3lb mono and should be perfectly acceptable to the tench. Nevertheless, I had to change something, and so both terminal rigs were retrieved. When they were recast, they were armed with 3lb mono hooklinks. It was, however, to no avail, if you ignore the bonus pound and a half perch. As dusk fell, the eels moved in, and I wound in for the night, tenchless.

Next morning, I was grimly determined that my fortunes had to change as I once again cast my feeders into position, still retaining the 3lb hooklinks. A couple of quiet hours passed and then, out of the blue, the left bobbin shot to the butt, the reel started to backwind, and a big tench was hooked. And I do mean big. Twice I saw it turn high in the water, and it was certainly a double. And then the hooklink parted. At that moment, I felt very low indeed, and shouted in frustration, "God, give me a break!"

It was time to take stock of what I was doing, and I sat over a cup of tea for fifteen minutes thinking out my options. The decision was made. I was not prepared to tolerate the heartbreak of losing another giant fish. If I hooked one, I wanted to land it, and immediately reverted back to 10lb Herculine links. As I cast the baits into position once more, I could not have known that I was about to make one of the greatest catches of giant tench in angling history.

It was about 6.30 am, I was fully alert as a tench had just rolled, and then the right bobbin crept to the butt ring. This was no smash and grab affair, this was from a fish in no particular hurry. That changed, however, the instant I set the hook, as something big and powerful surged right, trying to get around the little headland that had proved my undoing with the lost fish earlier. This time, however, I had the extra security of the Herculine and bent into the fish, successfully turning it so that it headed back from whence it came. It then developed into a straightforward pull and counterpull affair until, at long last, a massive fish wallowed in my net. I cannot adequately express the elation I felt when my Avons whipped round to 10lb 3oz.

After sacking the fish securely, I shot round to Clive Goode, who was fishing some sixty yards away, to give him the good news, and he promised to be round for photographs after the drizzle had abated.

Back at my bivvy, I basked in that lovely warm afterglow you get when a specially big fish has been landed, and then I leisurely recast my baits. I didn't need another bite, the trip was a resounding success already, but barely a minute after setting the bobbin, the reel was spinning furiously as another terrific tench zoomed off with the maggots. Five minutes later, I was recording a weight of 9lb 12oz. What a brace! A second carp sack was brought into play.

What happened next took the day deep into the realms of fantasy. I had just recast, placed the rod on the rest, and the rod shot forward and nearly flew out of my hands. I hadn't even set the bobbin. Whatever I hooked was rocketing right, past the little headland I mentioned earlier, and felt so big I was convinced it was a big pike. It made sense. Perhaps the terminal rig had landed across the pike's back, spooking it, and it had set off in panic. That would account for the phenomenal speed and power with which the fish was departing the scene.

Within two minutes, I had lost forty yards of line and worse, it was running through the branches of the scruffy little alder on the right hand edge of the swim. And still the fish ran like a mad thing. This had to be at least a mid-double figure pike and I decided to pile pressure on it. I was fully expecting to be broken or bitten off, so I had nothing to lose. A good ten minutes war of attrition followed, with me heaving line back onto the reel, expecting the branches through which it was being forced to catch and break it at any moment. But it held, and then, amazingly, pinged free as the fish shot back in front of me, about thirty yards out. For the first time, I had serious thoughts about landing it. As the fish came closer, I started to have doubts as to the species, and then it rolled. Before my astonished eyes was one awesome Goliath of a tench, and it was all I could do to hold myself together long enough to slide it over the net.

Never in my wildest dreams did I ever expect to catch a tench the size of the fish that now reposed on my unhooking mat. It was just gigantic, and when my scales pulled round to 11lb 11oz, I could only stare in disbelief. I was hoping for a double, but this was just different class altogether.

About an hour later, Clive and another friend Leon came round to witness the fish and do the honours with the camera, and I am indebted to Clive for the superb photographs he took. The shot of the three tench together is one of the most impressive big fish photographs I have ever seen.

But the day was far from over. After a lull in late morning, two more bites in quick succession in early afternoon led to me banking two more incredible fish of 9lb 2oz and 9lb 4oz, to be followed, at 5.30pm, by another unbelievable tench of exactly 10lb. And that was where the action stopped for the day, having banked six tench for an aggregate of exactly 60lb, which obviously is an average weight of dead on 10lb. As far as I am aware, no one has ever caught three doubles in a day before or since, or had six fish with such an incredible average. All my disappointments and frustrations of the previous two sessions had been repaid, in spades!

I had two more sessions for those tench, before the fish scattered and became more difficult to locate, but in those sessions managed two more over nine, at 9lb 5ozs and 9lb 6oz, as well as several more eights and lesser fish. I remember thinking, when I moved on to my barbel fishing, that I hoped the following summer would also be wet and windy so the water would stay full. What would the tench weigh then?

But there is, I'm afraid, a sad epitaph to this chapter. That catch of big tench was never reported at the time because of a publicity ban on the water, so why am I telling you about it now? The answer to that is simple. All those big tench are now dead.

In May 1999, things were looking good. The first week of the month was warm, but the water was brimming. The weed was already taking hold, the only problem being that we had an unusual amount of surface algae because of the early hot spell. That was our undoing. If you recall, the second week of May that year saw temperatures plummet. One week it was hot, in the upper seventies, the next we were having very late night frosts. The effect on the water was catastrophic. Overnight in mid-May, we experienced what the EA term an algae crash, in which the algae dies in the cold, and then sinks to the bottom, deoxygenating the water and killing everything as it does so. So absolute was the wipe out that we even had eels crawling out of the water to find air, and dying in the fields. It was truly heartbreaking. Severn Trent did all they could, with aerators and no shortage of volunteers helping us assess the devastation. But it was to no avail. The loss of fish was counted in tons, including over 400 big tench, 99% of all the big pike and virtually the entire stock of big roach. The only fish that seemed to survive were large shoals of small roach that took refuge in the feeder stream.

At the time of writing, August 2000, we have been able to assess the water one year on. Very hard fishing by the members has turned up a handful of average tench only, but the big pike are gone. It remains to be seen whether it will ever produce big roach again, but at the moment the water has been colonised by thousands of tiny roach from the stream.

I have fished and loved Stanford for almost thirty years, latterly as Secretary of the syndicate that controls the fishing. We will stay with it, in the hope that it can, one day, return to its former glory. But at the moment, and for the foreseeable future, it is a shadow of its former self. And that makes me intensely sad.

Past, Present & Future

The following was written in September 2000 and it is now March 2001, and the publishers have given me time to insert one last story which really brings this work to an explosive climax.

Having now read this book, you will know that my consuming passion is in big fish of all coarse species, except eels, although I have never fished for zander or catfish. This is an omission I hope to correct before too much longer. You have now shared the highlights of over forty wonderful years, but what of the present and the future.

You will be pleased to know that I am still going strong, keener and more obsessed than ever, if that is possible. It is September as I put the finishing touches to this book, and so far this season I have been chasing some particularly elusive carp, in a water known to hold fish to over 40lb. There is nothing spectacular to report, with only eight fish so far landed, smallest 17lb 10oz and largest 23lb 14oz, with two other twenties. So I've hardly set the carp world on fire, but I have enjoyed every last second of it.

This autumn and winter I have an exciting project in mind. Over the last two seasons, as you will have read, I have conducted extensive experiments with special barbel baits. I now intend to put that knowledge to good use on a stretch of river thought to hold monster fish, with a target certainly a personal best and hopefully a British best, the ultimate goal for a specimen hunter. One of my greatest thrills in angling is exploring relatively unknown waters and eventually catching big fish from them. I am proud of the fact that I have been involved in the initial explorations of many waters that are now renowned big fish waters. But, if I fail, will it really matter? The older I get, the more I realise that it is the being there that is most important.

The new venue mentioned above is a remote stretch, very difficult of access, that appears totally barren. Some three miles in extent between two areas known to contain good fish, it is hardly ever fished because it is apparently a blank waiting to happen. I had actually confirmed that diagnosis in the winter of 1996/97 when I fished the area for nine two-day sessions, day and night, and caught precisely one perch for my efforts. Despite that, I remained convinced that the potential was there.

At the start of the 2000 season, I had made a decision that I would give the stretch a determined campaign from autumn onwards, but with a very different game plan. In 1996, I had fished traditional methods, thinking that any barbel there must be unsophisticated as they were hardly ever fished for. So I had fished sweetcorn or meat over hemp, I had tried flavoured meat in high water, and mass baiting with maggots in normal conditions. But all were to no avail. So for the new campaign, I decided to apply what I had learned about designer bait application to the problem, and, after a lot of thought, came up with a bait that I thought would give me the dual benefits of a long term food source, hopefully for consistent results through the winter, plus an instant attraction combination that would give a reasonable chance of quick success. One of my experiments in 1999 at Adams Mill was centred round this dilemma. Most good baits will work if applied long enough, and most will work instantly if over flavoured, although the latter soon blow. But very few combine the best of both worlds. In July 1999, then, I arrived at Adams Mill with a bait that I thought was about there in achieving what I was after. As I arrived at the swim, my first act was to introduce ten baits where I intended fishing, and then the swim was left in peace for three hours. The water was clear, and I knew the fish were present under far bank foliage. For the whole of that day I fished fruitlessly, without a sign of a bite. As the time came to pack up, night fishing not being allowed at Adams, I introduced a further ten baits, in the hope of getting the swim the following day. In that I was lucky, and the following day I took three barbel, the best over thirteen pounds. That bait, therefore, had taken over 24 hours to work, nothing unusual for a new bait, but not quite what I was looking for. So, before the following week, I altered one ingredient, added another and adjusted my flavour levels. I followed exactly the same procedure, and this time the first barbel came only five minutes after the first cast, to be followed by three more throughout the day. This was what I was after. In an area of low population, almost certainly nomadic, I needed to know that my bait would be taken by a passing barbel, even if it had been only lightly prebaited.

My successful 1999 bait was based on one of John Baker's specialised mixes, and I spoke to John at length about my bait requirements, as well as discussing it with Stuart Morgan, himself very well advanced in barbel bait design. I was pleased to note that they both largely concurred with my findings, although both John and Stuart provided very valuable "fine tuning". John is an acknowledged expert in the field of bait design to meet differing needs, while Stuart's experience of bait application is second to none. My 2000 bait, therefore, was 90% the same as the previous year, but with vitally important modifications that I will keep secret for the time being. By the start of the season in June 2000, I knew exactly what bait I would be using from October onwards.

With that background, my first exploratory trip to the stretch was in mid-October, when I decided to split the three mile stretch into mile long segments for detailed investigation. Although the river has bends and some bankside foliage, and a couple of very obvious shallow areas, the rest of the river looks very uniform, preliminary findings showing little variation in depth. The last thing I wanted was to be fishing blind, so I had decided to spend a few hours with a plumbing rod, looking for any irregularity on the river bed. I was particularly interested in depressions, which would be important to know of in high water conditions. By midday on my first day, I had located five such areas, each being quite a narrow trench in the gravel, around two yards wide and between five and eight yards long. For the two days at my disposal, these five areas would suffice, and each was baited with a dozen freebies. It was now time to wait, and I spent a little while wandering further downstream with the plumbing rod, finding another three interesting areas in the process.

My first cast was at about 4.00pm, but it wasn't until about 7.30pm that I had my first indication, a real thump that produced a good chub of exactly five pounds. I was over the moon with that fish, for several reasons. First, I'm always pleased to land big fish, but to get a specimen fish on my first day, after the dour fishing I had experienced on my previous campaign on the stretch, was a very encouraging sign. Also, it's always a confidence booster when you've had your first fish on a new bait. No matter how good you know it is in theory, it's only when it has worked in practice that you mentally relax. Not long after taking that chub, I was to have another solid wrench, but this time the outcome was different. I only had the fish on for seconds before the line went limp, and I wound in a size 6 Drennan Continental with the hook point turned over. That is very unusual for that pattern, which is very strong, and I can only assume that I had either foul hooked a big barbel, with the hook point catching in bony gristle, or a very big chub had taken the hook to its throat teeth. I rather favour the latter explanation.

That was the only action I experienced on the first session, and two weeks later I arrived for my second investigation. I had decided beforehand to go back to the top section again, obviously giving the swim I'd caught the chub from some more attention, but when I arrived on the bank I decided to concentrate solely on the middle mile. It wasn't a conscious decision, just a gut feeling, but as I've often written before, I never ignore such feelings.

On the first trip, I had carried out some fairly sketchy plumbing in this area, so I knew where to start, and a couple of hours later I had uncovered three very sexy trenches in the gravel bed. Two looked absolute screamers, diving off at least two feet quite sharply. Barbel love to lie with their snouts up the slope, intercepting whatever passes. This week, each swim initially received eight baits, and then I left them alone while I took a long trek downstream to do more plumbing.

Eventually, I was set to go at mid-afternoon, and gently introduced a hookbait into the first prepared swim. I remember how wound up I was as I sat back in the chair, rod butt resting on my knee. I had a very powerful premonition. Tonight could be the night. The conditions were certainly favourable, two feet up but dropping, fairly well coloured, and with a water temperature of 53°F. As well as that, it was mild and heavily overcast, which would hold up air temperatures overnight.

An uneventful hour passed, other than plucks from tiny dace, and then suddenly the line tightened over my finger and the rod hooped over. Immediately, I knew this was no barbel, but a muscular chub gave a good account of itself despite the heavy tackle. I was soon returning a pristine fish of 4lb 10oz. Again, not an earth shattering specimen, but a confidence booster from an unknown swim on a new bait only introduced a few hours before.

After a further fruitless hour in that first swim, I moved down to the second, and in half an hour had two tremendous wrenches, again from chub. But what a brace! They weighed 5lb 2oz and 5lb 6oz. I was yet to tempt a barbel on the new bait, but I had certainly uncovered a concoction the chub appreciated.

Again, the early action was followed by a blank hour, and I moved into the third area where, incredibly, the same sequence of events transpired. The two chub this time weighed 4lb 14oz and 5lb 7oz, to give me a total in just five hours fishing of five big chub, including three fives. Whether I caught a barbel or not, it was already an incredible session.

By 10.15pm, I was back in the first swim, by now quite seriously tired and starving hungry as I had been up since well before dawn and not eaten for ten hours. By 10.50pm the thought of a hot curry and fresh tea in the van was becoming more appealing by the minute, especially as it was now raining steadily. Not so appealing was the thought of a two mile hike across muddy fields, through ditches and over fences. I remember glancing at my watch and saying to myself that I'd give it until 11.00pm and then turn in for the night. I normally fish much later, but I could hardly keep my eyes open. Seconds later, the rod nearly took off, as what was obviously a barbel snaffled the bait and then suddenly remembered an urgent appointment in St Neots! I've had some savage barbel bites in my time, but that was awesome! If I hadn't been holding the rod, I'd have lost it for sure.

The speed of the first run was tremendous, with twenty yards screaming off the spool in seconds, and it was this acceleration that led me to the initial conclusion that I'd hooked an average barbel only. The really big fish are usually much slower and give a dour but powerful battle. I wa,s therefore, not unduly excited at this stage, although obviously chuffed that I was in contact with my first barbel from the stretch.

Once the initial run had faltered, and I began pumping the fish back upstream, I began to revise my estimates. Although the fish came towards me steadily, in response to tremendous pressure from my Pulse rod, the rod was round to the corks. This barbel was a dead weight. Once under the rod top, it began those irresistible heavy lunges so typical of the bigger fish, but it never actually gave me any anxious moments. There were, thankfully, no snags to worry about, it was just a matter of keeping up the pressure and doing nothing stupid.

Eventually, perhaps ten minutes after I hooked it, the fish was circling just under the surface, and I switched on my head lamp ready for netting. A yard away from the net cord, it made one last desperate roll, and in that instant I caught my first good look at the fish. This barbel was not just big, in fact not just very big. This was monstrous, and I think I stopped breathing until the fish at last folded into the mesh.

As I hoisted the net up the bank I knew without doubt that this was a personal best, and moments later, seeing the full extent of the fish for the first time on the unhooking mat, thoughts of a potential British record were surfacing. I was trembling as I carefully zeroed the Avons against the wetted weigh sling, and then watched in ever increasing excitement as the needle raced round the dial to settle on 16lb 10oz. My target had been a new personal best, with hopefully a barbel of 15lb plus, but this awesome beast had just eclipsed all my expectations.

About an hour later, my good friend Adrian Busby, who had a long drive in the dark to get to me, and a wet, muddy walk across a swamp to boot, sat with me on the bank. It is the measure of a good friend that he was as delighted as I was, and for two hours we talked, as we got wetter and wetter under the incessant rain. He had witnessed the fish on his arrival and, by 2.00am, it was obvious the rain wasn't about to stop. We therefore elected the far from satisfactory ploy of taking flash photographs from under my umbrella, which I carry for that purpose but very rarely fish under when on a mobile session. In the circumstances, Adrian made a first class job of the photography, and I would like to record my eternal gratitude to him for leaving a warm fire to come out to me on such a foul night. I know that, when he eventually returned home, he was soaked and plastered in mud! Thanks, mate!

One of the most gratifying aspects of this wonderful sport of ours is that there are new targets appearing over the horizon constantly. Fish are getting bigger all the time and specimens that a few years ago were highly rated now come well down the pecking order.

For those interested in statistics, my personal best list currently reads as follows.

Roach   *2lb 11oz, with 121 two pounders*
Rudd   *3lb 5oz, with two other three pounders and many over 2lb*
Perch   *5lb 0oz, with another fish of 4lb 10oz and 32 others of 3lb+*
Chub   *6lb 12oz, with six other 6 pounders and 141 more over 5lb*
Barbel   *16lb 14oz**, with 68 others over 10lb*
Tench   *11lb 11oz, with two other doubles and nine others over 9lb*
Carp   *33lb 2oz, with another 63 over 20lb. In France, fish to 58lb at Cassien.*
Pike   *32lb 1oz, with another 41 over 20lb*
Crucian   *3lb 3oz, with two more over three pounds and numerous two pounders*
Dace   *1lb 0oz*
Bream   *15lb 2oz, with two more over 14lb.*
** The 16lb 10oz barbel described on these pages was re-caught at 16lb 14oz just as this book was going to production.

The dial settled on 16lb 10oz!

It is a chastening fact that no less than four of those personal bests are substantially bigger than the British record when I started out on my quest all those years ago.

When I'm not fishing, I'm writing, reading, talking or dreaming about it. With big fish angling, there is always a fresh challenge, a new personal best to pursue, and that is why I will only stop when these creaking old bones finally call a tortured halt. Until that day, I hope to experience the heart stopping thrill of that big fish sagging in the net many more times. In the meantime, let me wish you all a long life, good health and tight lines a-plenty.